India's Tryst with Destiny

Debunking Myths that Undermine Progress and Addressing New Challenges

JAGDISH BHAGWATI

ARVIND PANAGARIYA

HARPER BUSINESS

An Imprint of HarperCollins *Publishers*

First published in hardback in India in 2012 by Collins Business
An imprint of HarperCollins *Publishers*

HarperCollins Publishers India, Cyber City, Building 10-A, Gurugram,
Haryana-122002, India
www.harpercollins.co.in

4 6 8 10 9 7 5

First published in paperback in 2014

This edition published in India in 2018 by HarperCollins *Publishers*

P-ISBN: 978-93-5136-776-5
E-ISBN: 978-93-5029-932-6

Typeset in 12/16 Aldine401 BT at
SURYA

Printed and bound at
MicroPrints India, New Delhi

MIX
Paper
FSC FSC® C218906

This product is made of FSC®-certified and other controlled material.

HarperCollins Publishers, Macken House, 39/40 Mayor Street
Upper, Dublin 1, D01 C9W8, Ireland

Contents

PART II: THE NEW CHALLENGES— TRACK I REFORMS TO ACCELERATE GROWTH AND MAKE IT YET MORE INCLUSIVE

PART III: THE NEW CHALLENGES—TRACK II REFORMS TO MAKE REDISTRIBUTION MORE EFFECTIVE AND INCLUSIVE

Preface

Many of our readers are bound to ask why we have written another book. After all, both of us have written extensively on the economics of India, as evidenced by the list of references at the end of the book. Writings by Jagdish Bhagwati include *India: Planning for Industrialization* (with Padma Desai), *Foreign Trade Regimes and Economic Development: India* (with T. N. Srinivasan) and *India in Transition,* as also numerous articles. Bhagwati delivered a lecture to the joint session of the Parliament in 2010, which led to a major debate on the CUTS (Consumer Unity and Trust Society) forum with many leading economists participating, and resulted in an e-book as well as a hard copy edition, titled *Growth and Poverty: The Great Debate*. This has been followed by his centenary lecture under home ministry auspices on governance reforms, addressing topical issues such as corruption.

Arvind Panagariya has recently published *India: The Emerging Giant*, which *The Economist* magazine described as the 'capstone of a career, a sustained work of scholarship', and listed it as a top pick of 2008. He has also written numerous articles on Indian economic reforms published in journals and book volumes. Currently, he is co-editing (with Bhagwati) the book series *Studies in Indian Economic Policies* (Oxford University Press, USA), containing new scientific research. The first volume in this series, edited by him and Bhagwati, has just appeared under the title *India's Reforms: How They Produced*

Inclusive Growth. Panagariya is also one of the founding editors of *India Policy Forum,* jointly published by the Brookings Institution and the National Council of Applied Economic Research, which he continues to co-edit.

In addition, both of us have written numerous op-ed articles in our regular and occasional columns in newspapers such as *The Wall Street Journal, Financial Times*, *The Times of India*, *The Economic Times, The Hindu, Hindustan Times* and magazines such as *India Today, Business Today* and *Outlook*.

A hostile critic might say: Enough is enough! Yet, he would be wrong. For India has today reached a stage of political and economic development that needs a comprehensive, holistic look at what we have accomplished, where we have failed, where the popular and populist critiques are unwarranted and in need of refutation, and where the next set of challenges lie in India's continuing need and quest for reforms.

Some of this needs only systematic drawing together of what others and we have written earlier. But much requires research that has only begun to develop, as in the case of several studies with empirical data which have been undertaken by a remarkable group of young, technically proficient economists such as Anusha Chari, Rajeev Dehejia, Nandini Gupta, Poonam Gupta, Rana Hasan, Pravin Krishna, Devashish Mitra and Megha Mukim, all working singly or together under the direction of Arvind Panagariya in a substantial Program on Indian Economic Policies at Columbia University. As against assertions unconstrained by facts and analysis, we now have access to a substantial set of studies whose findings are overturning a number of generally left-wing populist fallacies that continue to plague our discourse and our efforts at continuing reforms.

The analysis in the present book stands on the shoulders of these many writings, synthesizing in a consistent and coherent treatment the lessons we have learnt and the old and new challenges that lie ahead.

Acknowledgements

In the course of finalizing this book, we benefited greatly from the comments by several panellists and participants at a pre-publication discussion of the book that the National Council of Applied Economic Research (NCAER) and the Columbia Program on Indian Economic Policies jointly organized at the India International Centre in New Delhi on 5 January 2012. Our thanks go to Rajesh Chadha, senior fellow, NCAER, who organized that event and oversaw its efficient execution.

The event brought together two panels, one consisting of intellectuals from various fields and the other comprising a group of leading journalists from Indian and Western newspapers. The comments and critiques we received at this meeting have resulted in many revisions in the final version of the book.

In particular, we are grateful to Bibek Debroy (professor, Centre for Policy Research), Jay Panda (member, Lok Sabha), Manish Sabharwal (CEO, TeamLease) and Shekhar Shah (director general, NCAER), who spoke on the first panel and Vikas Bajaj (*The New York Times*), Sunil Jain (*The Financial Express*), James Lamont (*Financial Times*) and T.N. Ninan (*Business Standard*), who served on the second panel. Bina Agarwal (Institute of Economic Growth), Bornali Bhandari (NCAER), Rajesh Chadha (NCAER), Shashanka Bhide (NCAER), Rana Hasan (Asian Development Bank), Vijay

Joshi (Oxford University) and Deepak Mishra (World Bank) offered additional comments from the floor.

The eminent historian, Ramachandra Guha, read all the chapters in Part I and provided detailed comments that have led to many improvements in the final draft. We also received positive feedback from Ashoka Mody of the International Monetary Fund and Swagato Ganguly of *The Times of India,* who read parts of the book.

A rather generous input came from a young scholar whom neither of us has as yet met—Manish Kumar of Jawaharlal Nehru College in Chakradharpur, Bihar. Manish researched virtually all publicly available volumes of speeches by prime ministers Jawaharlal Nehru, Indira Gandhi, P.V. Narasimha Rao, Atal Bihari Vajpayee and Manmohan Singh, and provided us literally dozens of pages worth of quotations to choose from. We are deeply indebted to him.

Zeenat Nazir, Shivam Srivastava and May Yang provided excellent research assistance at various stages of the work.

Finally, the book generously draws on the scientific research undertaken by a number of leading scholars of the Indian economy as a part of the Program on Indian Economic Policies under the joint auspices of the School of International and Public Affairs (SIPA) and the Institute for Social and Economic Research and Policy (ISERP) at Columbia University. The programme has been funded by a generous grant from the Templeton Foundation. While the views expressed in the book are solely ours, we take this opportunity to thank the Templeton Foundation for funding the programme and the ISERP staff, especially Michael Falco, Michael Higgins, Shelley Klein, Carmen Morillo, Andrew Ratanatharthorn and Kristen Van Leuven, for their excellent logistical support.

INTRODUCTION

The Tryst—The Vision and the Reality

When Jawaharlal Nehru, virtually handpicked by Mahatma Gandhi as India's first prime minister and the leader of a newly independent India, spoke to the nation at the 'stroke of the midnight hour' on 15 August 1947, he spoke in the tradition of the great orators over the ages: straight from the heart and in his own eloquent words, without the use of speechwriters[1] and the teleprompter that mars the impact that even gifted politicians have today.[2]

---

1. Winston Churchill was among the orators whose speeches were his own handiwork; as Lord Birkenhead remarked, 'Winston has spent the best years of his life writing impromptu speeches.' By contrast, John F. Kennedy flew to great heights on wings supplied by his speechwriter Ted Sorenson.
2. It is interesting, for example, that President Obama is notorious for the use of the teleprompter even though he won the White House with stirring speeches. This also means that he mispronounces names wherever he goes, obviously because his speechwriters do not take care to rehearse him in the names included in the speeches he reads. He did this several times, including in the address he gave to the Indian Parliament, leading the MPs to warn

(Contd....)

He dwelt upon all the great themes that had marked the independence movement, defining the tasks before the leaders of independent India and the vision that framed them. In particular, he singled out the two pillars on which he thought that India's destiny uniquely rested: the politics of democracy and the economics of poverty removal.

On democracy, it is clear that he defined it in the broadest sense in which we regard it today, not equating it simply with elections but rather spelling out what we would call today the institutions of a liberal democracy. Thus, he reminded his audience that 'our endeavour' should be '. . . to build up a prosperous, democratic and progressive nation, and to create social, economic and political institutions which will ensure justice and fullness of life to every man and woman'.[3]

Again, on secularism, he reiterated his conviction, no doubt against the backdrop of communal violence that would soon engulf the subcontinent and claim the life of Mahatma Gandhi, that India ought to embrace multi-ethnicity and multi-religiosity, that:

> All of us, to whatever religion we may belong, are equally the children of India with equal rights, privileges and obligations. We cannot encourage communalism or narrow-mindedness, for no nation can be great whose people are narrow in thought or in action.

(...contd.)

one of us (Bhagwati), who addressed the Parliament a few weeks later, to avoid reading a speech and to speak extempore and from the heart, with wit and humour. A Japanese diplomat also told us that Obama was mispronouncing names during his visit to Japan as well. One can only dread the prospect of his battling with the tonalities of Chinese names!

3. That electoral democracy without the institutions such as an independent judiciary and a free press would be hollow was not a thought that would have been foreign to Nehru's *Weltanschauung*.

On the economics of poverty removal, he was even more impassioned. After all, this son of Motilal Nehru, whose affluent lifestyle included sending shirts to Parisian laundries, had participated in India's independence struggle alongside Mahatma Gandhi, travelling the vast expanse of India's countryside and seeing poverty at first hand. So, his remarks on India's suffering masses and the immense task the nation faced in extending a generous hand to them, and on Mahatma Gandhi's ambitions in meeting that challenge, are particularly poignant:

> The service of India means the service of the millions who suffer. It means the ending of poverty and ignorance and disease and inequality of opportunity.
>
> The ambition of the greatest man of our generation (Mahatma Gandhi) has been to wipe every tear from every eye. That may be beyond us, but as long as there are tears and suffering, so long our work will not be over.

But by the strangest irony, while India began its tryst with democracy with advantages that were unique among the newly liberated developing countries—India was the 'exceptional nation' that maintained democratic institutions—its economics began (except till the end of the 1950s) with an embrace of an economic policy framework that was so counterproductive that it produced an abysmal growth rate and therefore little impact on poverty.

So, while India's democratic 'surplus' was initially in abundance and was frittered away due to poor governance only later, India's economics collapsed early into the disaster range. It is only after the reforms began in earnest in 1991 that India's growth rate emerged from the doldrums and the accelerated growth rate began to make a serious dent on poverty and on the fortunes of the marginalized groups.

This 'crossover' of the politics and the economics of India's post-independence history defines the backdrop against which we now proceed to analyse India's performance on the tasks set before it by Prime Minister Jawaharlal Nehru on the fateful dawn of 15 August 1947.

But while we leave the problems of politics aside,[4] concentrating on the appropriateness of Indian economic reforms (since 1991) and the challenges that face us as we take these reforms forward, we should not forget that the sorry state of current politics in India and the crisis of governance is not unrelated to the counterproductive economic policy framework that India had embraced prior to the 1991 reforms.

Institutions are not exogenous to policies, as many seem to believe; they change as a result of incentives that the policies provide. As we will often observe later, the licence-permit raj that undermined our economy was also the major cause of the degeneration of Indian politics. Thus, politicians discovered that they could make money by diverting remunerative licences to applicants offering cash, while senior bureaucrats enjoyed the power and patronage that licensing gave them. The economic policies clearly undermined the efficacy of India's political institutions that defined a 'liberal' democracy, taking them from an exceptional high to a commonplace low.

The conjunction of the politics of democracy and the economics of poverty reduction in Nehru's famous 'Tryst with Destiny' speech, therefore, is apt. It also provides us with the opening theme of our economic analysis: the role of Nehru's socialism in defining the politics and the economics of India after independence. It additionally provides us with an entry into a comprehensive analysis of several myths that have developed around both Nehru's ideas and policies, and around related critiques of our earliest approaches

---

4. We have written extensively on the subject elsewhere. See, in particular, Bhagwati (2011), Panagariya (2011e, 2011g) and Gupta and Panagariya (2011a, 2011b and 2012).

(or alleged lack thereof) to reducing poverty and improving health care and education of the poor and the underprivileged.

Debunking these myths—and clearing the debris of ex cathedra critiques of India's reforms—in the chapters that follow will then lay the groundwork for our analysis of the ways in which the reforms can now be broadened and deepened.

Part I

DEBUNKING THE MYTHS

1

The Myths Originating in the Ascendancy and Decline of Socialism

If we squander our resources in merely acquiring for the state existing industries (that we have acquired them may be for the nation's good), for the moment we may have no other resources left, and we would have spoiled the field for private enterprise too. So, it is far better for the state to concentrate on certain specific, vital, new industries than go about nationalizing many of the old ones, though, as I said, in the case of some specific vital industry of national importance, that might be done.

—Jawaharlal Nehru in a speech to the Constituent Assembly (Legislative), New Delhi, 17 February 1948.

I am saddened, though not surprised, to find that several critics of the NIP (New Industrial Policy) have denounced this as anti-Nehruvian, which only shows how little they knew of the dynamic mind of Pandit Nehru, who, faced with the havoc in the economy, would have been the first among the first to salute the NIP.

—J.R.D. Tata in 'Berlin Walls Should Fall,' *The Times of India*, 1 August 1991.

Socialism, which was part of the rhetoric under Prime Minister Jawaharlal Nehru (who could be described accurately as having been schooled in Fabian Socialism) did not fully dominate and constrain the actual policy framework that was adopted under his leadership.[1] Indeed, one of us (Bhagwati), who had been educated at Cambridge and was influenced by Joan Robinson, his tutor, went so far as to condemn the policy framework as deficient on socialism upon his return to India in 1961. While working on the economics of poverty at the Indian Planning Commission at the time, he went on to characterize the 'socialistic pattern of society', which the Parliament had adopted as the guiding principle of social and economic policy in December 1954, as mere 'socialist patter'.[2]

Socialism came to occupy a far more prominent place in the Indian policy framework only under Prime Minister Indira Gandhi, Nehru's daughter.[3] Whereas, for instance, Nehru had not embraced nationalization of existing private sector enterprises (including foreign multinationals) and instead had adopted a 'gradualist' policy of increasing the relative size of the public sector by planning a steady increase in the share of investment in it with presumably each Five-Year Plan, Indira Gandhi chose the more radical and rapid path of nationalization on the one hand and ever-tightening regulation of the private sector on the other.

Beginning with the dramatic decision to nationalize the fourteen largest banks in 1969, Indira Gandhi went on to nationalize general insurance, oil companies and coal mines in the following four years. Alongside, she went after the large private firms, both

---

1. We provide some historical details corroborating this proposition in Appendix 1.
2. See Bhagwati and Desai (1975).
3. 'Socialism' under Jawaharlal Nehru is set out in greater depth in Appendix 1 while 'socialism' under Indira Gandhi is discussed immediately below in the text. The former was like a medium Merlot while the latter was a full-bodied Cabernet Sauvignon.

domestic and foreign, with the stated objective of combating the concentration of wealth and economic power. Among the measures she took were forced dilution of foreign equity in virtually all firms to 40 per cent or less; confinement of investments by large domestic and foreign firms to nineteen narrowly defined highly capital-intensive industries; reservation of a large number of labour-intensive products for exclusive production by small-scale enterprises; strict limits on the size of urban land-holdings; and prohibitive restrictions on the layoff of workers in large firms. To further enhance government control, she extended government monopoly over the imports and exports of several new products. She also attempted a government takeover of wholesale trade in food grains but had to retreat midway once it became clear that this was beyond the government's capacity.

But this comprehensive turn to socialism was not to last. The economy took a nosedive with per capita incomes rising just 0.3 per cent per annum during 1965-75 and private final consumption rising even more slowly. By the mid-1970s, evidence that the rapidly expanding government controls had closed nearly all avenues to growth was visible and at least some within the government began to recognize the need for unwinding the system. A process of ad hoc and piecemeal liberalization strictly within the existing policy framework therefore soon got under way.

This process continued haltingly in the 1980s, with some acceleration under Prime Minister Rajiv Gandhi, especially in fiscal years 1985-86 (1 April 1985 to 31 March 1986) and 1986-87. The liberalization, complemented by large fiscal deficits, led to some acceleration in growth in the 1980s. But since the deficits had been financed through substantial external borrowing and the export earnings necessary to finance the resulting debt service payments were small due to inward-looking policies, the economy wound up facing a balance-of-payments crisis in 1991. That crisis provided the occasion for turning the ad hoc reforms into a more systematic and systemic process.

This happened to the chagrin of the intellectuals on the left. Indeed, during the first half of the 1970s, when Indira Gandhi was implementing her socialist agenda, these intellectuals had sought to justify her policy changes by propagating many critiques, indeed myths, about the development strategy that India had adopted at the time of independence. Principally, they had argued that India had pursued growth for its own sake; and that growth had failed to result in poverty alleviation. They had also insisted that redistribution offered the only effective avenue to poverty alleviation. These, and related critiques, would now be revived as weapons with which to undermine the reforms that were clearly a massive shift away from socialism.

These critics had little option but to retreat from reality into fantasy if they were to carry any conviction. For, by 1980, the wave, in fact a tsunami, of socialist measures had virtually drowned out the prospects for rapid growth of the economy. In turn, the long-standing commitment by Indian leaders to the objective of eradicating poverty had also been frustrated because (as we argue below) the lack of growth meant that a stagnant economy was failing to make a dent on poverty. It was abundantly clear to those who did not wear ideological blinders that the socialist path Indira Gandhi had chosen had failed to deliver on the promise forcefully conveyed in her memorable slogan 'Garibi Hatao' (End Poverty).

The shift to the 'liberal' (or 'neoliberal', which sounds more sinister) reforms meant that the myths that had fed the turn to socialism by Indira Gandhi now had to be revived to deride the shift away from the failed socialism that the reforms implied. The psychological need to do this, gathering steam since 1991, was all the greater precisely because the reforms were so successful, not merely in accelerating India's growth rate but also in finally reducing poverty.

These myths define a rich tapestry relating to growth, poverty and social goals. Among the litany of complaints, one can find passionate assertions that the reforms address growth but not poverty and social goals; that the growth they may generate is in any event not 'inclusive'; that the reforms have increased inequality; that they have increased corruption; that they even hurt the socially disadvantaged Scheduled Caste (SC) and Scheduled Tribe (ST) groups; and indeed much else that makes one wonder if the critics have let their ideology and political preferences entirely cloud their judgement.

Since these myths, endlessly repeated, muddy the discourse on the post-1991 reforms, and often are the weapons used to wound and maim the reforms in the public eye, it is important to sort them out, and refute them systematically with logic and facts. This is the task to which we turn in the following five chapters under various headings.

2

Development Strategy in Historical Perspective

Prime Minister Indira Gandhi came to power in 1966 with no real socialist convictions. At the time, a right-of-centre coterie of Congress leaders, known as the Syndicate, controlled the organizational wing of the party and it handpicked her for the country's top post following the sudden death of Prime Minister Lal Bahadur Shastri, the immediate successor to Nehru. The choice of the Syndicate had been based on two considerations. It saw Indira Gandhi's connection to Nehru as a major asset in the elections that were due in 1967; and the fact that she had no political base of her own offered the Syndicate the prospect of ruling the country by proxy.

But Indira Gandhi proved herself to be a determined, ambitious and skilful politician. She made common cause with the only substantial force within the Congress willing to openly challenge the Syndicate: the left wing of the party, loosely organized under the Congress Forum for Socialist Action, which included several firebrand young socialists known as 'Young Turks' at the time.

Within three years of becoming the prime minister, she successfully unseated the Syndicate, split the Congress party and firmly established control over the faction that stayed with her. But while doing so, she also made the socialist agenda of her socialist allies her own.

Known as the Ten-Point Programme, this agenda included the social control of banks, nationalization of insurance, nationalization of foreign trade, limits on urban incomes and property, tightening of controls on large firms, and an end to the privileges and privy purses of the former rulers of princely states. As Indira Gandhi proceeded to implement the agenda, many intellectuals on the left sought justification for it through the propagation of a number of myths about the nature of of the development strategy India had pursued during the preceding two decades. The exposure of five sets of these myths forms the subject matter of this chapter.

Myth 2.1: Indian planners pursued growth as an end in itself, ignoring poverty reduction (and other 'social' objectives).

As Indira Gandhi embarked upon her socialist agenda, many analysts came to argue that the development programmes initiated immediately after independence—the First Five-Year Plan spanned 1951-52 to 1955-56—had pursued growth for its own sake and had ignored poverty alleviation. This assertion would, of course, be revived later in the wake of the assault on socialism by the post-1991 reforms, with the critics arguing that the reforms were about growth per se and neglected the 'true' objectives of poverty reduction and other social goals, including the elimination of hunger and starvation and adequate provision of health and education.

The myth eventually found its way into the first Human Development Report published by the United Nations

Development Programme (UNDP 1990). Thus, in its technical note (p. 104), the report noted, 'While the pioneers of measurement of national output and income stressed the importance of social concerns, economic growth became the main focus after the Second World War . . . the growth rate of per capita GDP became the sole measure of development.' It added, 'As GNP became the goal of development in the 1950s and 1960s, the question of promoting individual well-being receded.'

But this narrative is wide off the mark, at least in the Indian context. The notion that during the 1950s and 1960s GNP became the 'sole measure of development' to the neglect of poverty and related 'social' objectives can only be made by ignorant critics. For growth was seen from the earliest times, even before independence, essentially as a strategy to achieve 'social' objectives, especially poverty reduction. And there is simply no evidence for the assertion that the Indian planners shifted away from these objectives during the 1950s and 1960s. In fact, there is plenty of evidence to the contrary from numerous 'evaluation' reports on these objectives, and from extended attention to these objectives in the texts of the First, Second and Third Five-Year Plans.

The immediate post-independence leadership in India had thought of, and indeed written about, growth as the *instrument,* with poverty alleviation as the *objective*. As early as 1938, the Indian National Congress had taken the initiative to appoint a fifteen-member National Planning Committee under Nehru's chairmanship to evolve the development strategy once independence was achieved. All of the members came from diverse disciplines and were important thinkers in their respective areas. They included three economists as well.[1]

In his monumental work, *The Discovery of India* (1946), Nehru offers the following fascinating account of the thinking behind the

1. For further details, see Chakrabarty (1992).

committee's decision in favour of a growth-centred strategy: 'Obviously we could not consider any problem, much less plan, without some definite aim and social objective. That aim was to ensure an adequate standard of living for the masses, in other words, to get rid of the appalling poverty of the people . . . To . . . ensure an irreducible minimum standard for everybody the national income had to be greatly increased. . . . We calculated that a really progressive standard of living would necessitate the increase of the national wealth by 500 or 600 per cent. That was, however, too big a jump for us, and we aimed at a 200 to 300 per cent increase within ten years.'[2]

The ideas developed by the planning committee eventually influenced the design of India's development plans. Growth remained the central (though not exclusive, since redistribution was regarded as a subsidiary) element in the strategy, with poverty alleviation and equity prominently figuring as the true goals.[3] For example, the First Five-Year Plan, spanning 1951-52 to 1955-56, stated at the outset: 'The urge for economic and social change under present conditions comes from the fact of poverty and of inequalities in income, wealth and opportunity. The elimination of poverty cannot, obviously, be achieved merely by redistributing existing wealth. Nor can a programme aiming only at raising production remove existing inequalities. The two have to be considered together; only a simultaneous advance along both these

2. Nehru (1946), pp. 437-38.
3. We say more on redistribution below. Our quote from the First Five-Year Plan, however, has it right. Redistribution was not regarded as a strategy that could take us far, given the extent of the poverty. The principal strategy had to be 'growing the pie'. Also, among the social objectives was not just poverty reduction, which was central, but other goals such as prevention of concentration of economic power which, in the wrong-headed way in which it was pursued, wound up detracting gratuitously from the poverty-reduction objective.

lines can create the conditions in which the community can put forth its best efforts for promoting development.'

Lest the reader doubt this, it is enough to read the Plan documents themselves on health, education and other social objectives: these are not cursory side remarks but get full-length treatment. There are also the programme evaluation reports, which address the progress and the shortfalls in reaching targets in these areas. We might add that the membership of the Planning Commission was quite a prestigious affair at the time; its members included Shrimati Durgabai Deshmukh, who was a child widow and an articulate and effective advocate for women's issues. There was also a health portfolio in the cabinet, and the incumbent was another remarkable woman, Rajkumari Amrit Kaur.

The evidence, therefore, lends no support to the claims that India pursued growth for its own sake, ignoring poverty reduction and related social objectives such as improved health and greater spread of education in the immediate post-independence era. Our discussion below will provide further details on health and education.

Nor did the objective shift from poverty alleviation to 'growth for its own sake' with the launch of the liberalizing reforms in 1991. If such a shift had taken place, the most likely document to carry the corroborating evidence would have to be the 2004 BJP election manifesto. After all, it is the BJP which has been blamed most vociferously for pursuing the 'India Shining' agenda to the neglect of the poor. A quick search through the Vision Document that the BJP issued in 2004 shows, however, that not only was BJP not guilty of this error but, like the early Five-Year Plans, it drew an explicit connection between growth as the instrument and poverty alleviation as the objective. Thus, when it comes to stating the key economic objective of the party, the document describes it thus: 'Further broadening and deepening of economic reforms, based on a self-reliant approach, for sustained double-digit GDP growth rate to achieve complete eradication of poverty and unemployment' and also to end 'regional and social disparities; and bridge the urban-rural divide'.[4]

Myth 2.2: Health and education were only recently thought of as objectives.

With the recent drives for the recognition of education and health as fundamental rights, culminating in the passage of the Right to Education Act of 2009 and proposals for a similar Act on health, it has been asserted by their proponents that even if the early leaders saw poverty eradication as a key goal of policy, they failed to recognize the importance of education, health and other similar determinants of human welfare. After all, like growth, even the eradication of poverty is fundamentally an *instrument* for providing a richer existence, of which education and health are important integral parts to the citizenry.

We have already indicated earlier that health and education of the poor, and indeed of all, were certainly among the objectives that the earliest Indian planners had embraced forcefully. But the assertion of neglect of these objectives is so insidious that fuller documentation of its absurdity needs to be provided.

Thus, the 1938 Planning Committee, to which we have already alluded above, explicitly considered virtually every economic aspect of human existence that determines welfare. The relevant part of the account that Nehru (1946) provides of these deliberations is once again worthy of reproduction. After explaining why a

4. Visit http://www.indian-elections.com/partymanifestoes/party-manifestoes04/bjp.html (accessed on 11 September 2011) for the BJP *Vision Document* from which this quotation is reproduced.

significant rise in the national income was essential to combating poverty, he goes on to state,

> We fixed a ten-year period for the plan, with control figures for different periods and different sectors of economic life.
>
> Certain objective tests were also suggested:
>
> (1) The improvement of nutrition—a balanced diet having calorific value of 2,400 to 2,800 units for an adult worker.
> (2) Improvement in clothing from the then consumption of about fifteen yards to at least thirty yards per capita per annum.
> (3) Housing standards to reach at least 100 square feet per capita.
>
> Further, certain indices of progress had to be kept in mind:
>
> (i) Increase in agricultural production (ii) Increase in industrial production (iii) Diminution of unemployment (iv) Increase in per capita income (v) Liquidation of illiteracy (vi) Increase in public utility services (vii) Provision of medical aid on the basis of one unit for 1,000 population (viii) Increase in the average expectation of life.

Clearly, the concerns of the committee went well beyond eradication of poverty by some monetary metric and explicitly included education, health, shelter and clothing. As in the case of growth and poverty, these concerns were subsequently incorporated into the Five-Year Plans. A detailed consideration of the contents of the First Five-Year Plan in health and education will demonstrate the depth and breadth of the planners' concerns.

After emphasizing the need for both growth and redistribution to eradicate poverty, Chapter 1 of the Plan document states that the objective of the policy is to remodel the socioeconomic framework to accommodate the impulses that express themselves 'in the demands for the right to work, the right to adequate income, the right to education and to a measure of insurance against old age, sickness and other disabilities'. Chapter 2 reiterates the importance of social objectives, stating, 'We have not only to build up a big productive machine—though this is no doubt a necessary condition of development—we have at the same time to improve health, sanitation and education and create social conditions for vigorous cultural advance.'

The Plan devotes Chapter 32 to health and Chapter 33 to education. These chapters are remarkable for the thoroughness of their coverage of the relevant policy issues and documentation of the existing conditions in the sectors. Chapter 32 begins by recognizing that 'health is fundamental to national progress' and that 'for the efficiency of industry and of agriculture, the health of the worker is an essential consideration'. It adds: 'Health is a positive state of well-being in which the harmonious development of physical and mental capacities of the individual lead to the enjoyment of a rich and full life.'

Citing data, the chapter explicitly discusses life expectancy, infant mortality, child mortality, maternal mortality and cause-specific mortality. It then addresses in careful detail the issues of medical personnel and physical facilities and identifies as policy priorities the provision of water supply and sanitation, control of malaria, preventive health care of the rural population through health units and mobile units, health services for mothers and children, health education, self-sufficiency in drugs and equipment and family planning and population control.

The chapter sets explicit targets for hospitals, rural and urban dispensaries and medical personnel and the number of beds in each of them by the end of the Plan period. It also contains a long section on nutrition, identifying the needs of cereals, pulses, fruits, vegetables, milk, sugar, eggs and meat for 300 million adult Indians. Finally, it discusses a number of specific diseases, including malaria, tuberculosis, venereal diseases, leprosy and even cancer, a disease barely known at the time.

Chapter 33 exhibits similar depth and breadth on education. It begins by noting that the existing enrolments at 40 per cent for children aged six to eleven, 10 per cent for persons aged eleven to seventeen and 0.9 per cent of those aged seventeen to twenty-three are highly inadequate. It goes on to note that the directive principles of the Constitution require that 'free and compulsory education should be provided for all children up to the age of fourteen within ten years of the commencement of the Constitution'. Thus, the concern for universal free education up to age fourteen, embodied in the Right to Education Act of 2009, has had a very long history.

The chapter proceeds to discuss the structure of the educational system at various levels and its internal consistency. It points out that the provision at the university level is larger than what the secondary and primary levels can profitably support. It finds the allocation of 34.2 per cent of the total educational expenditures to primary education in 1949-50 to be exceptionally low. It recommends shifting in favour of primary and secondary education and away from higher education. After a careful analysis, the Plan sets explicit goals for the expansion of primary and secondary enrolments to 60 and 15 per cent, respectively, by 1955-56. The Plan explicitly notes that no targets have been set for the university education because the problem here is mostly one of consolidation rather than expansion.

The subsequent Plans continued in a similar vein. In addition, a number of committees recommended key changes. For example, the recommendations of the Health Survey and Planning Committee (Mudaliar Committee 1961) led to the establishment and expansion of primary health care centres (PHCs) and sub-centres in the rural areas in the early 1960s. Likewise, the Kartar Singh Committee Report on Multipurpose Workers (1974) and the Srivastava Committee Report on Medical Education and Support Manpower (1975) provided recommendations on the distribution of the health cadres at the primary level. The build-up of rural health infrastructure got particular impetus during the Fifth Five-Year Plan (1974-75 to 1978-79) under its Minimum Needs Programme.[5]

In education, the goal of universal free education for children between six and fourteen years of age by 1960 was missed by a wide margin. Indeed, two national policy statements in 1968 and 1986 (revised in 1992) and the passage of another four decades still left India some distance away from the goal. In 2001, the country launched the Sarva Shiksha Abhiyan or the National Movement for Universal (Elementary) Education. The country even went on to adopt the 86th constitutional amendment, elevating the right to education from a directive principle of state policy to a fundamental right in 2002. Yet, the implementing legislation, the Right to Education Act, was not passed until 2009.

This brief review of very broad developments in health and education shows that the slow progress in health and education did not result from either a lack of awareness of the importance of these areas or the absence of good intentions. Instead, as we will argue more fully below, this outcome was ultimately the result of slow growth. With limited national income (due to very slow growth resulting from a counterproductive policy framework), the government could muster only limited revenues.[6]

Thus, in education, the government had amended the Constitution to make elementary education a fundamental right in 2002 and had prepared a first draft of implementing legislation as early as 2003. In 2005, the Central Advisory Board of Education Committee submitted the Right to Education Bill to the ministry of human resource development. But the Finance Committee and the Planning Commission rejected it, citing lack of funds. It took

5. See Nundy (2005) for further details.
6. Whether the revenues would have resulted in intended outcomes is a question that remains pertinent today.

another four years of negotiations among various constituencies to modify the bill in such a way that it could be financed.[7]

Similarly, following the recommendations of the report entitled 'Health for All: An Alternative Strategy,' jointly sponsored by the Indian Council of Medical Research and Indian Council of Social Science Research, the 1983 National Health Policy adopted the provision of universal, comprehensive primary health services as its goal. But it quickly became clear that financial resources for it were lacking.[8] The subsequent National Health Policy 2002 and the National Rural Health Mission 2005 stayed away from the goal of the provision of universal health care. The issue has forcefully returned lately. A right-to-health legislation is being actively discussed but financial resources, even with more revenues now available (thanks to acceleration of growth subsequent to the post-1991 reforms), remain a hurdle.[9]

Myth 2.3: Growth is not necessary for poverty alleviation; redistribution alone suffices.

Critics of a growth-centred poverty-reduction strategy assert that India need not have waited for growth to happen. It could have, instead, attacked poverty through redistribution from the rich to the poor. Now this proposition may have some salience in the

7. See Balachandran (2010) for details.
8. See Government of India (2005), p. 48.
9. We do not mean to imply that resources are a sufficient condition of improvement of health. They are, however, a necessary condition. How best to use the resources to get a good, if not the best, bang for the buck, is an extremely important issue today. We return to this issue in depth in Part III.

industrial countries, which have had the benefit of growth for more than a century. The high levels of income made possible by prior growth allow these countries to generate enough revenues to sustain large-scale anti-poverty programmes even if the economy were to fall into long-term stagnation.[10]

But the story is quite different for a country like India, which started with its overwhelming population in poverty at the time of independence. The option to eradicate (as against making a minuscule impact on) poverty through redistribution, even if politically feasible, was not available.

As the eminent Polish communist economist Mikhail Kalecki put it in 1962 when he was visiting the Indian Statistical Institute,[11] the trouble with India was that 'there were too many exploited and too few exploiters'. That is to say, there were too few from whom the government could take and too many to whom it needed to give. Furthermore, the government needed to attack poverty on a sustained basis rather than approach it as a one-shot affair. With a rising population and stagnant growth, any favourable effects of redistribution on poverty would have quickly eroded.

When the founding fathers of the country opted for a growth-centred strategy, they did so in the full knowledge that India's poverty problem was too immense to be solved by redistribution

---

10. Currently, of course, the crisis and the associated Great Recession, with the need to reduce huge debt overhang, has created a crying need for growth even in the developed countries so as to avoid having to cut spending on anti-poverty and other programmes.
11. Kalecki made the remark to Bhagwati, who was at the time a professor of economics at the Indian Statistical Institute, Delhi, and was on loan to the Planning Commission, where he worked with Pitambar Pant, the chief of the perspective planning division, on ways to bring the bottom 30 per cent of India's households up to a 'minimum standard of living'. Bhagwati was the first professional economist in the unit, with the eminent economists T.N. Srinivasan and B.S. Minhas joining him later.

alone. We just recalled Jawaharlal Nehru's statement in *The Discovery of India*, where he argued that the immense poverty of many Indians meant that 'to remove this lack and ensure an irreducible minimum standard for everybody, the national income had to be greatly increased.'

The issue of whether poverty could be overcome without growth figured again in the First Five-Year Plan, to be re-asserted in the Second Five-Year Plan, with the planners opting to endorse the critical role to be assigned to growth in the assault on poverty.[12] In the early 1960s, when poverty and income distribution became the subject of heated debates in the Parliament and Prime Minister Nehru became concerned with the question 'where the growing incomes were going', the Perspective Planning Division (PPD) of the Planning Commission took another careful look at the policy options. Among other things, the fifteen-year plan it produced offered a coherent and clear-headed analysis of why growth was necessary. It began by noting that the income and consumption distribution data showed that approximately 50 per cent of the population lived in abject poverty on Rs 20 or less per month at 1960-61 prices. It then proceeded to argue the necessity of growth in these words (Pant 1962, pp. 13-14):

> The minimum which can be guaranteed is limited by the size of the total product and the extent of redistribution which is feasible. If, at the current level of output, incomes could be redistributed equally among all the people, the condition of the poorest segments would no doubt improve materially but the average standard would still be pitifully low. Redistribution on this scale, however,

12. The underlying growth models used in the two Plans were, however, different. The First Five-Year Plan essentially worked with the 'flow' Harrod-Domar model, whereas the Second Five-Year Plan reflected the 'structural', 'putty-clay' model associated with the Soviet economist Feldman and the Indian statistician Professor Mahalanobis.

> is operationally meaningless unless revolutionary changes in property rights and scale and structure of wages and compensations are contemplated. Moreover, when even the topmost 30 per cent of the households have an average per capita expenditure of only Rs 62 per month, it is inconceivable that any large redistribution of income from the higher income groups to the other can be effected. To raise the standard of living of the vast masses of the people, output therefore would have to be increased very considerably.

Moreover, Pitambar Pant's document had a novel argument about the need to grow the pie rather than share it in a more fulsome way. Based on Bhagwati's work in Pant's division, the document went on to examine the income distribution data available at the time for several countries and argued that the distribution of incomes in countries at very different levels of income followed a remarkably similar pattern.[13] In particular, the proportion of incomes earned by the lowest three or four deciles of the population appeared to be stable across countries. Therefore, it followed that a strategy of redistribution, or changed political orientation, did not offer a panacea and that 'growing the pie' seemed to be the only effective way to bring the groups at the bottom of the distribution up to 'minimum' standards of living.

Since there were groups such as tribals that were outside the mainstream economy, the document recommended a strategy of poverty reduction that relied on growth for the population that was

---

13. Bhagwati produced two substantial papers, one on income distribution estimates for India, and one on the cross-country income distributions, when he worked for Pitambar Pant. The argument in the text was in the latter paper. Produced in the early 1960s before the advent of photocopy machines and computers, these two 'cyclostyled' papers were not preserved by Bhagwati due to a lack of storage space since he lived in different temporary locations. But they may still be gathering dust on the shelves in the Planning Commission or in the Indian Statistical Institute in Calcutta.

or could be potentially integrated into the mainstream of the economy, and on redistribution for those outside the mainstream. Using a formal model, it calculated that a 7 per cent growth, combined with redistribution to those outside the mainstream, could potentially eliminate abject poverty, measured by Rs 20 per capita per month income at 1960-61 prices, in fifteen years.

On the other hand, the argument that poverty could be overcome without growth acquired some salience among Indian intellectuals following its advocacy by Mahbub ul Haq, a Pakistani economist. In an article published in 1972 titled 'Let us stand economic theory on its head: joining the GNP rat race won't wipe out poverty,' Haq argued that whereas China had eradicated through redistribution the worst forms of poverty, illiteracy and malnutrition with only modest rates of growth, other countries, including India, which had focused on growth, had missed the boat.[14]

We now know that the premise on which Haq based his argument was false. On one hand, China had struggled to achieve speedy growth by extracting surplus from agriculture for investment in urban industry and, in the process, allowed millions of people to lose their lives. On the other hand, China was quite far from

---

14. Specifically, Haq (1972) wrote (as quoted in Sau, 1972, p. 1572), 'It appears that within a period of less than two decades, China has eradicated the worst forms of poverty; it has full employment, universal literacy and adequate health facilities; it suffers from no obvious malnutrition or squalor. What's more, it was my impression that China has achieved this at fairly modest rates of growth.' We might add also that the notion that 'economic theory' dictated that 'the GNP rat race (would) wipe out poverty' invites the comment that Haq obviously did not know economic theory. There are many theoretical models—especially the one on 'Immiserizing growth,' which one of us (Bhagwati, 1958) is known for, where growth actually immiserizes the country. This model has been used to argue that immiseration of the poor can also follow as a matter of theory from growth. We may also ask what Haq meant by the 'GNP rat race'; who were the rats he had in mind?

eradicating the worst forms of poverty, illiteracy and malnutrition as late as 1971.[15]

In India itself, despite the justified scepticism about redistribution as the route to take to assault poverty on a sustainable basis, modest redistribution did take place through expenditures on health and education. For instance, as the fifteen-year plan by Pitambar Pant noted, the 40 per cent increase in income between 1950-51 and 1960-61 had allowed improvements in the social sphere such as an 85 per cent increase in school enrolment and a 65 per cent increase in hospital beds. But this was hardly a drop in the ocean of poverty.

The situation did not much improve almost until the late 1970s. This is demonstrated by Figure 2.1, which shows countrywide per capita private final consumption expenditure (PFCE) per month from 1960-61 to 1979-80 at 1999-00 prices.[16] We can then see that the private final consumption expenditure rose from 564 rupees per capita per month in 1960-61 to just 597 rupees in 1976-77. This represented a mere 2 per cent increase in sixteen years! The scope for redistribution had scarcely risen beyond what was feasible in 1960-61.

15. Later, some anti-growth-strategy economists in India would shift to Kerala as their icon of development. And when 'Kerala Shining' became hard to argue plausibly, this group shifted to citing Bangladesh. On this issue, we will draw below on the claims to that effect by Amartya Sen (2011) recently and refutations thereof by Panagariya (2011a, 2011b).

16. The PFCE is estimated at 1999-2000 prices from the National Account Statistics (NAS). It consists of gross national product net of gross capital formation and current government spending. The average expenditures estimated by the National Sample Surveys are generally below the NAS expenditures.

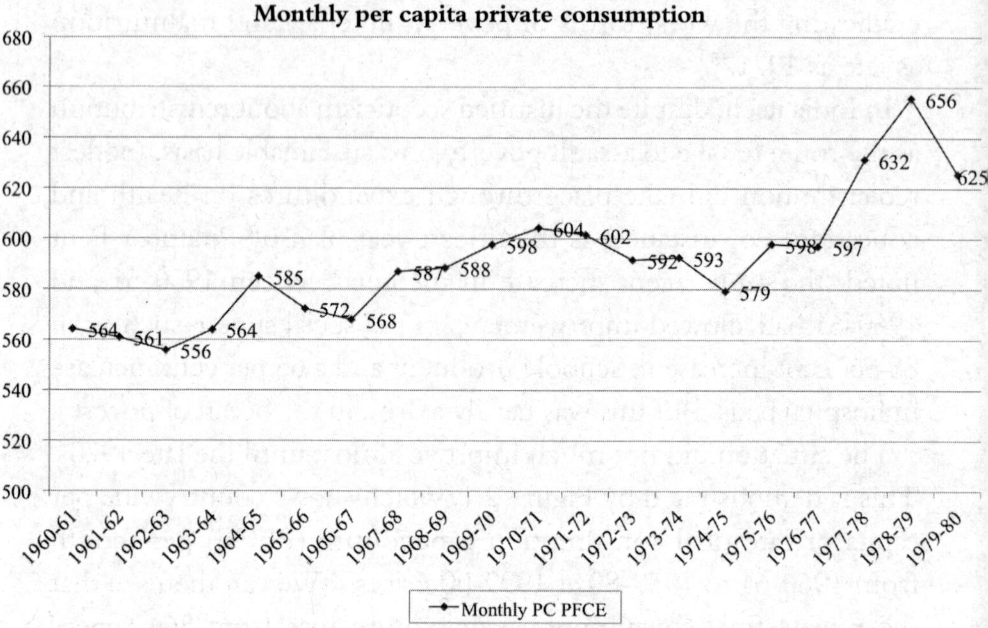

FIGURE 2.1: MONTHLY PER CAPITA PRIVATE CONSUMPTION EXPENDITURE, 1960-80

Source: Authors' construction based on data in the Handbook of Statistics on Indian Economy, *2010, Table 2.*

Myth 2.4: Since poverty did not fall through the 1970s, the growth strategy that had been adopted was in any event inappropriate for reducing poverty.

This myth is derived from the twin observations that India opted for a growth-centred strategy when planning began in the early 1950s and that no reduction in poverty took place until after 1980. While both these observations are correct, the inference from them is false.

The problem was that, thanks to our counterproductive policy framework, which the post-1991 breakthrough on major reforms effectively and progressively shattered, growth had not materialized. So, there was no way to test the proposition that growth would reduce poverty. But once growth began to accelerate through the 1980s and the decades thereafter, we could finally test the proposition that growth would dent poverty and hence would be 'inclusive'.

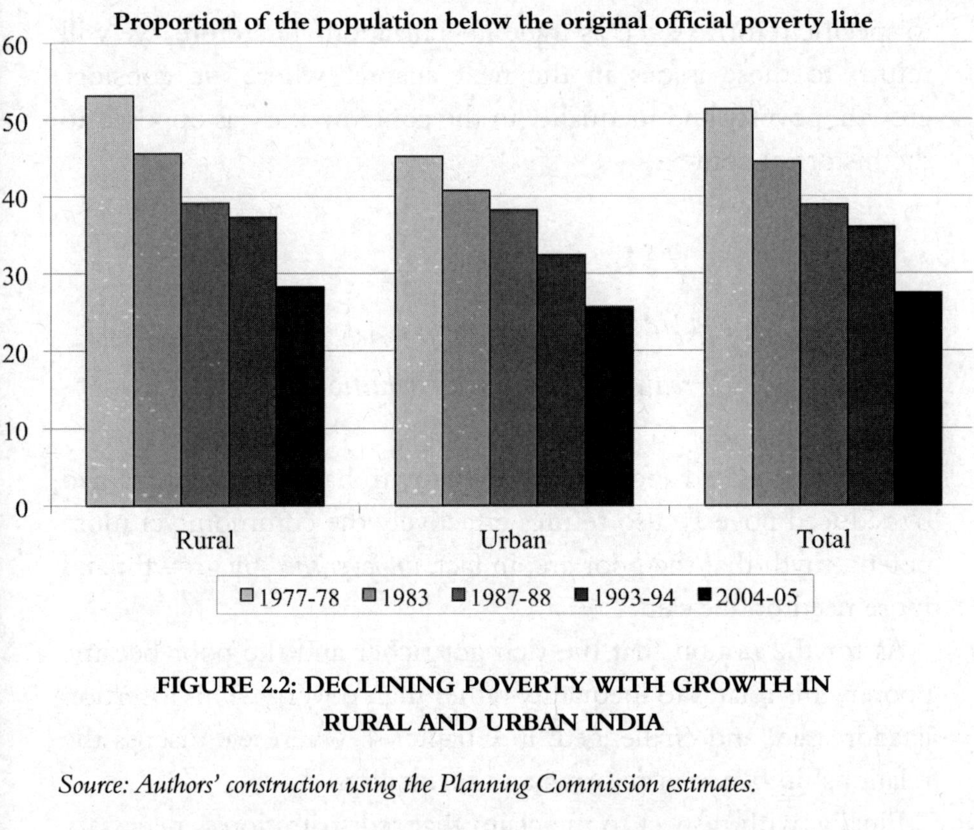

FIGURE 2.2: DECLINING POVERTY WITH GROWTH IN RURAL AND URBAN INDIA

Source: Authors' construction using the Planning Commission estimates.

It can now be asserted with empirical evidence that once growth picked up, poverty indeed declined. At the aggregate level, monthly per capita private final consumption expenditure at 1999-00 prices rose from 632 rupees in 1977-78 to 711 rupees in 1983-84, 840 rupees in 1993-94 and 1201 rupees in 2004-05. In parallel, the proportion of the nationwide population living below the poverty line fell from 51.3 per cent in 1977-78 to 44.5 per cent in 1983, 36 per cent in 1993-94 and 27.5 per cent in 2004-05.[17] As Figure 2.2 further demonstrates, a steady decline in poverty accompanied growth in both rural and urban areas.

Some critics are, of course, not satisfied with this evidence and continue to claim that poverty has failed to come down in the post-reform era. Others accept the decline but question its connection to specific reforms such as trade liberalization. Therefore, we will return to these issues in the next chapter where we consider growth, poverty and inequality in the contemporary as opposed to the historical context.

Myth 2.5: By itself, growth makes 'the rich richer and the poor poorer'. To reduce poverty, redistribution is necessary.

The evidence cited above as to how growth has been accompanied by reduced poverty also refutes effectively the common, yet more potent, myth that the poor are, in fact, *impoverished* by growth; and more need not be said.

As for the notion that the rich got richer and the poor became poorer, this relates to inequality rather than poverty. This assertion is addressed, and challenged, in Chapter 4, where we discuss the relationship between reforms and inequality.

Finally, with respect to the claim that redistribution is necessary to reduce poverty, we remind the reader that the Pakistani economist Mahbub ul Haq was the most prominent writer in the early 1970s to condemn the growth-centred strategy and celebrate the alternative

17. These poverty ratios are based on the original poverty lines and represent the official Planning Commission estimates.

policy of redistribution instead.[18] With India turning to socialism under Indira Gandhi, Haq found a constituency of left-wing journalists, academics and policymakers in the country eager to embrace him. A cottage industry under the self-congratulatory rubric of 'New Economics', whose basic premise was that growth by itself was not going to lead to any reduction in poverty, soon grew.[19]

Even Prime Minister Indira Gandhi seemed to give the premise a nod when she stated in her famous 25 March 1972 speech to the Federation of Indian Chambers of Commerce and Industry: 'Growthmanship which results in undivided attention to the maximization of GNP can be dangerous, for the results are almost always social and political unrest. Therefore, increase in the GNP must be considered only as one component of a multi-dimensional transformation of society.'[20] That this multiplicity of instruments (and a broad range of social objectives around the main theme of poverty reduction) was indeed what the Indian planners had long embraced (see our discussion of Myths 2.1 and 2.2 in particular) was lost in the novelty of her claims and the erroneous condemnation of what was the true situation earlier.

18. Maybe he was thinking of his native Pakistan where the army, as we know now, was siphoning off the gains from aid and growth to itself. But then one cannot help wondering why he went back from the US to join the cabinet under Zia's military dictatorship. It should be added in fairness to Haq that the world divides into those, like Solzhenitsyn, who confront dictatorships and those, like Tvardovsky, who work for reforms from within. The latter edited *Novy Mir* and in fact managed to publish Solzhenitsyn's *One Day in the Life of Ivan Denisovich* in *Novy Mir* in November 1962. A fascinating account of Solzhenitsyn's subsequent assault on Tvardovsky on this issue and a spirited defence of Tvardovsky appears in Vladimir Laksin, *Solzhenitsyn, Tvardovsaky and Novy Mir*, MIT Press: Cambridge, USA, October 1980.
19. See Sau (1972) and Ranadive (1973).
20. The quotation can be found in Ranadive (1973), p. 834.

True enough, as we have stressed, state-financed programmes to aid the poor can (when efficiently planned and run) help speed up poverty reduction in a growing economy that progressively enlarges the scope for such spending through increased revenues. Thus, remember that growth helps by drawing the poor into gainful employment; and it *additionally* helps by generating revenues that can be used to aid the poor through programmes targeted at the health and education of the poor.[21]

But we cannot emphasize enough that the view expressed by Indira Gandhi, that even without this revenue effect, if we had only growth by itself, it would do nothing for the poor (and would, in fact, be 'dangerous') finds little support in either conceptual analysis or empirical reality.

Conceptually, in an economy with widespread poverty, labour is cheap. Therefore, it has a comparative advantage in producing labour-intensive goods. Under pro-growth policies that include openness to trade (but are usually in tandem with other pro-growth policies), a growing economy will specialize in producing and exporting these goods and should create employment opportunities and (as growing demand for labour begins to cut into 'surplus' or 'underemployed' labour) also higher wages for the masses, with a concomitant decline in poverty.

Countries such as South Korea and Taiwan offer ample empirical evidence supporting precisely this argument. These countries managed to put in place the right mix of policies from the second half of the 1950s onwards and were able to achieve high rates of growth. In turn, they were able to pull workers from agriculture in the hinterland into labour-intensive manufacturing in ever-larger

---

21. This additional effect through easing of the revenue constraint was precisely what Bhagwati (1988) had pointed out almost a quarter of a century ago in the Vikram Sarabhai Lecture, in Ahmedabad, on 'Poverty and Public Policy'. Evidently, if the revenues are spent instead on other purposes, this additional effect on helping the poor will not follow.

volumes, resulting in steadily rising wages. The end result was a massive reduction of poverty. Rapid growth had 'pulled up' the poor into productive employment and out of poverty.[22]

In India, there has also been impact on poverty from the acceleration of growth. However, continuing regulations that have prevented this process from fully working its way has handicapped the linkage. In particular, as we document in Part II below, until at least 2000, the small-scale industries reservation, which required virtually all labour-intensive products to be produced in very small enterprises, kept India uncompetitive in these products in the world markets. But even after this regulation was considerably weakened by 2000, labour-intensive goods such as apparel, footwear, and light consumer goods failed to show rapid growth on account of continuing labour market inflexibilities.

The protection to labour in larger firms is extremely high in India and translates into excessively high effective labour costs. As an example, Chapter V.B of the Industrial Disputes Act of 1947 makes it nearly impossible for manufacturing firms with 100 or more employees to lay off workers under any circumstances. Such high protection makes large firms in labour-intensive sectors, in which labour accounts for 80 per cent or more of the costs, uncompetitive in the world markets. Small firms, on the other hand, are unable to export in large volumes.

Because of this limitation, growth in India has been driven by the capital- and skilled-labour-intensive sectors such as automobiles, two- and three-wheelers, engineering goods, petroleum refining, and software and telecommunications industries. In spite of this limitation, growth has successfully contributed to poverty alleviation

---

22. See the detailed evidence on South Korea in Panagariya (2008a, chapter 6) and on Taiwan in Panagariya (2011c). The same can be argued for China, whose phenomenal growth in the Guagdong province helped increase the demand for labour dramatically, raising wages and improving labour standards.

through an alternative mechanism. Rising incomes in the fast-growing sectors have led to expenditures that lead to gainful employment in the non-traded services sectors. Thus, for example, the proliferation of automobiles generates the demand for drivers and mechanics. As cell phones proliferate, retail outlets for their sales must expand. Rising demand for housing gives rise to employment opportunities in construction. Generally-rising expenditures also increase the demand for passenger travel; telecommunications, fax and courier services; tourism; restaurant food; beauty parlours; education; medical, nursing and veterinary services; and garbage collection. Employment in these non-traded services, thus, offers an alternative avenue to poverty reduction as growth accelerates.

Evidence linking poverty reduction to growth can also be gleaned from a comparison of per capita incomes and poverty rates across states in India. There is a strong negative correlation between per capita incomes of states and the poverty ratios. Making the plausible assumption that redistribution policies across states do not vary very much or that they are biased in favour of states with larger concentrations of poverty, this correlation would imply a positive relationship between per capita income and poverty reduction. In the same vein, given the fact that the truly substantial redistribution scheme—the Mahatma Gandhi National Rural Employment Guarantee Scheme (NREGS)—did not begin till 2006, it is difficult to imagine what factors other than the increases in per capita income could account for the significant reduction in poverty that has taken place between 1977-78 and 2004-05.[23]

23. Establishing causation that is beyond objection by econometricians on a relationship that does not lend itself to setting up a randomized experiment as is the case with most of the important issues of 'macro-level' economic policy is a very difficult task. But some suggestive evidence concerning causation between per capita income and poverty can be found in Cain,

(Contd.…)

Some critics, who acknowledge that growth has helped reduce poverty, ironically run down the reforms by arguing that poverty reduction associated with each percentage point of growth has been lower than that in other countries such as China. They fail to appreciate that it is not the reforms but the failure to extend them further to critical areas of inefficiency that accounts for the smaller effect of growth on poverty in India. As we have demonstrated, we have dragged our feet, for example, on critical labour market reforms that have handicapped, even crippled, the growth of labour-intensive manufacturing that is so critical to creating well-paid jobs for the poor.[24]

(...contd.)

Hasan and Mitra (2012) and Mukim and Panagariya (2012). We note as an aside that, while many 'micro-level' programmes on which many recent development economists like to concentrate do lend themselves to the randomized trials approach, the integral sum of their importance to development policy is far exceeded by that of big macro-level policy issues such as those relating to international trade.

24. Because this limitation of India's growth performance is extremely important, and since the reform of our labour laws still awaits political action, a fuller treatment of the issue is provided in Chapter 8.

3

Reforms and Their Impact on Growth and Poverty

This government is committed to removing the cobwebs that come in the way of rapid industrialization. We will work towards making India internationally competitive, taking full advantage of . . . opportunities offered by the evolving global economy . . . We also welcome foreign direct investment so as to accelerate the tempo of development, upgrade our technologies and to promote our exports. Obstacles that come in the way of allocating foreign investment on a sizable scale will be removed. A time-bound programme will be worked out to streamline our industrial policies and programmes to achieve the goal of a vibrant economy that rewards creativity, enterprise and innovativeness . . .

Our vision is to create employment, eradicate poverty and reduce inequality . . . (Mahatma) Gandhi said that it was his ambition to wipe every tear from every eye. That is the vision which will inspire the work of my government. Jai Hind.

—Prime Minister P. V. Narasimha Rao
in an address to the nation upon taking office, 22 June 1991.

We have seen how gross inefficiencies resulting from the introduction of wholesale controls on domestic and foreign investment, foreign trade and internal distribution during the first decade of Prime Minister Indira Gandhi's rule led to a sharp decline in the growth rate and set back the planned assault on poverty.

Recall also that by the second half of the 1970s, at least some within the government had begun to realize that the system was not working. But the grip of socialist rhetoric on the national psyche was so strong that few dared to challenge the policy framework itself. Therefore, the response was a very gradual, almost invisible, process of unwinding the controls without disturbing the underlying framework.[1] This process accelerated somewhat under Prime Minister Rajiv Gandhi, who took the reins of the government at the end of 1984, following the assassination of his mother, Indira Gandhi.

---

1. Marathe (1989, chapter 4), who retired as the secretary of industry in 1980, offers a fascinating insider's account of policymaking during this period. He states (pp. 91-92), 'By the early seventies there was sufficient evidence and a corresponding awareness of the inadequacy or ineffectiveness of some of the main elements of the industrial policy and particularly of the decision-making and administrative apparatus. The objective of "growth with social justice" . . . was beginning to run into difficulties. It was increasingly evident that there was a conflict between the number of individually desirable objectives of policy, . . . and that the system seemed incapable of resolving these conflicts with the result that in actual practice there was neither adequate growth nor was there a discernible move towards greater social justice.' Later in the chapter, referring to the liberalizing measures during 1975-76, the author states (p. 100), 'By far the most important reason why this phase of liberalization did not add up to much was that there was an unwillingness at the political level to recognize or accept that a change in direction was needed. . . . In the words of a distinguished civil servant who had retired by then, the attempt was "to go by stealth" and necessarily, therefore, the amount of good that could be done had to be modest.'

Through the 1980s, doubts concerning the controlled regime grew steadily, even if only gradually. But as the decade ended, the doubts were greatly heightened and confidence in the model India had followed was shaken by two external events: the success China had achieved after it turned outward, and the demise of the Soviet Union, which had served as the model for Indian planners. Therefore, when a balance-of-payments crisis in 1991 offered the opportunity to make more dramatic changes, the newly-elected prime minister, P.V. Narasimha Rao, who came to the helm due to the assassination of Rajiv Gandhi during the election campaign and who had experienced the tyranny of central controls as the chief minister of Andhra Pradesh in the early 1970s, did not hesitate. He launched a process of systemic reforms that firmly set India on a course dramatically different from the one Indira Gandhi had set for the nation.

These reforms posed the greatest challenge to the long-standing proponents of socialism, who now faced an existential threat. Unsurprisingly, their response has been to perpetuate yet new myths. In this chapter, we address the new myths that relate to the alleged malign impact of the reforms on growth, poverty and socially disadvantaged groups. Additional myths relating to the presumed deleterious impact of the reforms on inequality, education, health and related issues are treated in the rest of Part II.

Myth 3.1: Reforms do not explain the faster growth in India since 1991.

Perhaps the most surprising myth, current among a few economists, is that though growth did occur after reforms, it was not a result of the post-1991 reforms and that it could be traced back instead to the 1980s.

The command and control regime had, of course, peaked by the mid-1970s, and we have remarked how a quiet process of loosening some of the controls began soon after, accelerating somewhat in the 1980s, especially under Prime Minister Rajiv Gandhi in the second half of the decade. Recall also that this halting, partial process of reforms, introduced as it were 'by stealth', was replaced in 1991 by the reforms package that brought the liberalizing process frontally into the open, made reforms more comprehensive across important areas like industrial licensing, and represented a fundamental shift in the policy framework.[2]

So, we must ask: how can serious economists maintain that the reforms had no effect on the post-1991 acceleration of growth? Their argument takes one of two forms. First, they claim that the growth acceleration really started in the 1980s. Second, that even the acceleration of growth in the 1980s was a result not of the piecemeal reforms during the 1980s but of 'attitudinal changes' that trumped the effects of any 'specific' reform measures.

The economic historian Bradford DeLong (2003) was the first to argue that the post-1991 reforms followed, rather than preceded, the growth acceleration. But we note below that the growth acceleration of the 1980s has been greatly exaggerated so that it is misleading to argue that the true acceleration began in the 1980s rather than in the post-1991 reforms decade thereafter.

But DeLong did not argue that reforms as such had nothing to do with growth. DeLong acknowledged that the reforms in the 1980s might have led to the acceleration in growth in the 1980s and so one could not conclude that reforms and growth were delinked. In fact, DeLong also acknowledged that while the piecemeal reforms of the 1980s might have been behind that acceleration of growth in the 1980s, the 1980s growth acceleration might have proven to be

2. The details of these policy changes are set out in Panagariya (2008a, Chapters 2-5).

just 'a short-lived flash in the pan' in the absence of more comprehensive reforms of the post-1991 variety (as is indeed true, as we argue below).

The real problem lay with the separate assertion by Dani Rodrik (2003), in his editorial introduction to the volume carrying DeLong's paper, that the 1980s growth had little to do with reforms *anyway*. He argued that 'the *change in official attitudes* in the 1980s, towards encouraging rather than discouraging entrepreneurial activities and integration into the world economy, and a belief that the rules of the economic game had changed for good, may have had a bigger impact on growth than any specific policy reforms.' (Emphasis added.)[3]

Unfortunately, both the statistical assertion by DeLong about allegedly robust pre-1991 growth and its explanation by Rodrik are wrong.[4]

First, the claim that growth in the 1990s was no higher than in the 1980s carries what might be called a fallacy of aggregation. The acceleration in the early 1980s was in fact quite modest, with the bulk of the growth in the 1980s back-loaded in the last three years. Once we exclude the years 1988-91, growth in the remaining years—1980-81 to 1987-88—turns out to be just 4.6 per cent, which is closer to the 4.1 per cent growth that had already been achieved between 1951-52 and 1964-65, and perceptibly lower than the 6.3 per cent growth between 1992-93 and 1999-2000.[5]

Interestingly, Chetan Ghate and Stephen Wright (2008) have recently applied state-of-the-art techniques to detailed state- and

3. Rodrik and Subramanian (2005) further develop this point. Srinivasan (2005) offers a scathing critique of these authors.
4. The discussion below also draws on Panagariya (2004 and 2008a, Chapter 1) among others.
5. The year 1991-92 is excluded here because this was the crisis year for which the reforms could not be blamed.

industry-level data to identify the turning point of the economy. The careful and comprehensive work of these authors places the turning point at fiscal year 1987-88, just as did Panagariya (2004).[6]

Second, the 'super-high' annual growth of 7.2 per cent during 1988-91 was preceded by significant, though partial, reforms, especially in the years 1985-86 and 1986-87. It was also helped by significant depreciation of the rupee in the second half of the 1980s.[7] But, more important, this growth was also driven by fiscal expansion and external borrowing that were not sustainable. Unsurprisingly, the surge ended in a balance-of-payments crisis in June 1991.

Therefore, even if we ignore the differences in the growth rates in the 1980s and 1990s, the 1980s growth could not have been sustained without the post-1991 reforms.

Third, the shift to 8.5 per cent growth during the eight years between 2003-04 and 2010-11 represents a significant jump in the growth rate following the post-1991 systematic reforms. Surely, attributing this latest acceleration to some kind of 'attitudinal' change in the 1980s, as also saying that 'attitudinal' changes rather than the partial reforms at that time accounted even for the modest growth in the 1980s, strains credulity.

Finally, we must also note that many of the structural changes that have taken place since 1991 have a direct link to the liberalizing

---

6. We may mention here the earlier work of Wallack (2003), which tries to divide the years between 1951-52 and 2001-02 into two or more periods on the basis of statistically significant differences in growth rates. She finds one such breakpoint, which is 1980-81 if we consider the GDP series and 1987-88 if we consider the GNP series. Given that the GDP and GNP growth-rate series are virtually identical, the vast differences between the cutoff points in the two series indicate extreme sensitivity of her statistical method to small variations in the data. In contrast, the method used by Ghate and Wright is robust.
7. See Panagariya (2004) for details.

reforms. Could the trade-to-GDP ratio have risen from 17 per cent in 1990-91 to more than 50 per cent by the later 2000s without steady trade liberalization? Could foreign investment have risen from $100 million in 1990-91 to more than $60 billion in 2007-08 without the liberalization of the foreign investment regime? Could the number of phones have risen from 5 million at the end of 1990-91 to new additions of over 15 million every month without the liberalization of telecommunications? Could the automobile production have risen from 180,000 in 1990-91 to 2 million in 2009-10 without de-licensing of investment and opening up to foreign investment? The list goes on.[8] Policies matter; 'changes in bureaucratic attitudes' in the absence of policy changes are ephemeral.

Myth 3.2: There has been no reduction in poverty as a result of post-1991 reforms.

This myth challenges not the link between reforms and growth but the link between growth and poverty, by asserting that poverty did not decline after the acceleration of growth subsequent to the post-1991 reforms.

In our discussion of Myth 2.4, which included Figure 2.2, we cited evidence of declining poverty as per capita GNP grew. But some critics reject this evidence by arguing that there has not been a major dent in the absolute number of people living below the 'poverty line' and that this undermines the claim that poverty fell after the reforms. According to the Planning Commission data, at

8. Two additional contributions in a vein similar to Rodrik (2003) and Rodrik and Subramanian (2005) are Kohli (2006) and Nayyar (2006). Panagariya (2008a, pp. 16-21) provides a critique of each of these contributions.

the traditional poverty line, the Indiawide absolute number of poor was 323 million in 1983, 320 million in 1993-94 and 302 million in 2004-05. Presumably, therefore, the number of poor has at best declined marginally.[9]

Once popularized by the World Bank, going by the absolute number of poor is nevertheless a flawed method of measuring the evolution of poverty in the face of a rising population.[10] This approach to measuring poverty will in fact downplay the decline in poverty because it does not distinguish between the changes in the absolute and in the relative or proportionate number of poor.

This biases the poverty measure towards exaggerating poverty. One might therefore conclude cynically that the biased measure was popular at the World Bank and diffused to the client nations, so as to increase the alarm over poverty, and bolster the critiques of a reforms-oriented developmental strategy. In fact, the World Bank was being increasingly taken over by populist economists and non-economists, especially under President James Wolfensohn.[11]

---

9. For example, in an op-ed entitled 'Two decades of a misplaced idea' in the newspaper *Mint* (16 September 2011), the anti-reform commentator Himanshu argues that if the reforms are judged by what they have done for the poor, the results are at best mixed. He then cites the following numbers based on the revised, higher official poverty line, 'The number of absolute poor in the country, which was 404.9 million in 1993-94 and 406.6 million in 2004-05, has come down marginally to 397 million by 2009-10.'
10. For example, in its *1999 Annual Review of Development Effectiveness*, the World Bank (1999) noted, 'The number of poor people living on less than US$1 a day rose from 1,197 million in 1987 to 1,214 million in 1998. Excluding China, there are 100 million more poor people in developing countries than a decade ago.'
11. Wolfensohn's trusted consultants among the economists were also anti-growth and anti-reforms economists such as Joseph Stiglitz (who was also the World Bank chief economist and vice-president) and Amartya Sen. See, for example, Wolfensohn and Stiglitz (1999) and Sen and Wolfensohn (1999).

Shifting, however, to the 'proportionate' measure of poverty, we get a more meaningful insight into what happened to it. According to Planning Commission estimates, the proportion of the population below the poverty line in India was 44.5 per cent in 1983. Between 1983 and 2004-05, the population rose by 374 million to 1.1 billion. A reasonable assumption would be that, in the absence of an effective poverty alleviation strategy, the poor would have been 44.5 per cent of the additional 374 million individuals.[12] This assumption translates into the addition of 166.5 million to the existing population of the poor. Therefore, if the absolute number of poor were to remain unchanged at 323 million between 1983 and 2004-05, it would imply the exit of 166.5 million individuals from poverty. In reality, the number of poor in 2004-05 turned out to be 302 million, implying that India had successfully pulled as many as 187.5 million people out of poverty.

This substantial decline is properly captured by what economists call the 'poverty ratio', which fell to 27.5 per cent in 2004-05 from 44.5 per cent in 1983. This makes a mockery of the contention that the unchanged absolute number of poor people is equivalent to no change in poverty. This erroneous inference implies that we expected the entire net addition of 374 million to the population to be non-poor!

Faced with the critique above, the proponents of the 'there is no reduction of poverty' myth shift the argument to a variant of Myths 2.3 and 2.5, denying the link between the reforms and poverty alleviation (rather than denying the reduction of poverty itself). They argue that since the annual percentage-point reduction in poverty between 1993-94 and 2004-05 has not been perceptibly

---

12. We assume here a uniform increase in the population across rich and poor and no movement into and out of poverty. Insofar as population growth might be faster among the poor than the rich, the number of poor in the additional population of 475 million may turn out to be even larger than in the text.

higher than that between 1983 and 1993-94, reforms cannot be credited with adding to poverty reduction.

There are at least three serious problems even with this argument. First and foremost, the periods from 1983 to 1993-94 and 1993-94 to 2004-05 are both characterized by a shift to pro-market policies, though the pro-market reforms after 1991 were deeper and broader. Therefore, they both represent post-reform periods. Any serious comparison of the effectiveness of pro-market and socialist policies must juxtapose the pre-1980 and the post-1980 poverty reductions. If the socialist policies are truly efficacious, we must observe the most rapid reductions in poverty during the late 1960s and the 1970s. But this period turns out to be characterized by ultra-high poverty rates and we can find no trend towards poverty reduction whatsoever.

Second, there is a technical argument working against the critics. There is now agreement among most experts that the expenditure surveys of the National Sample Survey Organization (NSSO) have been overstating the poverty ratio by progressively larger margins over time. This naturally underestimates the reduction of poverty over time.[13]

13. 'This is because the surveys are underestimating the consumption expenditure by a progressively larger margin. The ratio of the mean expenditure as measured by the expenditure surveys and that measured by the National Accounts Statistics (NAS) has been progressively declining. According to an expert group set up by the Government of India (2008), this ratio fell from 0.75 in 1983-84 to 0.62 in 1993-94 and to 0.50 in 2004-05. What this means is that the mean per capita expenditure according to the expenditure surveys was 75 per cent of that according to the NAS estimates in 1983-84. It fell to 62 per cent in 1993-94 and only 50 per cent in 2004-05. Thus, by 2004-05, per capita expenditure according to the expenditure surveys was only half of that according to the NAS. Unless we assume that this entire difference originates in the non-poor population, the expenditures by the poor are being understated and therefore poverty is being overstated in progressively larger volumes.

Finally, poverty figures based on the latest survey, conducted in 2009-10, show that poverty reduction between 2004-05 and 2009-10, a period during which growth accelerated to 8.5 per cent, has indeed accelerated over what had been achieved between 1993-94 and 2004-05. Data show that poverty reduction during 2004-05 to 2009-10 was 1.5 percentage points per year compared with just 0.74 percentage points per year between 1993-94 and 2004-05.[14] Critics have tried to discredit this acceleration by arguing that the Planning Commission has cooked up its numbers by tampering with the poverty lines themselves. But as we explain in Myth 3.4 below, this is an entirely false claim.

Civil society groups also argue that poverty among certain individuals or groups of individuals has not declined or has even increased after reforms. But this will not work either since we discuss below that poverty has gone down amongst all broad-based groups such as the Scheduled Caste and Scheduled Tribe and across all states.

There is no doubt that there are many who were poor prior to the reforms and remain so today. And we also cannot rule out the possibility that reforms have impoverished some individuals, such as those who were displaced from land to make way for alternative activities without proper compensation.[15] However, this approach to the criticism of reforms is ill-conceived since we can measure the efficacy of a set of policies only at some aggregate level, even when we disaggregate the effects by groups such as the Scheduled

---

14. For example, see the report 'Poverty decline rate doubled during UPA regime: Montek Singh Ahluwalia' in *The Times of India*, 7 April 2012 available at http://articles.timesofindia.indiatimes.com/2012-04-07/india/31304633_1_poverty-line-bpl-people-upa-regime (accessed on 9 April 2012).
15. The question of compensation is a valid one. Those whose lands are taken for eminent domain, that is, for a social purpose, need to be compensated. This also raises questions as to what is a valid 'social purpose', which individuals must be compensated and by how much.

Castes and Scheduled Tribes (the impact on whom we examine in Myth 3.3 below). We know of no policy that makes everyone within each disaggregated group better off and hurts literally no one.

To repeat, the reality is that our track record is one where, in regard to poverty reduction, the regime of socialist policies did far less good for (and indeed even inflicted harm on) the poor and the underprivileged groups than turned out to be the case under the regime of reformed policies. India ultimately moved away from the old policies precisely because those policies, with their deleterious effect on economic performance, had failed to deliver on poverty reduction and other social goals.

Myth 3.3: Reforms have bypassed, even hurt, the socially disadvantaged groups.

Some NGOs and journalists argue that reform-led growth may have reduced poverty in aggregate but that it has not helped bring down the poverty among the socially disadvantaged groups, principally the Scheduled Castes and Scheduled Tribes, but perhaps also Other Backward Castes (OBC).

For example, a submission by the National Campaign on Dalit Human Rights to the House of Commons of the UK Parliament, published on 14 January 2011, states:

> In spite of high economic growth rate the poverty rate among excluded communities in India has increased, coupled with the insecurity of livelihoods.

In a similar vein, writing in *The Financial Chronicle* (29 December 2010), the journalist Praful Bidwai argues,

> Rising inequalities highlight what is wrong with India's growth trajectory, driven as it is by elite consumption and sectoral imbalances, *which exclude disadvantaged groups from the benefit of rising GDP*, while aggravating income disparities. (Emphasis added.)[16]

Once again, there is now irrefutable evidence that sustained growth alongside liberalizing reforms has reduced poverty not just among the better-off castes but across all broadly defined groups. It is true that the poverty ratios were, and still remain, significantly higher among the disadvantaged groups, reflecting historical injustices, but it is not true that these groups have not benefited from the recent growth. Indeed, evidence along all dimensions shows the Scheduled Caste and Scheduled Tribe gaining alongside the OBC and 'forward' castes. We cite now some of the compelling recent empirical studies that demonstrate our contention.

Mukim and Panagariya (2012) calculate the poverty ratios by social groups from the expenditure surveys conducted by the NSSO in years 1983, 1987-88, 1993-94 and 2004-05. The calculations show that the poverty ratios for the Scheduled Castes and for the Scheduled Tribes fell between every pair of successive surveys in rural as well as urban areas. For the Scheduled Castes, the nationwide (rural plus urban) poverty ratio fell from 58.5 per cent in 1983 to 48.9 per cent in 1993-94 and 38 per cent in 2004-05. For the Scheduled Tribes, the ratio fell from 64.4 per cent in 1983 to 51.2 per cent in 1993-94 and to 46.3 per cent in 2004-05. The authors also calculate the poverty ratios by states and find that they fell between 1983 and 2004-05 for each of Scheduled

16. For the document with the statement by the National Campaign on Dalit Human Rights, see <http://www.publications.parliament.uk/pa/cm201011/cmselect/cmintdev/writev/616/m02.htm> (accessed on 3 June 2011). The statement by Bidwai can be found in the article 'Equity, not growth, is the key' posted at <http://www.mydigitalfc.com/op-ed/equity-not-growth-key-359> (accessed on 3 June 2011).

Castes and Scheduled Tribes in each of the ten largest states they consider.[17]

Figure 3.1 shows the poverty ratios for the Scheduled Castes, Scheduled Tribes, Non-Scheduled Castes and all groups taken together at the national level for years 1983, 1987-88, 1993-94 and 2004-05. While poverty rates are higher for the disadvantaged groups, they steadily decline for each single group. This pattern repeats itself when we break up the data for rural and urban areas. The pattern has held up, with poverty reduction accelerating for every single social group between 2004-05 and 2009-10 (Thorat and Dubey 2012, Tables 1 and 3).

There is an impression among some scholars that growth acceleration has not helped the Scheduled Tribes. This impression has derived partially from the existence of the Maoist insurgency in certain regions where the tribes are concentrated, and partially from a sense that when displacement happens from projects involving mineral extraction, tribes are not adequately compensated. While the adverse impact of these factors on the tribes can be scarcely denied, the evidence of the decline in poverty among the Scheduled Tribes is quite unequivocal. In this regard, two factors must be kept in mind. First, while the beginning of the poverty decline can be traced to the early 1980s, as demonstrated by Figure 3.1, the Maoist insurgency, and even the acceleration in mineral extraction activity, are of more recent origin. And second, the states with the largest populations of Scheduled Tribes, including Madhya Pradesh, Maharashtra, Rajasthan and Gujarat, have not been the hotbeds of the Maoist insurgency.

---

17. They define the size of the state according to SC population when considering poverty among the SC; and by ST population when considering poverty among the ST.

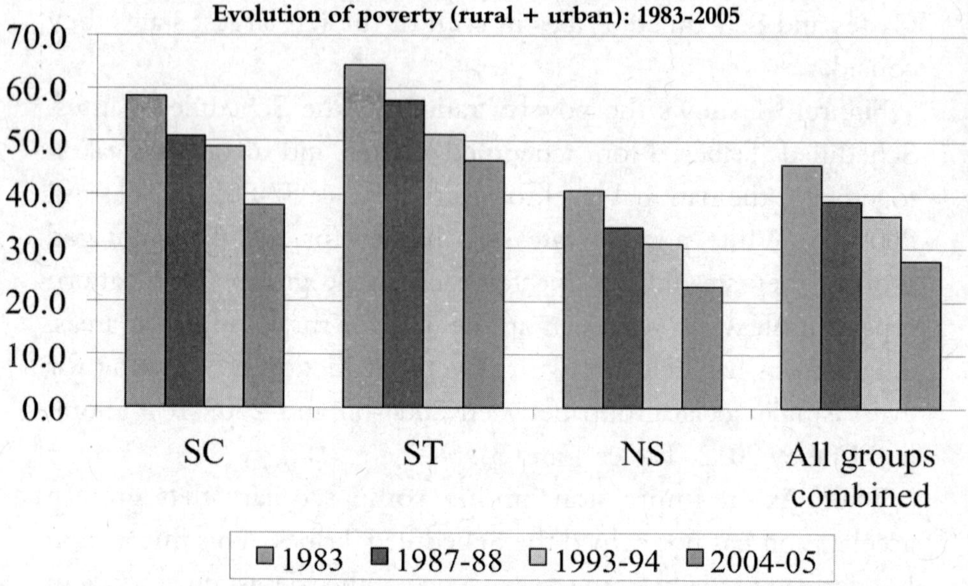

FIGURE 3.1: EVOLUTION OF THE POVERTY RATIO FOR VARIOUS SOCIAL GROUPS

Dehejia and Panagariya (2012) take a different route to analysing the impact of liberalization on different social groups. They consider the status of entrepreneurship among the Scheduled Caste and Scheduled Tribe groups in the service sectors, using the data gathered by the NSSO in two surveys conducted in 2001-02 and 2006-07.[18] They find for entrepreneurship a pattern very similar to the one found by Mukim and Panagariya (2012) for poverty. The share of each of the Scheduled Caste and Scheduled Tribe groups, according to the value added and the number of workers employed in the enterprises, was and remains well below its corresponding

18. These surveys identify the ownership of proprietary and partnership enterprises by social group, though not of cooperative and corporate enterprises. Therefore, it is possible to study the evolution of entrepreneurship by social groups within the proprietary and partnership enterprises.

share in the population, reflecting the historical injustices. But each social group experiences healthy growth in the output and in the number of workers employed in the enterprises owned by its members.[19]

It is worth emphasizing that even though the private sector has no caste-based reservations, the Scheduled Caste and Scheduled Tribe entrepreneurs have experienced healthy growth in their enterprises. We might add that some anecdotal evidence is now beginning to appear even on the rise of Dalits (among the Scheduled Caste group) to large fortunes. In particular, newspapers have widely reported on thirty 'Dalit crorepatis', almost all of them first-generation entrepreneurs, who were invited for a meeting to the Planning Commission specially organized for them in January 2011.[20] The groups included Milind Kamble, who serves as chairman of the Dalit Indian Chamber of Commerce and Industry (DICCI), formed in 2005. According to him, 'Including mine, most of the big Dalit-owned businesses are fifteen years old. With the emergence of globalization and the disappearance of the licence-permit raj, many opportunities appeared and many of us jumped on them.' Referring to the meeting at the Planning Commission, he is reported to have stated: 'The Planning Commission was stunned when they asked how many of us used government schemes

19. In the case of the Scheduled Tribe-owned enterprises, value-added as well as the number of workers employed grows faster than the corresponding average growth for all groups taken together. Therefore, shares of the Scheduled Tribe-owned enterprises in the value-added and the number of workers employed grow larger between 2001-02 and 2006-07. For the Scheduled Castes, the growth in value added is slightly below the average for all groups and that for workers significantly above it. Consequently, despite healthy growth, its share shows a tiny decline in value added and a rise in the number of workers employed.

20. A 'crore' equals 10 million and a 'crorepati' refers to someone having an accumulated wealth of 10 million rupees or more.

to build their businesses. Only one entrepreneur from Mumbai raised his hand and described how he'd applied for $20,000 (Rs 10 lakh), spent three years visiting government offices to chase his money and finally got $15,000 (Rs 7.5 lakh).'

Thus, contrary to general impression and especially the *a priori* fears of some critics, reforms and growth, rather than governmental assistance, seem to have opened opportunities for the Scheduled Caste and Scheduled Tribe entrepreneurs to seize, and these too not just in small enterprises but the larger ones as well.

Myth 3.4: The Planning Commission plays politics with poverty lines, arbitrarily lowering them to exaggerate the achievements in poverty reduction and setting them too low to understate the incidence of poverty.

All three claims underlying this myth require close examination.[21] First, the suggestion that the Planning Commission plays fast and loose with the poverty lines couldn't be farther from the truth. In setting the poverty lines, India has adhered to the highest standards of professionalism throughout its history. The official poverty lines we have used until they were revised in 2011 were based entirely on the recommendations of the Lakdawala Committee of 1993. Not only was Professor D.T. Lakdawala a leading scholar of poverty, he also stood on the broad shoulders of such stalwarts as Pitamber Pant, once handpicked by Prime Minister Jawaharlal Nehru to head the Perspective Planning Division of the Planning Commission, and V.M. Dandekar and Nilakant Rath, both

21. The following discussion heavily draws on Panagariya (2012a).

pioneering scholars of poverty in post-independence India.[22]

In a nutshell, these poverty lines had been set such that anyone above them would be able to afford consumption equivalent to 2,400 and 2,100 calories in rural and urban areas respectively, in addition to subsistence-level clothing and shelter. A committee headed by the late Professor Suresh Tendulkar was likewise behind the revisions to the Lakdawala poverty lines adopted in 2011 and reported to the Supreme Court by the Planning Commission. The integrity and qualifications of Tendulkar are beyond reproach.

Second, the claim that the Planning Commission has time and again lowered the poverty lines to make exaggerated claims of poverty reduction is equally false. In the second half of 2011, the media created the distinct impression that the Planning Commission, in its affidavit to the Supreme Court, had deliberately lowered the poverty lines to exclude many genuinely poor from the benefits reserved for the poor. The same impression was conveyed yet again when the Planning Commission released a report in March 2012 showing acceleration in poverty reduction between 2004-05 and 2009-10 as compared to the period between 1993-94 and 2004-05.

In both cases, media claims were outright false. In the first case, the Planning Commission had actually raised the poverty line, while in the second it had made no change. In 2011, the Planning Commission had reported to the Supreme Court poverty lines based on the Tendulkar Committee report. In turn, that committee had recommended raising the rural poverty line from the original level based on the Lakdawala Committee recommendations while keeping the urban poverty line at its previous level. After extensive

22. Although Professor Lakdawala passed away before the report of his committee was submitted, the report was largely the result of his work with other committee members.

consultation and careful analysis, the Tendulkar Committee reached the conclusion that while those living above the Lakdawala urban poverty line continued to be able to afford 2,100 calories, the rural poverty line needed upward adjustment so as to be aligned to its urban counterpart. This is what the committee recommended and the Planning Commission simply complied with it.

The claims of reductions in the poverty lines prominently surfaced yet again when the Planning Commission reported in March 2012 that poverty reduction had accelerated between 2004-05 and 2009-10 over that between 1993-94 and 2004-05. For instance, a headline on the NDTV website declared, 'Planning Commission further lowers the (urban) poverty line to Rs 28 (from Rs 32 in the Supreme Court filing).' But, once again, the Planning Commission had done no such thing. The Rs 32 line, reported to the Supreme Court, related to the year 2010-11 and Rs 28 to 2009-10, with the difference fully accounted for by the higher price level in 2010-11.

Finally, consider the claim that the Planning Commission has set the poverty lines at ultra-low levels so that it may exclude a large part of the population from benefiting from the government's redistribution programmes. While reasonable people may differ on whether it is desirable to further raise the poverty line, the subject is far more complex than commonly appreciated. The guiding objective behind the poverty line in India, and indeed worldwide, has been to monitor progress in combating destitution. Therefore, poverty line expenditures have been traditionally set at levels just sufficient to allow for above-subsistence existence.

The dilemma in raising the poverty lines is best brought out by considering the implications of poverty lines that are significantly higher than those currently in use and are advocated by many of the current critics of the Planning Commission. Thus, for example, suppose we raise the rural poverty line to Rs 80 and the urban one to Rs 100 at 2009-10 prices. What would these lines imply?

First, based on the expenditure survey of 2009-10, they would designate 95 per cent of the rural population and 85 per cent of the urban population poor. But few analysts would suggest that all but the top 15 per cent of the urban and 5 per cent of the rural population live in destitution today. Even if we were to argue that poverty goes beyond the destitute, measuring progress at 85th percentile in the urban and 95th percentile in the rural areas is unlikely to tell us very much about success in combating poverty.

Second, turning to the implications for redistribution, how much good to the bottom 30 or 40 per cent, who represent the truly destitute, will we do if the tax revenues raised from the top 15 per cent urban population were spread evenly over 95 per cent of the rural and 85 per cent of the urban population? With the tax revenues still relatively modest, significant redistribution in favour of the destitute requires limiting such redistributions to the bottom 40 per cent or so of the population. Spreading them thinly over a vast population will give too little to the destitute to make a major dent in poverty.

To dramatize this argument, suppose we were to redistribute all expenditures, as reported in the 2009-10 expenditure survey, equally across the population. Astonishingly, such redistribution would leave each individual with just Rs 45 per day in expenditure. This level is well below even the lowest poverty line any critic of the Planning Commission has advocated.

Myth 3.5: Trade openness has exacerbated poverty.

This argument is a part of the criticism that globalization is bad for the poor. It also links a specific policy reform, that is, increased openness to trade, to increase in poverty. It got a boost from a study by the International Monetary Fund economist Petia Topalova (2007), who argued that enhanced openness had adversely impacted poverty in India.[23]

It turns out, however, that several economists have successfully challenged her findings, showing that increased openness has reduced poverty instead. Given the importance of this issue, and the Topalova Myth, we provide below a summary of these studies (which can be skipped by readers not interested in the necessary technical arguments).

Using the expenditure survey data collected by the NSSO, Topalova asked whether rural and urban districts, which have different degrees of exposure to trade, experienced increased or reduced poverty as a result of trade liberalization in India. She measured openness by employment-weighted average of tariffs, assigning zero tariffs to exportable and non-traded sectors and positive tariffs to sectors producing importables. Working at the district level, she found that increased openness had been associated with, and had presumably led to, increased incidence of poverty in the rural districts but had no statistically significant effect in the urban districts. She found no evidence in either rural or urban India that openness was associated with poverty alleviation. These were startling results because, as we argued earlier, trade openness in a labour-abundant economy stimulates growth in general and the expansion of labour-intensive industries in particular so that it is expected to lower rather than raise poverty.

Hasan, Mitra and Beyza Ural (2006-07) have therefore revisited this question. They note that the analysis of poverty and trade openness at the level of the district poses several problems. For example, the data from the 1993-94 NSSO survey do not readily allow the identification of urban districts. District boundaries also shift over time. There are also questions of randomness of the

23. Our discussion of this myth is substantially borrowed from Bhagwati and Panagariya (2012).

sample at the level of the district. Finally, sometimes the number of observations in a district is insufficiently large to yield a reliable estimate of poverty.

Therefore, these authors study the question at the level of the state and NSS-identified regions within states. There being one or more regions within a state, regions are higher in number than states and therefore allow larger degrees of freedom. As such, these authors' research offers an improvement over the Topalova approach: their focus on regions allows for a tighter estimation of poverty than the district-focused approach and also allows for a tighter estimation of regression equations than a pure state-focused approach.

These authors also note that assigning zero tariffs to non-traded sectors in measuring openness, as done by Topalova, is erroneous. Many goods and services may be non-traded precisely because the barriers to trade are prohibitive. So they defined openness as an employment-weighted sum of tariffs such that only exportable products are assigned zero tariffs, with non-traded sectors entirely excluded from the calculation. These authors also take into account non-tariff barriers, which Topalova had ignored.

In sharp contrast to the claim by Topalova that trade openness was not associated with reduced poverty, the superior methodology of these authors failed to encounter even a single case in which reductions in trade protection worsened poverty at the state or regional level. Instead, they found that states more exposed to foreign competition had lower rural, urban and overall poverty ratios, with this beneficial effect being more pronounced in states that had more flexible labour market institutions. The authors also found that trade liberalization led to greater poverty reduction in states more fully exposed to foreign competition. The results held for overall urban and rural poverty, with varying strengths and statistical significance.

Moreover, Jewel Cain, Hasan and Mitra (2012) have also revisited the issue and reinforced the findings of Hasan, Mitra and Ural, using data from the more recent round of the sample survey conducted in 2004-05. They find that every percentage point reduction in the weighted tariff rate led to 0.57 per cent reduction in the poverty ratio on average. This implies that of the overall reduction in poverty during 1987-2004, on average, 38 per cent can be attributed to change in the exposure to foreign trade. The econometric technique used by the authors allows them to infer that the greater exposure of the labour force to foreign competition speeded up poverty reduction. The magnitude of impact and its statistical significance naturally vary across rural and urban sectors and the two sectors considered together, as also across the different tariff and non-tariff measures used. However, in no case do these authors find that increased openness results in increased poverty.

Finally, Mukim and Panagariya (2012) split the NSSO sample by social groups and analyse the impact of trade openness on poverty within each of the social groups in rural and urban areas. They find no evidence whatsoever in favour of the hypothesis that rising incomes or openness have adversely impacted poverty among any one of the groups. They also find that one or more measures of openness have had a statistically significant and favourable impact on poverty levels among the Scheduled Castes and non-Scheduled Castes in rural and urban regions and in both regions taken together. As regards the Scheduled Tribes, they find a statistically significant effect of openness on poverty in urban areas only.

4

Reforms and Inequality

One of the problems which immediately comes to us is that of controls. I think the correct problem is not that of controls but the question of controls versus controls. What has happened is that we have got numerous controls. But the fact is we have no control on what is happening in industry. We are doing absolutely what they like, whether it is MRTP (Monopolies and Restrictive Trade Practices Act of 1969) for big business houses or some other thing. But what has MRTP done? Has it prevented the big houses from growing bigger! Has it, in any way, given protection to the middle- and small-scale sector? All it has in fact done is that it has protected the large monopoly houses from anybody else entering the field. This is exactly the opposite of what it was meant to do. If this is what controls are to be, and we have to lose control of what we want to do, I think we are going down a totally wrong road. When we thought of controls, it was to guide the economy in a certain direction. But are we able to do it with what we have on the slate today? I feel that we are tremendously hampered and we need to look at it afresh, not to throw it out of the window because that is not the answer, but to look at it and see whether we are achieving what we set out to achieve. Perhaps in some areas we would have achieved something, but in others we will find shortcomings. So we must have the courage to correct it.

—Prime Minister Rajiv Gandhi in an address to the conference of state industry ministers, New Delhi, 10 December 1986.

Recall that the growth rate during the eight years beginning in 2003-04 has jumped to 8.5 per cent from less than 4 per cent until 1980. This has meant the creation of very substantial wealth. For example, while there were no billionaires in dollar terms in India as recently as 2000, the 2007 list by *Forbes* reports as many as fifty-five of them.

The addition of this new wealth has in turn led to claims that reforms have generated massive income inequalities and that India has entered a state similar to the American Gilded Age in the late nineteenth century. We argue here that while these claims may appear superficially plausible, they crumble in the face of close scrutiny.

Myth 4.1: Reforms have led to increased inequality.

At the outset, we need to emphasize that what is an appropriate measure of inequality is not simply a technical issue—for example, whether the index of inequality should be the economists' measure of what is called the Gini coefficient (explained below and more fully in Appendix 2), which is widely used by economists studying inequality in India and indeed elsewhere. An appropriate measure of inequality must also reflect broader questions of relevance to the popular concerns.

Thus, for a measure to be relevant to the public-policy discussion, it must have political and social salience. For example, if incomes increase in Mumbai but not in the Ratnagiri district of Maharashtra, evidently inequality of income has increased between Mumbai and Ratnagiri. But if those living in Ratnagiri are not comparing themselves to what is happening in Mumbai, why is this inequality measure of any relevance? So, measures of urban-rural inequality may have little relevance as well.

On the other hand, when *within* Mumbai inequality becomes more acute, the poor there are more likely to notice as they compare themselves with the rich in their own neighbourhoods. Similarly, within our own university (which happens to be Columbia University in New York), the inequality between the top salaries—the president enjoys the highest salary—and the lowest salaries is a salient issue, but what is not an issue (at least as of now) is how our salaries compare to those on Wall Street.[1] In short, an increase in inequality within one's own village or institution is likely to raise hackles but not inequality between groups that have little relationship or contact with one another.

Then again, the political and social implications of any increase in appropriately measured inequality would depend on the social context in which it occurs. Thus, if inequality increases and the rich spend money on conspicuous consumption, that could become socially explosive. But if mobility is high, the poor may react by celebrating the conspicuous inequality, rather than resenting it, in the hope that they too may some day 'make it' big in that way.

Keeping these caveats in mind, consider some general economic arguments that bear on income distribution between the rich and the poor in an economy such as India's. First, some forms of inequality can be expected to rise in a rapidly growing economy. Growth involves wealth creation. Insofar as a small number of entrepreneurs leads this wealth creation—and those creating wealth are unlikely to redistribute all of it in an act of altruism—disparity

1. Thus, economists' salaries are particularly high owing to the opportunities they enjoy outside of the academe. Hence, there are resentments by academics from lesser-paid disciplines such as anthropology, philosophy and comparative literature. An insider joke is that if you wanted academic signatures on an anti-liberal or anti-establishment petition, you were assured of many signatures if you went to these lower-paid departments: their resentments would prompt them to sign any such petition in huge numbers!

between the richest and the rest of the population in both income and expenditure is likely to rise.

Likewise, rapid growth is often led by the formation of a small number of agglomerations, which will generally concentrate in urban centres, leading to urban-rural as well as regional inequality. On the other hand, in a labour-abundant economy, pro-growth policies are also expected to lead to specialization in the labour-intensive goods, which raises employment and wages of the poor. The poor can move from lower-paid jobs in the countryside to the higher-paid jobs in rapidly growing urban agglomerations, thereby producing less inequality.

Against this background, what has been the Indian experience? As it happens, the evidence we discuss below shows that contrary to widespread impressions, inequality measures do not point to an unambiguously rising trend in inequality and even on a net basis, the rise in it has been at best modest.

Thus, Krishna and Sethupathy (2012) have recently measured inequality in India, using the household expenditure survey data from the NSS rounds conducted in 1987-88, 1993-94, 1999-2000 and 2004-05.[2] Interestingly, these authors show that inequality between states and between urban and rural areas is dwarfed by the inequality among households within each of these aggregates. For example, within-states inequality accounts for more than 90 per cent of the total inequality over the country (see Figure 4.1). Between-states inequality accounts for less than 10 per cent of the

2. They use, not the Gini measure, which is explained in Appendix 2, but what economists know as the Theil index. The latter has the advantage that it allows overall inequality in a population to be decomposed into inequality within and across sub-populations of that population. Thus, for example, it allows inequality among households within a country to be decomposed into inequality among households within states and that across states. Like the Gini coefficient, the Theil index varies between 0 and 1.

total inequality across the country. Likewise, within-rural and within-urban inequality accounts for 90 per cent or more of the total inequality across the nation.

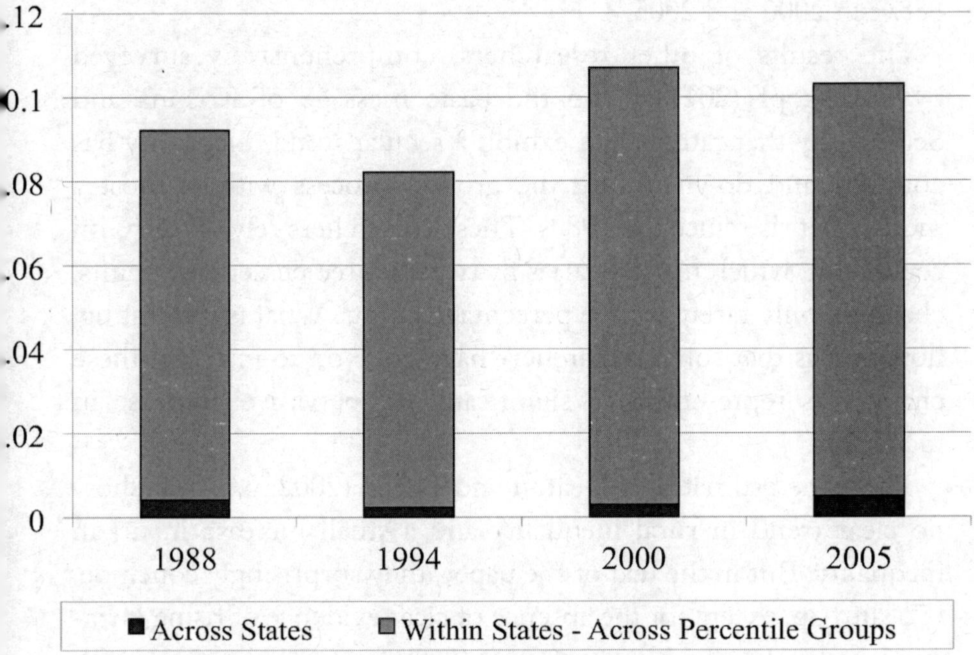

FIGURE 4.1: CHANGES IN INEQUALITY OVER TIME AND WITHIN HOUSEHOLDS VERSUS ACROSS-STATES INEQUALITY

Source: Krishna and Sethupathy (2012, Figure 6.9).

Importantly, the overall inequality exhibits only modest variation over the period, rising slightly between 1988 and 1994 and again between 1994 and 2000, but dropping by 2005 to a level slightly above that in 1988 (see Figure 4.1). Inequality trends within states mirror the national experience: it rose between 1994 and 2000 and then fell between 2000 and 2005 in most states. Indeed, between 2000 and 2005, only four states—Mizoram,

Maharashtra, Orissa, and Haryana—experienced significant increases in inequality. The picture is almost exactly the same for rural and urban areas within states; the vast majority experienced rising inequality between 1994 and 2000 but falling inequality between 2000 and 2005.

The results of other researchers, comprehensively surveyed by Weisskopf (2011), echo the basic message of Krishna and Sethupathy that rather than exhibit a secular trend, inequality has gone up and down during the growth process with at most a modest net rise since the 1980s. These researchers rely on the Gini coefficient, which usually varies by two or three percentage points, changing only rarely by five percentage points. What is interesting, however, is that some researchers have gone on to interpret these changes as representing a 'significant' or 'pervasive' increase in inequality.

Thus, the estimates in Deaton and Dreze (2002, p. 3740) show no clear trend in rural inequality and a small increase in urban inequality. But in the text of the paper, they surprisingly conclude, 'To sum up, except for the absence of clear evidence of rising intra-rural inequality within states, we find strong indications of a pervasive increase in economic inequality in the nineties. This is a new development in the Indian economy: until 1993-94, the all-India Gini coefficients of per capita consumer expenditure in rural and urban areas were fairly stable.' Evidently, their stark conclusion is not consistent with their statistical findings.

In almost an identical spirit, Weisskopf (p. 46) quotes Patia Topalova approvingly as stating that 'all measures point to significant increase in overall inequality in the 1990s'. Yet, the Gini coefficient calculated by Topalova and reported by Weisskopf changes from 31.9 in 1983-84 to just 30.3 in 1993-94 and 32.5 in 2004-05. One would think that the difference between 31.9 and 32.5, which may not even be statistically significant, would hardly warrant the inference that there has been a *significant* increase in inequality.[3]

Returning to Krishna and Sethupathy, an extra dividend from their analysis is the finding that there is no correlation between the change in inequality across households within states and the change in state-level measures of tariff and non-tariff protection. Trade openness is not linked to increased inequality.

The critics of reforms have also raised a different concern: that growth has been uneven across states and that this has resulted in increased inequality among them. This is correct since richer states have grown faster than the poorer states *on average*. This phenomenon may have political salience if it leads to resentment by the states lagging behind, which are poor to begin with. But four qualifying facts must be kept in view.

First, as Panagariya (2010a) and Chakraborty et al. (2011) show, the years 2003-04 to 2010-11 have seen nearly all states growing significantly faster than they did in any prior period. Therefore, the rise in interstate inequality does not reflect the poorer states remaining poor or being further impoverished. Instead, it represents the richer states growing faster than the poorer states in an environment in which all states are growing faster.

Second, two of the poorer states—Bihar and Orissa—are among the fastest growing states today. Their success shows that when the national policies are conducive to growth (as they have been after the significant reforms began) and some of the states grow rapidly, the door to poorer states achieving similar success is also opened wider. As Bhagwati and Panagariya (2004) and Panagariya (2009a)

3. Some analysts rest their assertion of a large increase in inequality on the ground that the NSS expenditure surveys on which all estimates of expenditure inequality are based are characterized by a systematic under-reporting at the top of the distribution relative to the bottom end and that this under-reporting has been getting worse over time. But without some hard evidence, we cannot be sure that this bias is large and that it is getting exponentially worse over time.

have argued and Gupta and Panagariya (2012) have analysed in detail, there will likely be a diffusion effect: when the rest of the economy is growing rapidly, the electorate in the poorer states will demand more from its leaders, prompting policy changes that increase prosperity. Both Bihar and Orissa have elected and re-elected chief ministers who have performed well.

Third, faster growth in some states opens the scope for larger-scale redistribution programmes in favour of poorer states. A programme such as the National Rural Employment Guarantee Scheme, which benefits the poorer states proportionately more, would not be feasible without certain states having large enough incomes to make the necessary revenues available.

Finally, labour is not immobile across states. It is well known that labour from Bihar has traditionally moved to Mumbai and to Kolkata for jobs, as have people from the Punjab and from the hills. That means that faster growth will attract migrants from the slower-growth states and regions, so that prosperity (as distinct from growth) will diffuse to the slower-growth areas through the usual channels such as remittances.

Yet another dimension of inequality relates to the socially disadvantaged groups. Once again, critics often assert that the income differences between the Scheduled Castes and Scheduled Tribes on one hand and non-Scheduled Castes on the other have gone up during the years of rapid growth. But in a comprehensive analysis, Hnatkovska, Lahiri and Paul (2012) show that such claims are not supported by empirical evidence.

Using Employment-Unemployment Survey data from the NSS rounds conducted in 1983, 1987-88, 1993-94, 1999-2000 and 2004-05, they show that the wages of the Scheduled Castes and Scheduled Tribes have been converging with those of non-Scheduled Castes since 1983. They demonstrate also that differential education levels of the two groups drive most of this convergence. Likewise, the occupation structure of the Scheduled Castes and Scheduled Tribes has also been converging towards that of non-Scheduled Castes. The Scheduled Castes and Scheduled Tribes have been able to take advantage of the rapid growth and structural changes in India during the post-reforms period and have rapidly narrowed their huge historical economic disparities with non-Scheduled Castes and Tribes.

Myth 4.2: Thanks to the reforms, India is now in the Gilded Age that obtained in the late nineteenth century in the United States.

The emergence of billionaires and the exposure of some mega corruption cases have led some, especially Sinha and Varshney (2011), to argue that India has now entered a Gilded Age much like the United States in the late nineteenth century.[4]

During this period in the United States, four main strands of criticism were rampant. First, that American business elites had succumbed to 'gross materialism', which was manifest in conspicuous consumption and crass displays of wealth. Second, that this was made possible by the accumulation of great wealth, while the vast masses toiled for minuscule wages for the likes of John D. Rockefeller and Dale Carnegie, and indeed many others. Third, that these tycoons were not 'captains of industry' to be admired but were rather 'robber barons' who had built their fortunes on abusive business practices and high-handed suppression of attempts at unionization of labour. Fourth, that (in modern terminology) there was a business-politics nexus, such that these

4. Some identify the precise period of the high point of the American Gilded Age as 1869-77, which coincided with the administration of President Ulysses Grant, with many writers including 1878-1889 in it as well.

robber barons and corrupt politicians had greased one another's palms and defrauded the nation.

The phrase Gilded Age was the creation of Mark Twain, the celebrated author, whose 1873 novel with Charles Dudley Warner was titled *The Gilded Age*.[5] It was a reaction to the excesses that accompanied the remarkable growth of the American economy as the production of iron and steel took off with rail transport expanding rapidly to bring primary resources from the expanding Western frontier to the East. Oil and banking grew at unprecedented pace as well, leading to massive fortunes for tycoons such as John D. Rockefeller and Cornelius Vanderbilt.

Vignettes from this Gilded Age amply illustrate the criticisms that attended the extraordinary growth.Thus, lavish parties were a way of life for the nouveau riche. An account of the time records: 'Sherry's Restaurant hosted formal horseback dinners for the New York Riding Club. Mrs Stuyvesant Fish once threw a dinner party to honour her dog who arrived sporting a $15,000 diamond collar.'[6]

Again, there was also a populist resentment of the extreme wealth contrasted with the tragic reality of slums and subsistence wages in the overcrowded tenements in the growing urban towns and cities. The general perception, reflecting that contrast, was that while the rich wore pearls, the poor were in rags. There was growing talk of retribution through emerging violence: fears grew of 'carnivals of revenge'.

Against this backdrop, labour began to organize against long hours and low wages; and the robber barons occasionally reacted by breaking the strikes brutally. Thus, even Andrew Carnegie, who professed sympathy for the poor, reacted to the Homestead

5. *The Gilded Age* prompted several writers, such as Upton Sinclair, to write novels about the abysmal social conditions afflicting the poor. These writers were called the 'muckrakers'.
6. Cf. www.pbs.org.

Strike of 1892 by supporting his manager, Henry Frick, who locked out workers and hired Pinkerton musclemen to threaten them. This was no isolated incident.

The robber barons also operated in a governance vacuum regarding business practices that they pursued to gain monopoly control. Notorious for such business practices was John D. Rockefeller of Standard Oil Company, who turned his company in 1870 into one of the nation's first notorious monopolistic trusts. The anti-trust legislations came later: the Sherman Anti-Trust Act of 1890 and the later, tougher and more effective Clayton Anti-Trust Act of 1914.

The era was also marked by corruption at the highest levels of government, including the office of the president, but more typically at the levels of local governance where, as today, businesses and governments shared the spoils from local grants of cash subsidies and land gifts, presumably for a 'social purpose' (such as constructing a railroad) but in fact for the sole purpose of defrauding the commonwealth.

Is India today in such a Gilded Age? There are superficial similarities, for sure. It is true that just as fast growth in the nineteenth-century US created the Vanderbilts, Carnegies, Rockefellers and Morgans, it has created a large number of billionaires in India. Again, like the robber barons of the American Gilded Age, Indian billionaires have tilted the playing field to their advantage through securing mining and land resources, seeking regulations favourable to them and blocking foreign entry. But the similarity ends there: today's India is no Gilded Age.[7]

First, the initial conditions characterizing the American Gilded Age and current-day India are vastly different. At the beginning of the Gilded Age, the dominant economic philosophy in the US was laissez faire. There was virtually no effective regulatory, labour or

7. See Panagariya (2011d).

social legislation at the federal level. Two key pieces of regulatory legislation, the Interstate Commerce Act of 1887, which aimed to limit the monopoly power of the railways, and the Sherman Act of 1890, which provided for anti-trust action against businesses, were enacted during and not before this period. Key laws providing protection to industrial labour, the poor and the elderly also came much later. With rare exceptions, only white males enjoyed voting rights.

In contrast, the post-reforms India and its growth explosion have been preceded by several decades of a command-and-control system complemented by stringent legislation in favour of industrial workers so that it is impossible to have business tycoons breaking strikes the way the American robber barons did. India, it may be recalled, has had a long-standing national commitment to the eradication of poverty and universal adult suffrage since independence. The country has all elements of a liberal democracy with the poor and the underprivileged having access to effective politics at the ballot box.

The economic reforms have allowed freer play to private entrepreneurs but can hardly be characterized as *laissez faire* (see our discussion below of Myth 6.4, according to which reforms have led India to shift to 'market fundamentalism'). For example, the railways remains a public sector monopoly and the government remains a major player in such key sectors as steel, coal, petroleum and engineering goods. Despite private sector entry in airlines, telecom, insurance and electricity, the public sector players have remained active in these sectors. In banking, the role of domestic and foreign private players has been expanded but the public sector again remains dominant. And several sectoral regulatory agencies, topped by an all-encompassing Competition Commission of India, oversee business practices.

Second, whereas during America's Gilded Age, major sectors such as steel, oil, sugar, meatpacking and the manufacture of agriculture machinery came to be dominated by 'trusts', the opposite is true for India today. We have multiple domestic firms within many sectors, competing against one another as well as with imports and foreign investors. Increased competitive pressures have led to reduced prices and improved quality of products and services in such diverse sectors as airlines, telecommunications, automobiles, two-wheelers, refrigerators and air-conditioners.

Third, the treatment of industrial workers in India today stands in sharp contrast to that in late nineteenth-century America. During the Gilded Age, factory workers toiled 60-hour weeks without pensions, compensation for job-related injuries or insurance against layoffs. In contrast to the strike-breaking actions of the robber barons at the Homestead Steel Mill in 1892 and George Pullman's railroad in 1894, labour laws in India provide a high degree of protection to industrial workers.

Finally, whereas the state provided no protection to those at the bottom of the income distribution, including farmers, in the US during its Gilded Age, the government in present-day India is sensitive to the fate of the poor. Indeed, growth and the social programmes it has made feasible have helped bring poverty significantly down. The changes have also benefited the underprivileged groups, as we have already documented in discussing Myth 3.3; and, as we noted, we now even have a handful of dalit 'crorepatis' among us.

But what about the corruption of the American Gilded Age? How does today's India compare? The critics contend that the post-reform era has been driven by 'crony capitalism'. This implies that Indian entrepreneurs have accumulated wealth mostly by redistributing it in their favour through outright fraud in collaboration with politicians, rather than by creating it.[8] But the

8. The businessmen who profit thus are 'cronies' of the politicians who favour them. But, of course, the bribes that are involved need not go to 'cronies'.

allegation is not persuasive. Unlike Mexico, for instance, where the billionaire Carlos Slim has used every conceivable means to generate monopoly profits for himself, most Indian entrepreneurs have become rich by creating wealth while operating in a highly competitive market. Recent empirical work by Alfaro and Chari (2012) also points to the existence of a highly competitive market in India with substantial entry of new firms on the margin. To be sure, one can find examples such as those of the Reddy brothers who, according to their recent indictment, have accumulated wealth from illegal mining; but that is not the case with the vast majority of Indian entrepreneurs from the information technology, telecommunications, pharmaceuticals or engineering goods industries.[9]

So, while the American Gilded Age produced the robber barons Rockefeller and Vanderbilt, India today has given rise to N.R. Narayana Murthy of Infosys, Azim Premji of Wipro and Uday Kotak of Kotak Mahindra Bank. There is not a hint of corruption or shady practices by these successful Indian tycoons. Besides, all are associated with extensive engagement with society, and have embraced Corporate Social Responsibility (CSR) and Private Social Responsibility (PSR). Whereas Carnegie and Rockefeller gave away their fortunes on their death, the Indian tycoons have given away massive sums of money even as they have earned them. Besides their lifestyles are simple, not extravagant.

In fact, we may remark that while the tycoon Mukesh Ambani has built a much-condemned high-rise in Mumbai, the display of personal wealth and 'gross materialism' is far less rampant in India than in nineteenth-century America or in the New York of the 1970s and even today, after the financial sector's recovery. Perhaps

9. Interestingly, Slim is a major donor to the Clinton Global Initiative, which provides political cover from a grateful former president of the United States.

the worst displays take the form of flamboyant and unseemly weddings costing millions, going back to a long-standing cultural tradition. But even here, American politicians and tycoons have caught up with the phenomenon. What is one to make of the wedding of Chelsea Clinton, daughter of Bill and Hillary Clinton, where over $2 million were reportedly spent at a time of deep recession?

5

Reforms and Their Impact on Health and Education

But if the critics of reforms cannot get traction by claiming adverse effects of reforms on growth, poverty and inequality, can they grasp at straws and contend that the reforms and consequent growth have failed to promote education and health? In fact, the critics have done so.

They have suggested that India lags behind much poorer countries in these areas; that states such as Kerala, which chose an alternative path, have performed much better; and that states such as Gujarat, which have relied on growth, have fallen short of satisfactory progress. But as we argue below, even these claims fail to stand up to careful examination of data.

Myth 5.1: Poverty may have come down but India scores poorly on health and education even when compared with much poorer countries.

The recent focus of the media on child nutrition indicators, which place India below virtually all sub-Saharan African countries, has created the widely-shared impression that India has performed poorly not just in nutrition but in health *in general* relative to these countries.

On the one hand, India is compared by the critics to the much richer China and on the other, to the significantly poorer Bangladesh to drive home the message that whether one takes rich or poor countries for comparison, India is a serious laggard in health achievements despite growth and successful poverty alleviation.[1] But these inferences are little more than myths propagated wittingly or unwittingly by the critics of the reforms.

We will have more to say (in the discussion of Myth 5.2 below) about problems with the indicators showing ultra-high levels of malnutrition among children and adults. Here, however, we wish to make the simple but important point that India is by no stretch of the imagination an exceptional underachiever in health generally. In fact, India is hardly out of line with other countries with similar per capita income levels.

Moreover, when countries with similar or lower per capita incomes outperform India along a specific indicator such as life expectancy, it is often because they started well ahead in the race: the current lead of these countries in terms of levels of the indicators reflects their past progress. Therefore, what we must compare is not the *level* of the indicators but *change* in level during the period under consideration (what economists call 'first difference').

1. In the op-ed mentioned earlier, Amartya Sen (2011) puts the matter thus, 'India's per capita income is now comfortably more than double that of Bangladesh. How well is India's income advantage reflected in our lead in those things that really matter? I fear not very well—indeed not well at all.' In this op-ed, Sen also cites an op-ed by Jean Dreze (2004) entitled 'Bangladesh Shows the Way,' which implictly suggests that Bangladesh has moved ahead of India in health outcomes. Most recently, the themes of these articles have again been repeated in Dreze and Sen (2011).

At the outset, we should dispel any lingering doubts about India having done poorly relative to the countries in sub-Saharan Africa in terms of vital statistics in the context of its per capita income. We show the position of India relative to that of all sub-Saharan African countries along four different indicators of health plotted against per capita income in 2009 in Figure 5.1. The indicators are: life expectancy, infant mortality, maternal mortality and deaths due to malaria. As is readily seen, India scores very well relative to the countries with the same per capita income or less and, indeed, in many cases relative to countries with higher per capita incomes as well.

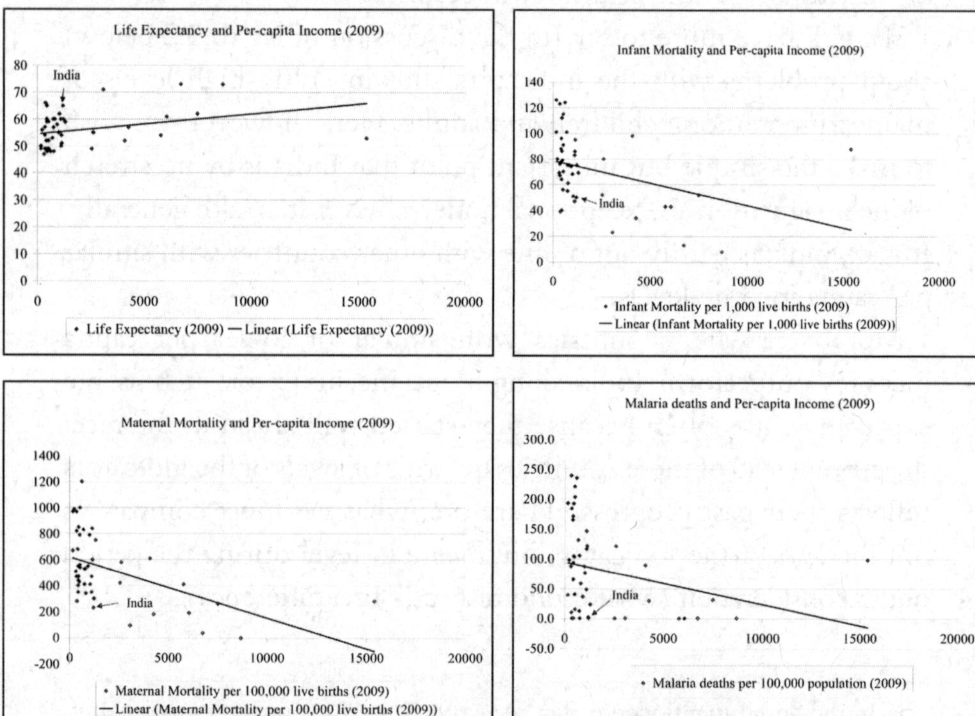

FIGURE 5.1: COMPARING INDIA TO THE COUNTRIES IN SUB-SAHARAN AFRICA IN TERMS OF LIFE EXPECTANCY, INFANT MORTALITY, MATERNAL MORTALITY AND DEATHS DUE TO MALARIA

Source: World Development Indicators for per capita incomes and WHO (2011) for other indicators.

But how does India compare with the critics' favourite countries—Bangladesh and China? Table 5.1 provides vital statistics for these countries and India, as reported in the 2011 World Health Organization (WHO) publication.

TABLE 5.1: SELECTED INDICATORS: BANGLADESH, CHINA AND INDIA, 2009

Health Indicator	*India*	*China*	*Bangladesh*
Per capita income, 2009 (current dollars)	1192	3744	551
Life expectancy at birth in 2009 (years)	65	74	65
Stillbirth rate (per 1000 total births)	22	10	36
Infant mortality, 2009 (per 1000 live births)	50	17	41
Maternal mortality, 2008 (per 100,000 live births)	230	38	340
Death from malaria, 2008 (per 100,000 population)	1.9	0	1.8
Per cent children stunted, 2000-09	47.9	11.7	43.2
Per cent children underweight, 2000-09	43.5	4.5	41.3

Source: WDI of the World Bank for per capita GDP and World Health Organization (2011) for the remaining indicators.

Take Bangladesh first. Without discounting its achievements, we must deflate them relative to those of India, refuting the unwarranted encomiums for Bangladesh and the exaggerated criticisms directed at India.

The performance of Bangladesh relative to that of India in terms of health indicators is significantly more equivocal than has been reported by the critics. India and Bangladesh enjoy the same life expectancy at birth. Bangladesh has a lower infant mortality rate than India (41 per 1000 live births against the latter's 50) but its rate of stillbirth more than offsets the difference (36 per 1000 births against India's 22): an inconvenient fact that almost all observers emphasizing the lower infant mortality in Bangladesh ignore.[2] The maternal mortality rate in Bangladesh is, in fact, much higher than in India. Mortality due to malaria is almost similar while Bangladesh edges out India only marginally on nutrition indicators.

In comparing Bangladesh and India, we must also take into account history. According to the United Nations (World Population Prospects, the 2010 revision), life expectancy in Bangladesh during 1950-55 was forty-five years compared to just thirty-eight years in India. The 1971 war led to a major dip in most health indicators of Bangladesh but they recovered in the following decades. At least some of the accelerated progress Bangladesh has achieved during the 1980s and beyond is therefore to be attributed to its return to the initial conditions.

This point is reinforced when we compare Bangladesh to West Bengal, with which it has a shared history and geography. Not only are the two entities located in the same region; they were once part of the same larger state in pre-independence India. It turns out that West Bengal outperforms Bangladesh in terms of health indicators. During 2002-06, it enjoyed a life expectancy at birth equalling sixty-five years. And its infant mortality rate at 33 per 1000 live births in 2009 and maternal mortality of 141 during 2004-06 were considerably lower than the corresponding rates reported for Bangladesh in Table 5.1.[3]

---

2. For example, see the recent attack by Dreze and Sen (2011) on the health achievements of India as compared to Bangladesh and other South Asian countries.
3. We may also add that in terms of the United Nations Human Development Index (HDI), India ranks ahead of Bangladesh by ten places. It may be recalled in this context that it was Amartya Sen, a leading proponent of the

(Contd....)

Turn next to the India-China comparison. Some critics of Indian performance on health argue that despite acceleration in growth since the 1980s, India has done poorly relative to China in improving its health indicators. Such assertions are misleading for at least two reasons. First, growth in the 1980s, 1990s and early 2000s has been much faster in China than in India.[4] And second, like Bangladesh, China has enjoyed a historical advantage over India. For example, China had already gained much of its lead over India in life expectancy by the early 1970s (See Figure 5.2).

Indeed, the gap in life expectancy between China and India has steadily declined in recent decades, falling from 13.2 years at its peak in 1971 to 9.3 years in 2009. It is ironic that Amartya Sen, who has been deploring India for its poor achievements in health vis-à-vis China, had himself made this point in 2005 stating, 'The gap between India and China has gone from fourteen years to seven (since 1979) because of (China) moving from a Canada-like system to a US- like system.'[5]

(...contd.)

view that Bangladesh has outdone India in terms of human development, who helped the United Nations Development Programme design the HDI. Oddly, as Panagariya (2011b) pointed out, Sen (2011) neglects to cite this statistic in his critique of India in relation to Bangladesh. Indeed, any references to the index remain conspicuously missing even from Dreze and Sen (2011), which was published well after Panagariya (2011b).

4. It is odd that authors disparaging India often applaud Bangladesh for doing well in health outcomes despite its lower per capita income but gloss over the much larger per capita-income gap India suffers vis-à-vis China when they compare it to the latter.
5. See 'An *Annie Hall* Moment: A Nobel Prize-winning economist spouts off, and a Chinese survivor sets him straight,' originally published in *The Wall Street Journal*, 21 February 2005, and available at http://www.parrikar.org/misc/amartya-wsj.pdf (accessed on 3 March 2012). According to the report, speaking in Hong Kong, Sen had argued that while China had made great

(Contd....)

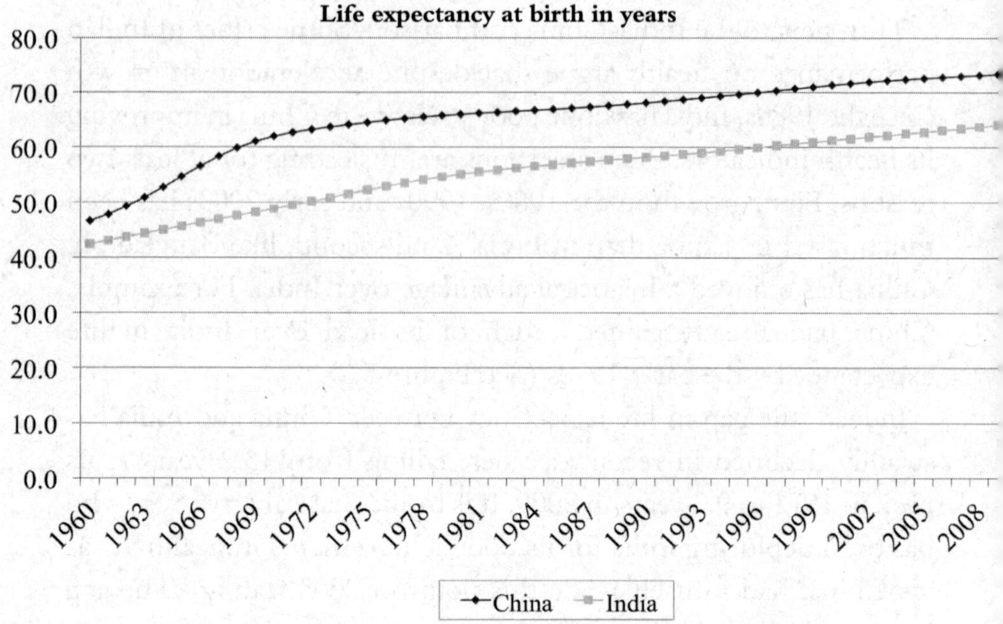

FIGURE 5.2: LIFE EXPECTANCY IN INDIA AND CHINA, 1960-2009

Source: Based on the data from World Development Indicators of the World Bank.

(…contd.)

strides in medicine during the Cultural Revolution, the move to a privatized system in recent years had made the system less fair and efficient. It so happened, however, that the audience included a Hong Kong banker, Weijian Shan, who had lived through the Cultural Revolution and had been one of Mao's 'barefoot doctors'. The report notes that Shan was surprised by Sen's comments and went on to state to the audience, 'I observed with my own eyes the total absence of medicine in some parts of China. The system was totally unsustainable. We used to admire India.' He added that when he observed medical school graduates in Taiwan serving in the countryside in the 1980s during a visit there, he thought, 'China ought to copy Taiwan.' Shan further stated that had Mao's medicine system been made optional, 'nobody would have opted for it.'

As a concluding thought, we state that there is little doubt that India has some ways to go in the area of health. But this requires a realistic assessment of both achievements and failures. If income increases have indeed helped in improving health outcomes, this needs to be recognized. Otherwise we would erroneously conclude that income increases are not crucial to improving human welfare after all.

~

Myth 5.2: India suffers from the worst malnutrition anywhere in the world, including the much poorer countries in sub-Saharan Africa.

There is constant repetition by Indian as well as foreign-based civil society groups, journalists, international institutions, bloggers and even academics that India suffers from the worst malnutrition anywhere in the world. Some also contend that the country is making no progress in bringing malnutrition down. Indeed, this has been the latest illusion to which the critics of Indian reforms are clinging.

As a representative example, the headline of a blog post by Meg Towle on the website of Columbia University's Earth Institute asks, 'India is booming—so why are nearly half of its children malnourished?' Towle opens the article thus, 'India has more hungry people—and the highest burden of child malnutrition—than any country in the world. The 2010 Global Hunger Index designates national levels of hunger as *alarming*, and India scores lower than many sub-Saharan African countries despite having a considerably higher GDP.' She adds, 'The percentage of children under age three who are underweight has virtually not changed between 1998-1999 and 2005-2006, hovering under 50 per cent.'[6]

Indeed, nutrition among children as well as adults is an important and urgent problem in India. This being said, addressing it effectively also requires proper analysis. To date, however, rhetoric and journalistic assertions such as that of Meg Towle, which are unfortunately carried on websites of institutions that claim to be scientific but fall short in practice, have filled the public policy space, misleading many. Our critique below shows why.

Begin with child nutrition. There are very serious measurement issues with translating the heights and weights of children into stunting (low height for age) and underweight (low weight for age).[7] Before we discuss them, however, it is useful to consider the evidence, such as there is, which is being currently utilized to reach judgements on the issue.

At the outset, we must recall our earlier documentation of the fact that health as an objective had received ample attention from the beginning of development planning in India. Nutrition, within health, was no exception: the First Five-Year Plan (1951-56) had devoted a substantial separate section to it. More importantly, India is perhaps the only developing country where systematic and comparable surveys at regular intervals aimed at measuring nutrition among children as well as adults were conducted since the 1970s.

As early as 1972, the Indian Council of Medical Research, Hyderabad had established the National Nutritional Monitoring Bureau (NNMB), which has conducted regular nutrition surveys of rural populations in nine states. The NNMB surveys provide

---

6. The post is at http://blogs.ei.columbia.edu/2011/03/24/india-is-booming-so-why-are-nearly-half-of-its-children-malnourished-part-1/ (accessed on 21 September 2011).
7. There is a third measure of child nutrition known as wasting, which measures weight for height. The problem with this measure is that even if the height-for-age and weight-for-age measures are showing improvements, it will show deterioration if the former improvement is sufficiently faster. Because of this strange characteristic of this measure, we do not discuss it.

comparable nutrition indicators for the periods 1975-79, 1988-90, 1996-97 and 2003-06.

Figure 5.3 depicts the evolution of the proportions of the underweight and stunted children between ages one and five years according to these surveys. The estimates are based on pooled observations from all nine NNMB states. We cannot overemphasize the fact that both measures show a *steady improvement* in child nutrition status, contrary to Meg Towle's claim (though that improvement is accompanied by India still showing exceptionally high levels of malnutrition, a separate issue over which Towle chides India and which we address below).

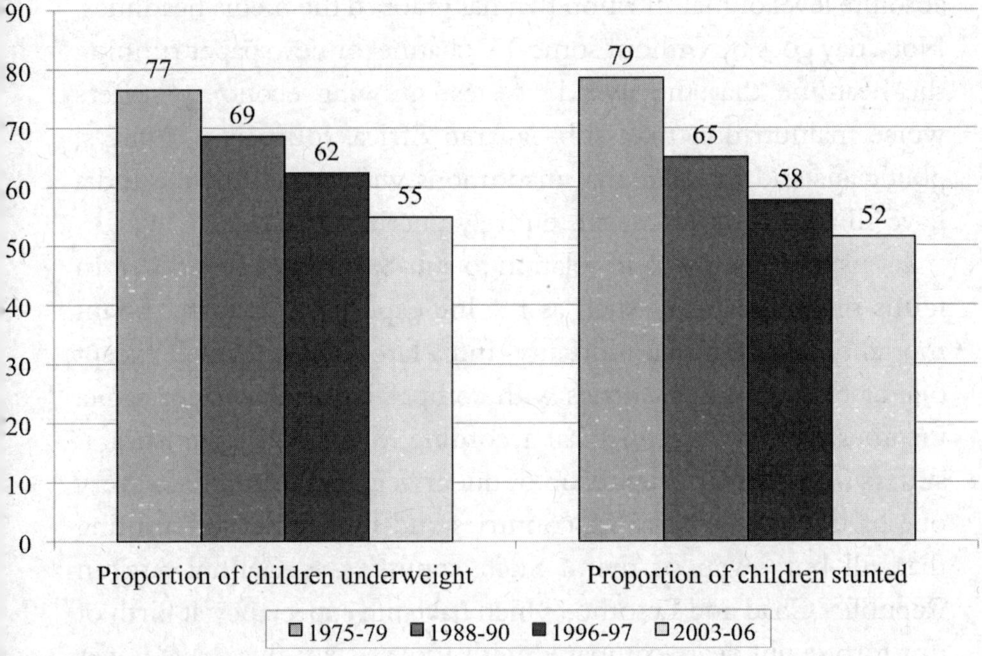

FIGURE 5.3: MALNOURISHMENT AMONG CHILDREN ABOVE ONE AND BELOW FIVE YEARS OF AGE IN RURAL AREAS OF NINE STATES

Source: Authors' construction based on NNMB (1999), Report of Second Repeat Survey-Rural, Indian Council of Medical Research, Hyderabad, Table 19 and NNMB Fact Sheet 2003-06 at http://www.nnmbindia.org/downloads.html (accessed 27 June 2011).

Evidence from a more recent comprehensive source, the National Family Health Survey (International Institute for Population Sciences and Macro International 2007), corroborates the trend indicated by the NNMB estimates. This newer source covers virtually all states and rural as well as urban areas and has conducted three rounds of surveys in 1992-93, 1998-99 and 2005-06. Comparable child nutrition estimates are available for children under three years of age for 1998-99 and 2005-06. It turns out that the proportion of the stunted children fell from 51 to 45 per cent and that of underweight children from 43 to 40 per cent between these two years.

The decline in malnutrition notwithstanding, it is the high absolute level of malnutrition that has grabbed the media headlines. Not a day goes by without some TV channel or newspaper running the headline that the world's fastest growing economy suffers worse malnutrition than sub-Saharan Africa. Journalists, NGOs, politicians and international institutions within and outside India have all accepted these levels entirely uncritically.

Let us consider India in relation to sub-Saharan Africa (SSA). In terms of vital statistics such as the life expectancy at birth, infant mortality and maternal mortality, India fares better than all except one or two of SSA countries with comparable or lower per capita incomes. So it is puzzling that according to the WHO statistics, it suffers from higher proportion of underweight children than every one of the forty-eight SSA countries and higher rate of stunting than all but seven of them. Such countries as Central African Republic, Chad and Lesotho, which have life expectancy at birth of just forty-eight years compared with India's sixty-five, have lower rates of stunted and underweight children.

To further underline the absurdity of the malnutrition numbers for India, compare Kerala and Senegal. Kerala exhibits vital statistics edging towards those in the developed countries: life expectancy of seventy-four years, infant mortality rate of 12 per 1000 live births and maternal mortality rate of 95 per 100,000 live births. The corresponding figures for Senegal are far worse at 62, 51 and 410 respectively. But nutrition statistics say that Kerala has 25 per cent stunted children compared to 20 per cent of Senegal and 23 per cent underweight children relative to 14.5 per cent of the latter. In Punjab, which has a life expectancy of seventy years and is the breadbasket and milk dairy of India, 37 per cent of the children are stunted and 25 per cent underweight.

It is tempting to argue that indicators other than child malnutrition are poorer in sub-Saharan Africa due to the toll taken by HIV/AIDS. But it is hard to believe that AIDS would affect infant mortality adversely but not measures of nutrition. Moreover, at least in Senegal, HIV prevalence has been stable at under 1 per cent of the population since 1997. Therefore, the differences between this country and Kerala cannot be attributed to HIV-related factors.

To make sense of this nonsense, we must look at how the stunting rates are calculated (the procedure for determining underweight children is identical). To classify a child of a given age and sex as stunted, we must compare his or her height to a pre-specified standard. The WHO sets this standard. In the early 2000s, it collected a sample of 8,440 children representing a population of healthy breastfed infants and young children in Brazil, Ghana, India, Norway, Oman and the United States. This 'reference' population provided the basis for setting the standards.

As expected, when comparing children of a given age and sex even within this healthy sample, heights and weights differed due to genetic differences. Therefore, some criterion was required to identify stunting among these children. In each group, identified by age and sex, the WHO defined the bottom 2.25 per cent of the children as stunted according to height. The height of the child at 2.25 percentile then became the standard against which children of the same age and sex in other populations were to be compared to identify stunting. A similar procedure applied to setting the standard for the identification of underweight children.

The key assumption underlying this methodology is that *if properly nourished*, all child populations would produce outcomes similar to the WHO reference population, with only 2.25 per cent of the children at the bottom remaining stunted and underweight. Higher rates of stunting would indicate above-normal malnutrition. So the million-dollar question is whether this assumption really holds for the population of children from which the estimate of half of Indian children being stunted is derived?

As it happens, the answer to the question can be found buried in a recent study published by the Government of India (2009a). The latest estimate for stunting in India has been derived from the third National Family Health Survey (NFHS-3) mentioned earlier. The report draws a highly restricted sample from the fuller NFHS-3 sample consisting of *elite* children, defined as those 'whose mothers and fathers have secondary or higher education, who live in households with electricity, a refrigerator, a TV, and an automobile or truck, who did not have diarrhoea or a cough or fever in the two weeks preceding the survey, who were exclusively breastfed if they were less than five months old, and who received complementary foods if they were at least five months old' (Government of India 2009a, p. 10).

If the assumption that proper nutrition guarantees the same outcome in every population as in the WHO reference population is valid, the proportion of stunted children in this sample should be 2.25 per cent. But the study reports this proportion to be above 15 per cent! The assumption is violated by a wide margin.

The implication of this and other facts is that Indian children are genetically smaller on average. A competing hypothesis, which says that it may take several generations before nutrition levels improve, fails to explain how, without a genetic advantage, the far poorer sub-Saharan African countries, which lag behind India in almost all vital statistics, could have pulled so far ahead of India in child nutrition. Moreover, the trend of the stunting proportions shown in Figure 5.3 would suggest that nearly all those born in the 1950s and before are stunted! This is as absurd as it gets.

We note here with some puzzlement the uneven treatment of child malnutrition by prominent activist-economist Jean Dreze in his different writings. Thus, in the article with Angus Deaton in the *Economic and Political Weekly* (Deaton and Dreze 2008), Dreze discusses at length the finding that even the elite Indian children fail to attain the high nutrition levels exhibited by the WHO 2006 population. Yet, when writing in the *Outlook* magazine with Amartya Sen on the same issue, he makes no mention whatsoever of the qualifications this finding implies. In the latter article, the authors begin with two opposite narratives of the post-reform India, a brighter one based on accelerated growth and a gloomy one rooted in poor performance in education and health. In articulating the gloomy narrative, the authors regurgitate the malnutrition indicators that place India below nearly all sub-Saharan African countries without indicating any of the qualifications discussed in Deaton and Dreze (2008).

Turning briefly to adult malnutrition (as distinct from child malnutrition that we have addressed already) next, the story told by the critics is equally suspect. The source of alarm here is the steady decline in per capita calorie consumption in rural India, with no clear trend in urban India during the last twenty-five years. Deaton and Dreze (2008), who provide a comprehensive survey of the evidence, point to per capita calorie consumption and the proportion of the population reporting lack of food as sending conflicting signals on hunger. On one hand, per capita calorie consumption fell from 2240 in 1983 to between 2000 and 2100 in the first half of the 2000s. On the other, the proportion of those reporting lack of food fell from 17.3 per cent in 1983 to just 2.5 per cent in 2004-05. Alongside, per capita protein consumption has declined while per capita fat consumption rose in both rural and urban areas.

There are several possible explanations for the decline in calorie consumption while the proportion of the population reporting lack of food drops dramatically. One is that increased mechanization in agriculture, improved means of transportation and improved absorption due to improved epidemiological environment (better child and adult health and better access to safe drinking water) have curtailed the need for calorie consumption. Another possible explanation is a shift from more nutritious coarse grains, such as millet and sorghum, to less nutritious but finer ones such as rice, wheat and fruits.

Adult weights and heights, which are more direct measures of nutrition, do show steady, even if slow, improvements. According to the NNMB surveys to which we have previously alluded, the population with below-normal Body Mass Index (BMI) of 18.5 fell from 56 per cent to 33 per cent for men and from 52 to 36 per cent for women between 1975-79 and 2004-05 (Deaton and Dreze 2008, Table 10). In absolute terms, the proportions of men and women with below-normal BMI prevailing in 2004-05 are high when seen in the international context. But this is an issue relating to the *level*, not *change*, which is the centre of concern of those focusing on increased hunger.

In conclusion, we remind that the purpose of our critique is not to suggest for a moment that all is well with child and adult nutrition in India. We fully appreciate that despite the progress it has made, India remains very far from the progress made by the developed countries in all aspects of health, including child and adult nutrition, and therefore has a long way to go.

But this requires a proper assessment of where precisely the greatest deficiencies are so that scarce revenues are spent prudently. Overstating problems has its own hazards: if healthy children are designated as malnourished, we might push them towards obesity and, likewise, if we misdiagnose the problem of a lack of proper balance in diet as one of low calorie consumption, we would erroneously push calorie consumption.

Myth 5.3: The Kerala Model has yielded superior education and health outcomes.

The evidence is unequivocal that Kerala has the best all-round education and health indicators amongst all Indian states. Its literacy rates for both males and females and life expectancy are higher and the rates of infant mortality, maternal mortality and malnutrition are lower than for all other states in India. Therefore, the superior education and health outcomes in Kerala are not in question.

But the evidence that there is a clearly identifiable Kerala Model to which these superior outcomes can be attributed is absent. Authors Richard Frank and Barbara Chasin offer a definition, but beyond the redistribution of land, it is descriptive of the Kerala experience rather than a set of policies that other states could potentially emulate.[8] As we noted earlier, land redistribution as an instrument of poverty alleviation was well known to Indian planners and was tried all over India but its implementation failed due to political opposition.[9]

Amartya Sen is also said to have talked about a Kerala Model but George Mathew (2001) has contradicted this by stating: 'Dr Amartya Sen during his recent visit to Kerala repudiated the argument that there is what is called a Kerala Model, and disclaimed

8. The interested reader may look up the details and references in the entry Kerala Model in Wikipedia (accessed on 23 September 2011).
9. The nature of the redistribution in different parts of the country depended on the land tenure system in place. The different land tenure systems came from different ideas and philosophies of the British in the different presidencies, as brilliantly documented by the historian Eric Stokes.

that he had ever used the term. At best, what has happened is Kerala's experience of development.' One has also to ask why the UNDP, where Haq and Sen were influential, embraced Kerala as its icon if it was not regarded as a 'developmental model'.[10]

Nonetheless, we may make four observations about Kerala's developmental approach and outcomes.

First, if redistribution has been at the heart of its achievements, as it is widely believed, we should find a relatively low level of, and a significantly declining trend in, inequality in the state. Yet, in regard to the level, according to the 2004-05 NSSO expenditure survey, Kerala exhibits the highest degree of inequality among the fifteen largest Indian states. It is possible that Kerala had greater success in redistributing land than other states but that has certainly not translated into a more egalitarian distribution of expenditures than in the rest of the country. Likewise, inequality fails to show a declining trend. Rural and urban inequalities in Kerala did fall between 1983 and 1993-94 but they rose back in 2004-05 to levels well above those in 1983. The significant decline in poverty between 1983 and 2004-05 could not be explained by the trend in inequality.

Second, Kerala began with a huge advantage in literacy over the rest of the country at independence. Since then, it is hard to find anything spectacular or unique in outcomes in Kerala. This is shown in Figure 5.4, which plots the evolution of literacy rates in Kerala, Maharashtra, Gujarat and India. Maharashtra began with a 20-percentage-points disadvantage vis-à-vis Kerala in 1951. By 2011, the disadvantage had been reduced to 11 percentage points. Gujarat began with a 25-percentage-points gap but narrowed it to 15 percentage points. Similar narrowing of the gap can be observed with respect to the Indiawide average.

---

10. An early influential case study of Kerala in this context was done by the Centre for Development Studies at Thiruvananthapuram for the Department of Economic and Social Affairs of the United Nations (1975).

The historical advantage of Kerala can also be observed in the indicators of health. Here we do not have ready access to the data from 1951 but we do have the series on life expectancy and infant mortality rates beginning in the early 1970s.

In Figure 5.5, we show the life expectancy at birth from 1970-75 to 2001-05 at five-year intervals in three high-achiever states: Kerala, Maharashtra and Tamil Nadu. Maharashtra begins with an eight-year disadvantage and Tamil Nadu with a twelve-year disadvantage vis-à-vis Kerala. But the gap narrows to approximately seven years in each case by 2001-05. A similar story unfolds in the infant mortality rate. The gap of more than 45 deaths per 1000 live births vis-à-vis Kerala in Maharashtra and Tamil Nadu in 1971 is reduced to less than twenty in 2009 in each case.

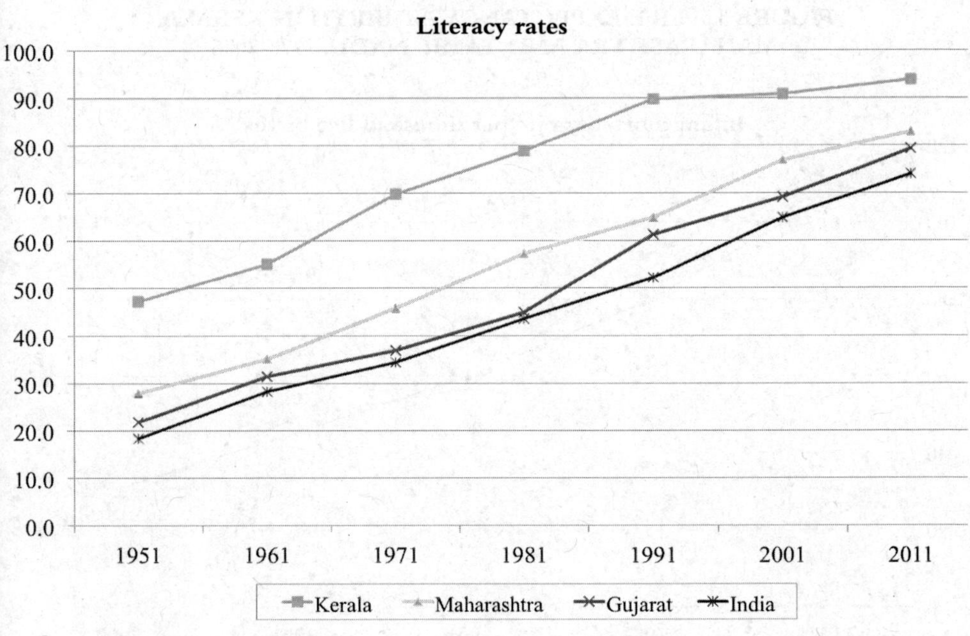

FIGURE 5.4: LITERACY RATES IN KERALA, GUJARAT, MAHARASHTRA AND INDIA, 1951-2011

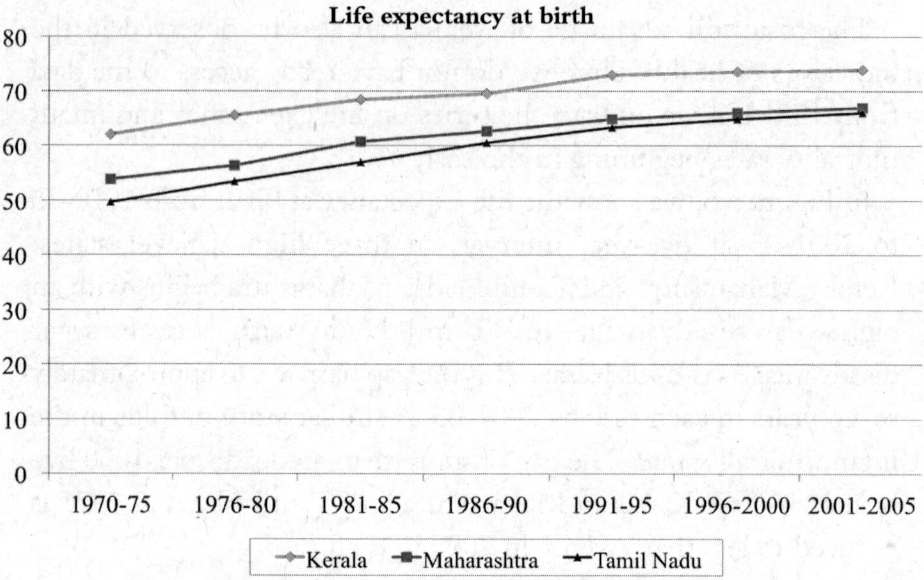

FIGURE 5.5: LIFE EXPECTANCY AT BIRTH IN KERALA, MAHARASHTRA AND TAMIL NADU, 1970-2006

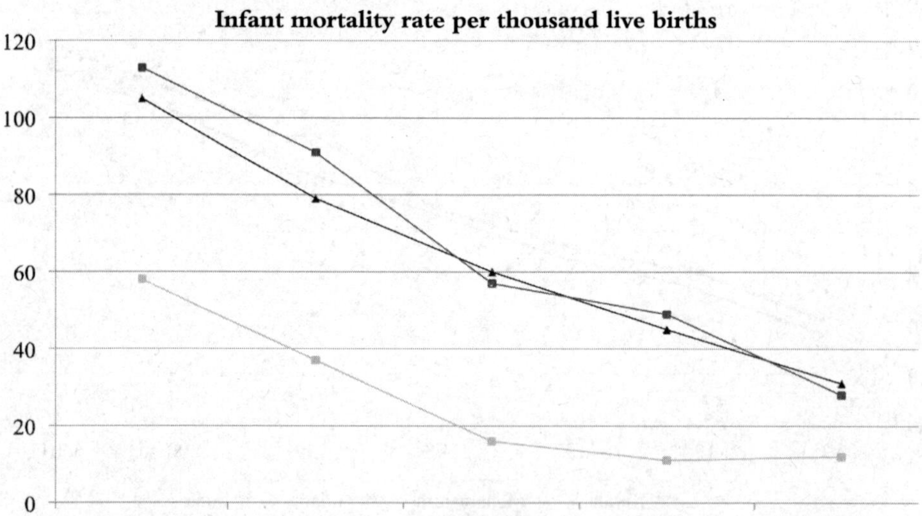

FIGURE 5.6: INFANT MORTALITY RATE PER THOUSAND LIVE BIRTHS IN KERALA, MAHARASHTRA AND TAMIL NADU, 1971-2009

Third, the advocates of the 'Kerala Model' argue that the achievements of the state with respect to poverty, education and health are to be distinguished from those of other states because it has done so despite its low per capita income and poor growth performance. Clearly, low per capita income and a high Gini coefficient (that is, unequal distribution of expenditures) and yet low levels of poverty in relation to other states cannot all be true simultaneously!

What gives way is the per capita income. As Chakraborty et al. (2011) show, once the available state per capita Gross State Domestic Product (GSDP) data are converted to the common 2004-05 base, Kerala has consistently ranked among the top five of the largest fifteen states by per capita GSDP since 1980-81, the year from which the GSDP series are available on a continuous and consistent basis.[11] The picture is even more dramatic when we consider per capita expenditure. According to the latest large-scale expenditure survey conducted in 2009-10, Kerala tops the list of the largest fifteen states ranked by per capita expenditures in both rural and urban areas. High achievements of Kerala in poverty alleviation, health and education are associated with high, not low, per capita incomes and expenditures.

Finally, the claim by the proponents of the 'Kerala Model' that the state achieved superior health and education outcomes through significantly more activist state interventions also turns out to be implausible. Once again, at least the available data do not reveal anything out of the ordinary. During the twenty years from 1991-92 to 2010-11 for which we are able to obtain public-health expenditures data for the states, per capita public expenditures on health turn out to be by far the highest in Goa. Indeed, it is

---

11. For consistency over time, Uttar Pradesh, Madhya Pradesh and Bihar are defined to include Uttarakhand, Chhattisgarh and Jharkhand, respectively, in these data. The latter three states were carved out of their mother states in 2000.

consistently three times the per capita public health expenditure in Kerala. Excluding Goa, Kerala spends more than its nearest rival state in eleven out of the twenty years. This may give some credence to the 'Kerala Model' except that the expenditures themselves are not all that large: but for the recent three or four years, they rarely exceed 1 per cent of the GSDP.

Far more impressive for Kerala are its private health expenditures. These data are available for each state for two years and they are by far the highest of any state (including Goa) in Kerala both on a per capita basis and as per cent of the GSDP. Thus, for example, in 2004-05, per capita private expenditure in Kerala was 2663 rupees per annum with the nearest rival Punjab spending only 1112 rupees. In comparison, per capita public expenditures of the two states in the same year were 280 and 234 rupees, respectively. Good health in Kerala is being financed predominantly by private expenditures (and this may have something to do also with the influx of massive remittances from the Middle East, which again would call into question the generally anti-globalization attitudes of the proponents of the 'Kerala Model').

This dominance of the private sector in the health sector is also observed in education. The NGO Pratham has been conducting extensive surveys of schoolchildren up to sixteen years of age in rural India in recent years. In its latest report (ASER 2010), it finds that with the exception of two or three tiny northeastern states, Kerala has the highest proportion of students between ages seven and sixteen in *private schools* in rural areas. At 53 per cent, it leads its nearest rival, Haryana, by a margin of 13 percentage points. The conventional and dominant story of Kerala as a *state-led* success in the post-independence era simply does not stand up to a careful empirical investigation.

When confronted with the evidence contained in our second observation above relating to the lacklustre performance of Kerala in terms of the *progress* in the social indicators in the post-independence era, proponents of the 'Kerala Model' counter that this comparison is misleading because each percentage-point improvement gets harder as we reach higher and higher level of achievement. For example, it is much harder to improve literacy from 50 to 60 per cent than from 20 to 30 per cent.

But there are at least three reasons why this defence is unconvincing:

- There is no compelling reason why the going should get rougher as the level of an indicator rises. True, the *scope* for improvement in literacy is less as the level of literacy gets closer to 100 per cent, but this need not translate into slower progress on the margin. Indeed, one can think of many reasons why the going might get easier as the literacy rate rises. The social pressure on a family to impart literacy to its children is higher, the larger the proportion of literate children in its neighbourhood. As the level of literacy rises, the pressure on the government to do something about those left behind also rises. Besides, at low levels of literacy, teachers are not easy to find since the handful of the literate are much in demand in other occupations.
- Again, if the 'Kerala Model' is that much more effective, it should be able to overcome a higher barrier and still deliver a superior outcome. In effect, resorting to the argument that the performance looks poorer because a higher starting point gives the state a handicap seems like an admission that the model is as mortal as any after all.
- Finally there is an objective way to test whether the higher starting point was truly a handicap or the 'Kerala Model' has indeed been overrated. We can accomplish this by assigning Kerala and the other states the same starting point and then evaluating who wins the race. In Figure 5.7, we depict the progress in literacy in Kerala, Maharashtra, Gujarat and India with their starting years being 1951, 1971, 1981 and 1981, respectively. These starting years assign the four entities as

close a starting literacy rate as data would permit.[12] We depict the literacy rates at four points in time since this is as far as we can go for Gujarat and India, whose starting point is 1981.

- Gujarat unambiguously beats Kerala: it starts more than two percentage points below Kerala in Year 0 but ends up a hair's breadth above it in Year 30. Both Maharashtra and India as a whole perform only slightly worse than Kerala. For example, Maharashtra is 1.4 percentage points below Kerala in year 0, and 2 percentage points below it in Year 30. India as a whole performs almost similarly.

The discussion up to this point has focused on the developments in health and education in Kerala in the post-independence era. An interesting and important unanswered question, however, is what accounts for Kerala having acquired its gigantic lead over much of the rest of India at independence. Even here the conventional story that this was to be attributed to the movements for social justice and social programmes by the rulers of Travancore and Cochin is quite incomplete. A careful scrutiny gives way to a more complex explanation that includes important links of the early success of Kerala to globalization.

---

12. Unfortunately, there still remains one small element of non-comparability due to the fact that the literacy rates for years 1951, 1961 and 1971 relate to rates for the above-five-years of population while those for subsequent years to above-seven-years of population. This makes the starting-year literacy rates for Kerala and Maharashtra as having been calculated on above-five-population basis and that for Gujarat and India on above-seven-population basis. Insofar as the literacy rate among children of five-to-seven years' age is likely to be lower than that for the above-seven population, if calculated on above-seven-population basis, the starting-year literacy rate of Kerala (and Maharashtra) would be higher than that shown in Figure 7.6. This would make the gains in Kerala by Year 30 even less impressive. We suspect, however, that since the population between five to seven years is a small proportion of the total above-five population, any bias on this account is likely to be tiny.

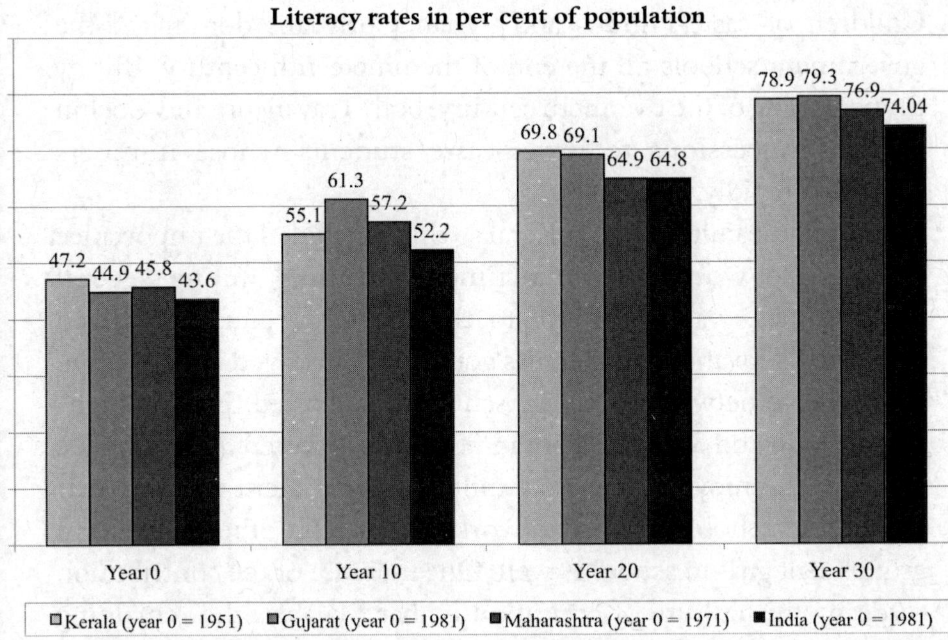

FIGURE 5.7: COMPARING PROGRESS IN LITERACY RATES IN KERALA TO THOSE IN GUJARAT, MAHARASHTRA AND INDIA BEGINNING AT APPROXIMATELY THE SAME LEVEL

While we have been unable to find reliable accounts of developments in the health sector in pre-independence Kerala, Robin Jeffrey (1992), who has spent many years living in various parts of India since the 1960s, offers a detailed account of the socioeconomic-political developments that contributed to the spread of literacy in Kerala in the second half of the nineteenth and first half of the twentieth century. Based on his account, four key factors can be highlighted.

First, the rulers in Travancore and Cochin played an important role in the spread of education. The Travancore maharajas began investing in the spread of vernacular primary schools in the 1860s. The maharajas of Cochin followed suit, beginning in the 1890s. Their objective was to spread modern knowledge to the widest circle of people through the use of the mother tongue, Malayalam.

Children of caste-Hindus and Syrian Christians dominated the government schools till the end of the nineteenth century. But by the beginning of the twentieth century, both Travancore and Cochin offered concessions to lower-caste students whose numbers expanded rapidly.

Second, the culture of old Kerala, which included the importance assigned to women by matrilineal tradition among several communities, was conducive to the spread of education. Even before the Travancore maharajas got actively involved in education, an extensive network of village schools had existed. Landed high-caste Hindu and Syrian Christian families supported these schools. The wealth enjoyed by these families allowed them to send their children to school rather than work. Nayars and other matrilineal groups sent girls to school as well. One measure of the contribution made by this culture of education is that Malabar, the remaining Malayalam-speaking district, which was administered by the Madras Presidency and had no princely government to promote education, never fell below the third place within the presidency overall and consistently ranked No.1 in female literacy.

Third, caste- and religion-based groups also played some role in the spread of education. Among the upper-caste groups, the Nair Service Society (NSS), which was founded in 1914, promoted education through the so-called Nair schools. The Sri Narayana Dharma Paripalana Yogam that the widely revered Sri Narayan Guru founded in 1903 played the same role among the lower-caste Ezhavas, though with less success since the community was much poorer and lacked resources. The Christian missionaries also helped accelerate the process of the spread of education. Protestant missionaries made their debut in Travancore with the arrival of Tobias Ringeltaube in 1806. He quickly got permission from the maharaja to open a few schools. According to Jeffrey (1992, p. 97), by the middle of the nineteenth century, Travancore had a higher density of Protestant missionaries than any other part of India. They not only actively promoted literacy directly, especially among the lower-caste Nadars, but also greatly influenced the largest Christian group, the Syrian Catholics, who started establishing formal, literacy-oriented schools in the early 1880s.

The fourth and last factor, which gets rarely highlighted in the spread of education in Kerala prior to independence, is economic. A necessary condition for all of the above agents of the spread of literacy to succeed was the availability of necessary resources. Those building schools had to have the necessary revenues and the parents sending children to school had to have enough income to make ends meet without the use of their children's labour. To sustain the process, it was also necessary that those acquiring education would have prospects for jobs commensurate with their qualifications.

This is where globalization played a key role. Roman coins commonly found in Kerala testify to its trade links abroad through pepper and cardamom exports going back 2000 years. Jeffrey suggests that this trade link is a plausible explanation for the early presence of Jews, Muslims and Christians—they came to trade and chose to stay. 'Long before Britain or America, Kerala was a part of a "world economic system".' (Jeffrey 1992, p. 72)

Beginning in the 1830s, cash crops saw a boom in Kerala. Europeans began establishing plantations to grow crops of interest to Europe and America. First came coffee; after its destruction by a leaf disease in 1880, came tea; and in the 1920s, cashew. Alongside, coconut, with its varied uses, turned into the most important cash crop with coconut trees springing up everywhere. Jeffrey (1992, p. 73) quotes the collector of Malabar in the mid-1930s as reporting to his superiors, 'All but the poorest Malabar ryots (peasants) have their own compounds of fruit trees.' Since coconut could not serve as a staple food, it had to be converted into money and money into food. This fact contributed in a big way to both the growth of trade as well as the conversion of Kerala into a cash economy. Jeffrey (1992, p. 73) writes, 'In this way, cash-oriented agriculture spread. Before about 1810, Kerala was, to be sure, part of a world market, but few Malayalis had to deal with it directly; but by the 1920s, few Malayalis could avoid it.'

The growth of commercial houses and estates created job opportunities for the educated, making education attractive. Cash crops also served as an excellent source of revenue to finance schools for the state as well larger landowners. Prosperity brought by the spread of cash crops made it possible for civic organizations to raise funds to open schools as well. There was thus an important link of the early spread of education in Kerala to markets and globalization.

The historic origin of pre-independence success of Kerala therefore owes as little to the 'Kerala Model' as does its post-independence performance.

Myth 5.4: Despite high growth, Gujarat has performed poorly in health and education.

This myth is the mirror image of the previous one, whereby rapid growth in Gujarat is alleged to have not translated into rapid progress in social indicators. The problem once again lies in inference on the basis of the *levels* of the indicators rather than the *change* in them achieved during the high-growth phase. Gujarat began with low social indicators but its progress has not been poor by any means.

We have already alluded to the superior performance of Gujarat in raising literacy rates in our discussion of the 'Kerala Model'. When compared with Kerala, Maharashtra and the Indiawide average, Gujarat made by far the largest percentage-points gain in literacy rates between 1951 and 2011. Additionally, even when we take approximately the same starting level of literacy as in Figure 5.7, the gains made by Gujarat exceed those made by Kerala, Maharashtra and the Indiawide average.

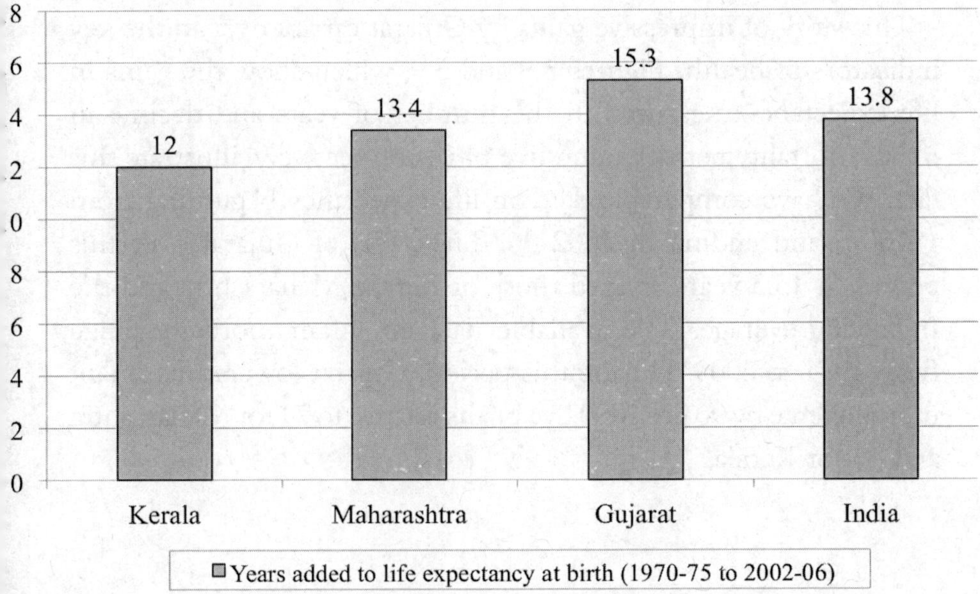

FIGURE 5.8: ADDITIONS TO LIFE EXPECTANCY IN YEARS: 1970-75 TO 2002-06

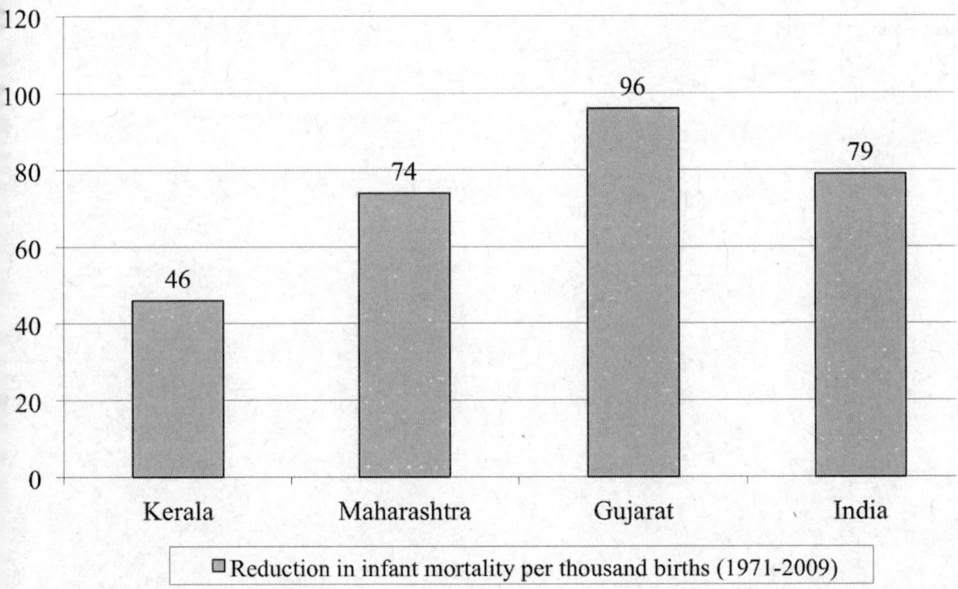

FIGURE 5.9: REDUCTIONS IN INFANT MORTALITY PER THOUSAND LIVE BIRTHS: 1971-2009

This story of impressive gains by Gujarat carries over to the key indicators of health. Figures 5.8 and 5.9, which show the gains in life expectancy measured in the number of years and decline in infant mortality per thousand live births respectively, illustrate this fact. We have comparable data on life expectancy beginning from 1970-75 and ending in 2002-06. The gains of Gujarat over this period, at 15.3 years, exceed those of Kerala, Maharashtra and the Indiawide average. The available data on infant mortality range from 1971 to 2009. During this period, Gujarat lowered its infant mortality rate by 96 per 1000 live births relative to 74 for Maharashtra and 46 for Kerala.

6

Yet Other Myths

We have now seen that growth, poverty, inequality, education and health are the key areas where the critics of reforms have tried to mobilize their opposition. But they have failed. So they have turned to a potpourri of yet other myths. Chief among them are the following five.

Myth 6.1: Reforms have led to increased suicides by Indian farmers.

Recent farmer suicides have properly been an emotionally charged issue in India. The result has been that new myths have arisen, condemning both the use of new GM (genetically modified) and BT (*Bacillus thuringiensis*) seeds in particular and Indian reforms in general.

Influential journalists such as P. Sainath (2009) of the newspaper

The Hindu, and activists such as Vandana Shiva (2004) have contributed to these concerns.[1] But the evidence they provide, and the explanations they advance, fail to substantiate the case they seek to make. This is not surprising since suicide is a complex phenomenon with multiple causes and, in the case of farmer suicides, even the basic facts are treacherous to analyse.

In the following analysis, we first look broadly at the problems afflicting the data on suicides, whether overall or among farmers. Next, we address the issue whether overall and farmer suicides are correlated with Indian reforms generally. We then assess the specific issue whether the new BT seeds have resulted in accelerated farmer suicides.

To begin with, data on suicides in general and by farmers in particular are not entirely reliable. In the latter case, the most commonly used series is also very short. The source on which most scholars rely is the annual publication, *Accidental Deaths and Suicides in India,* brought out by the National Crime Records Bureau (NCRB), ministry of home affairs. According to Nagaraj (2008), the chiefs of police of all states, Union territories and mega cities furnish data to NCRB, which in turn compiles and publishes them. Although NCRB has published the basic data since 1967, it began to provide details that allow farmer suicides to be identified

---

1. One of us (Bhagwati) has appeared on two prominent TV shows in the USA—the PBS and the Christianne Amanpour show—where Sainath was cited and Vandana Shiva made cameo appearances with claims about farmer suicides and their causes (such as the use of new BT seeds), which Bhagwati challenged. Interestingly, the PBS documentary, which was produced with great finesse, concentrated on one suicide, attributed to the use of the new BT seeds; later, on a panel discussion of the film at the Asia Society in New York where Bhagwati appeared, the producer made a frank admission: that they had discovered that this suicide had nothing to do with the farmer's use of the new seeds.

only in 1995. But the data for 1995 and 1996 are incomplete; the consistent series begins only in 1997.

Figure 6.1 plots the data reported by Nagaraj (2008). Three observations follow immediately. First, since the data begin only in 1997, strictly speaking, we cannot connect suicides to reforms generally. To do so convincingly, we must have the pre-reforms data going back to at least the 1970s and 1980s. It is quite remarkable that the critics of the Indian reforms have ignored this simple fact and gone about claiming such a link as if farmer suicides today are a new phenomenon (absent prior to their explicit identification by NCRB beginning in 1995).[2]

Second, we might hypothesize that since major additional reforms took place in the late 1990s and early 2000s and growth accelerated in 2003-04, a connection may still be forged through a comparison of suicide rates prior to 2003 and later. But whereas the general suicide rates do show a mildly rising trend in the last three years shown, farmer suicides rose in 2004 but fell in 2005 and 2006, dropping below their 2002 level.

Finally, and most intriguingly, we may compare the levels of farmer suicides relative to suicides in the general population. At their peak, reached in 2002, they were 16.3 per cent of the latter. But at least half of the Indian workforce is engaged in farming. This fact points to a much lower suicide rate per 100,000 individuals for farmers than in the general population. Given this fact, one might well be agitated—less about the farmer suicides than about why the suicide rate in the general population is so much higher and how we could bring it down to the levels prevailing among

2. This issue was raised on the previously-cited Christianne Amanpour TV show by Bhagwati when he observed that suicides by indebted farmers had been part of what he had read about in Indian agriculture when he was a student almost half a century ago; and suicides by farmers were not a new phenomenon.

farmers. On the other hand, the difference is so huge between the measured farmer and non-farmer suicide rates that one may question the validity of the data.[3]

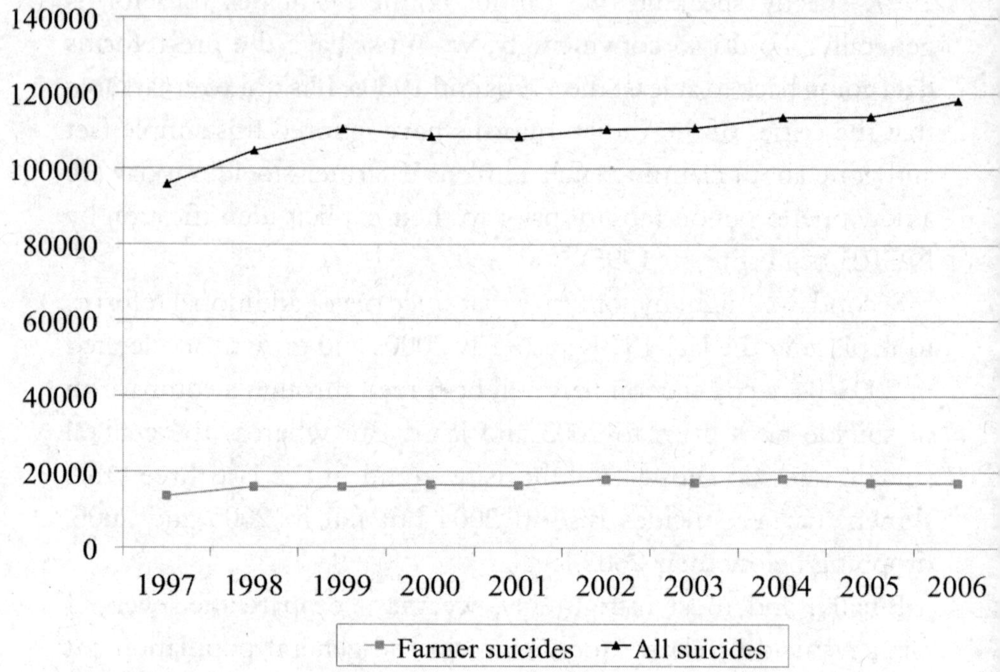

FIGURE 6.1: SUICIDES IN THE GENERAL POPULATION AND AMONG FARMERS

Source: Authors' construction using data in Nagaraj (2008).

3. We may note that Nagaraj calculates suicide rates per 100,000 farmers and finds them substantially higher than the suicide rates in the general population per 100,000 people. But in doing so, he is comparing apples and oranges. To be consistent, farmer suicides per 100,000 farmers should be compared to suicides in the general population per 100,000 working, rather than the entire, population.

But while there is no evidence for the link between reforms and suicides in general and farmer suicides in particular, it leaves open the narrower and more explosive issue of whether the introduction of BT seeds in cotton in 2002 led to an acceleration of suicides among farmers.

Contrary to what the critics assert, however, it is evident from Figure 6.1 that farmer suicide rates show no accelerating trend from 2002. Yet, according to Gruere, Mehta-Bhatt and Sengupta (2008, Figure 11), the area under BT cotton expanded from nil in 2002 to more than 3.5 million hectares in 2006. These authors also look at individual states such as Maharashtra and Andhra Pradesh and fail to find any correlations between rising trends in farmer suicides and the expansion of the area cultivated under BT cotton.

Gujarat provides the most compelling example from this perspective. It was the first state to adopt BT cotton, and the third largest after Maharashtra and Andhra Pradesh. By 2006, 25 per cent of its total area under cotton had come under BT cotton. At the same time, it has the lowest numbers of reported farmer suicides at approximately 500 per year with the number slightly lower on average during 2003-06 than in the preceding five years.[4]

Then again, the causes of suicides are many. This is so even in the case of farmer suicides. It is, therefore, unlikely that a single cause like BT seeds would emerge as the main factor. A study by Deshpande (2002) that examined in depth ninety-nine cases of farmer suicides in Karnataka underlines the need for this caution. Deshpande extensively interviewed the friends and relatives of the victims and considered a long list of proximate causes, including the volume and the terms of debt, crop failures, dowry burden and

4. None of this is to deny the existence of problems that would accompany any new technology that shows promise. Therefore, there have been problems with fake seeds being sold and farmers lacking proper information on the use of pesticide.

drinking problems. He did not find a single case in which one reason accounted for the fateful event. On the average, there were three to four reasons in each case. Farm-related reasons get cited only approximately 25 per cent of the time as reasons for suicide. Even more surprisingly, he notes (p. 2608): 'Debt burden and the price crash, which have been quite commonly referred as important factors by the media and public personalities, happen to score 6 per cent probability of being prominent reasons for suicides along with other reasons.'

Nonetheless, we may observe that in the few regions where farmer suicides have followed the introduction of BT seeds, the cause could well be that small, highly-indebted farmers are bamboozled by salesmen employed by the corporations producing the seeds into buying and using the seeds, using high-cost loans, on the promise that this investment will produce high returns to relieve the debts under which they labour. This is then a casino-type bet. When that fails, for reasons such as poorly implemented planting or teething problems endemic to the region or simply a bad harvest, the distress rises to a level that prompts a suicide.

It is noteworthy that the earlier green revolution was not a result of privately invented and propagated seeds; that a proper government-financed and organized extension service aimed at educating farmers in the application of scientific research and knowledge to agricultural practices, for which Dr Swaminathan deservedly became famous, complemented it. This also meant that the larger farms, with more resources and ability to take the risk of failure, used the new seeds while the small farmers did not.

This time around, in the few regions where farmer suicides have occurred, the small farmers who have been misled by the salesmen peddling the new seeds unscrupulously (much like the salesmen who were peddling risky housing mortgages to undeserving mortgage buyers in the US and feeding the housing bubble, whose collapse forced these victims into distress sales) are the victims. The answer then appears to be a regulation of these salesmen and measures such as the setting up of an extension service for the BT seeds, whose cost should be charged to the corporations that are selling the BT seeds.

Myth 6.2: The post-1991 reforms have led to increased corruption.

A common refrain of the left-wing critics is that the post-1991 'neo-liberal' reforms have led to an exponential increase in corruption. For example, in an article entitled 'Economic Reforms: Fountainhead of Corruption' in the *New Age Weekly*, the central organ of the Communist Party of India, R.S. Yadav writes: 'The early stage of liberalization process in the 1980s was accompanied by (the) Bofors scandal, which for the first time in independent India, put the prime minister and the prime minister's office in the centre of the scandal. After the full-fledged adoption of neo-liberal reforms in 1991, the country came across a wave of scams and scandals, every scandal bigger in magnitude, and more bold, and involved people at the helm of governance, administration and industry.'[5]

Among such critics, the young are blissfully ignorant of history while the old probably suffer from amnesia.[6] The near-absence of corruption was among the hallmarks of the Indian political virtue in the 1950s.[7] Corruption broke out, not with the liberal reforms

---

5. See http://www.newageweekly.com/2011/09/economic-reforms-fountain-head-of.html (accessed on 5 October 2011).
6. The following discussion draws on Panagariya (2011e).
7. Recall our discussion in Part I.

of the 1980s, but under the licence-permit raj that peaked in the 1970s during the socialist-era policies of Prime Minister Indira Gandhi. With the government controlling the manufacture, distribution and price of numerous major commodities, bribes became virtually the only means of accessing the latter within a reasonable timeframe. Thus, for example, if you wanted a phone, car or scooter, you had to choose between a many-years-long queue and a bribe. If you were among the lucky few to have a phone, a bribe was still necessary to receive the dial tone. If you wanted an airline ticket or a reserved railway seat, your choice was to take a chance and stand in a long queue or resort to 'baksheesh'. It was no different for a bag of cement. God forbid, if you had to travel abroad, many-hours-long queues and unfriendly customs officials would be awaiting you upon return. As an entrepreneur, if you wanted an investment or import licence or to stop your competitor from getting one, bribing a senior official in the relevant ministry would do it.

It was the reforms, initially carried out on an ad hoc basis but made more systemic in 1991, which freed the ordinary citizens and entrepreneurs from their daily travails and humiliations at the hands of the petty government officials. This may not be obvious to the young, who probably do not even know what the licence-permit raj was, but those of us who lived through this history know that reforms bid goodbye to many forms of corruption.

The critical question then is: why have we witnessed so many mega corruption cases recently? The success of reforms has opened up new opportunities in several areas to make profits. But because the reforms have still not been extended to these new areas, new avenues for corruption of the older variety have now multiplied.

Thus, reforms (which include opening up our access to the world markets) and the growth resulting from them have pushed up the prices of scarce resources such as minerals and land. These price increases have multiplied the scope for government officials (and colluding businessmen) to make vast sums of illegal money through the pre-reforms-type arbitrary and opaque allocations of the rights to extract minerals and the acquisition and resale of land.

The 2G scandal offers a dramatic example of how the success of past reforms (in opening up new opportunities to make profits) and the failure to extend them (to cover these new opportunities) have combined to produce a mega scandal. With the telephone arriving in India in the early 1880s, it had taken the country 110 years to reach five million phones in 1990-91. But the spectacular success of telecom reforms brought the number to 300 million at the end of 2007-08 with the rate of expansion reaching 6.25 million per month. This turned the spectrum on which cell calls travel into a resource worth tens of billions of dollars. That allegedly allowed the then telecom minister, A. Raja, to make handsome sums for himself and his friends when allocating the spectrum to his wealthy friends for a small 'fee' in January 2008. Had reforms been extended to government procurement and sales policies, Raja would not have had the freedom to allocate the spectrum at a pre-specified low price to his friends with bribes allegedly provided in return.

The most effective course of action available to the government to curb corruption, therefore, is clearly the deepening and the broadening of the reforms to new areas. The reform of the antiquated Land Acquisition Act of 1894, the issuance of land titles that would improve access to credit,[8] transparency in government procurement and competitive auctions of mineral rights and telecom spectrum are among such measures.

---

8. This reform has been most associated with the Peruvian intellectual Hernando de Soto. Whereas the micro-credit programme, which Ilabehn Bhatt pioneered and promoted through SEWA (Self-Employed Women's Association) two years earlier than Mohammad Yunus, and the priority-sector lending programme of the Reserve Bank of India, initiated even earlier, provide loans to very small, poor borrowers without collateral, de Soto intriguingly argued that the poor did, in fact, have assets but that the lack of clear titles prevented them from turning them into effective collateral.

Myth 6.3: Focus on growth and policies to promote it, such as opening up the country to inward direct investment, crowd out discussion of the really important questions that should concern us because of our poverty.

Of course, the growth strategy was designed precisely to lift the poor and the underprivileged out of poverty. And, as we have demonstrated, the strategy did work and helped the poor and the underprivileged once the counterproductive policy framework began to be dismantled and finally growth materialized. So it would seem astonishing that any serious analyst would claim that we 'crowd out' discussion of poverty!

Yet, Jean Dreze and Amartya Sen (1995, p. vii) have argued recently:

> Debates on such questions as the details of tax concessions to multinationals, or whether Indians should drink Coca-Cola, or whether the private sector should be allowed to operate city buses, tend to 'crowd out' the time that is left to discuss the abysmal situation of basic education and elementary health care, or the persistence of debilitating social inequalities, or other issues that have a crucial bearing on the well-being and freedom of the population.

In reviewing the Dreze and Sen book, one of us (Bhagwati 1998, p. 199) responded sharply:

> Much is wrong here. No one can seriously argue that there is a crowding out when the articulation of Indians is manifest in multiplying newspapers, magazines and books and the expression of a whole spectrum of views on economics and politics; this reviewer has noticed no particular shyness in discussing social issues, including inequality and poverty in India . . . But, more

> important, the put-down of attention to multinationals misses the point that India's economic reforms require precisely that India join the Global Age and that India's inward direct investments were ridiculously small in 1991, around $100 million, and that this was an important deficiency that had to be fixed.
>
> The reference to Coca-Cola is no better, serving as a cheap shot against multinational investment; but it also betrays the assumption that Coca-Cola is drunk by the elite or the Westernized middle class, not by the truly poor. It is more likely, however, that the former derive their caffeine from espresso coffee as well whereas the poor are the ones who must depend on Coke instead!

In fact, we would go further and argue that the inefficiencies caused by pre-reform policies hurt, not the rich, but the poor and the lower middle class. This is because the rich manage to insulate themselves against the inefficiencies. Thus, take the Dreze-Sen derision of concern with the question of whether private operators should be allowed to run city buses. Anyone who has had to ride for an hour-and-a-half in a Delhi bus—as one of us (Bhagwati) did twice a day, from his small sublet in the suburb of Motibagh to Delhi University—will not scoff at the notion that one might improve the service by letting in the private sector; only those who enjoyed high salaries and consulting incomes and drove a Fiat could insulate themselves from the question of efficient city bus service. Similarly, reforms could help reduce the frequent interruptions in electricity supply, thus giving respite to the poor man who slept on a charpoy and used a small Usha fan to cope with the heat of the Delhi summer. The rich, on the other hand, had their own generators that took over during the interruptions of electricity supply, so that they could continue sleeping in their air-conditioned bedrooms.

Myth 6.4: The reforms have been characterized by 'market fundamentalism'.

That the reforms meant that India had embraced 'market fundamentalism' is an oft-repeated charge. In fact, the phrase 'market fundamentalism' has become an epithet levelled in the US by the populists such as the financier George Soros[9] and our colleague, the economist Joseph Stiglitz, at anyone who says anything in favour of markets, just as the word 'liberal' is an epithet hurled at those who ask for government interventions.

The 'M-word' is, in terms of abuse that obfuscates and prevents informed discourse, on a par with the 'L-word'. So is the use of the word 'neoliberal', which sounds more sinister than 'liberal'. When described pejoratively as a 'neoliberal' in a debate, one of us (Bhagwati) has successfully countered by saying: 'If you call me a neoliberal, I will call you a Neanderthal. We can debate on that basis if you insist. But I would rather win by debating you on specific policies where we have disagreements.'

In the case of India, the M-word betrays yet more folly. Outsiders are often ignorant of where we have come from. They assume that India has moved from pragmatism to market fundamentalism (construed as libertarianism or opposition to all intervention). But we really had, as we have documented here, what we can appropriately call 'anti-market' fundamentalism. Markets were virtually rejected, the private sector was steadily handicapped, and the use of foreign trade and inflows of foreign investment were strongly discouraged. With reforms, we then moved to pragmatism. In fact, we have nowhere completed our reforms: the legacy of the

---

9. Soros, whose conviction in Europe for insider trading has just been upheld on appeal, is of course known for having played the market himself for his huge profits from speculation on currencies.

'anti-market' fundamentalism still lingers since reformers must contend with the institutions and the interests (that is, lobbies) that grew up over the years around that economic philosophy and, in democratic societies, they can move only slowly.

Myth 6.5: The reforms were forced on India by conditionality from Bretton Woods institutions, who were captive to the 'Washington Consensus'.

Yet another populist myth, propagated in the Western media and repeated often by left-wing commentators in India, is that the International Monetary Fund (IMF) and the World Bank, which were captive to the so-called 'Washington Consensus', imposed the reforms on India.[10] The 'Washington Consenus' is, of course, yet another epithet used by Stiglitz who, we may recall, was vice president of the World Bank and oversaw its activities in many developing countries.[11]

Two points must be made. First, the Washington Consensus is nothing but Washington Conceit. Proposals for freer trade worldwide, and for promoting prosperity in India and other developing countries, owed to theoretical and empirical work that was developed in the early 1960s by Indian economists, and then

10. The term 'Washington Consensus' was originally introduced to refer to a set of relatively noncontroversial pro-market policy measures, including trade liberalization, fiscal discipline and tax reform but not capital-account convertibility. But it has now come to be used in the same pejorative sense as the terms 'neo-liberalism' and 'market-fundamentalism'.
11. He also has edited with Narcis Serra a book of essays, with a contribution by Deepak Nayyar at Jawaharlal Nehru University, who clearly shares Stiglitz's views, titled *The Washington Consensus Reconsidered*, Oxford University Press: 2009.

influenced thinking and policy at the World Bank.[12] Dani Rodrik, in one of his early papers written before he became sceptical of free trade, has said that the World Bank had produced no basic research: he was indeed right.

Of course, if one could say that our reforms were a result of something called the Washington Consensus, it would lend an extra edge in India, where many of us are keenly aware of our sovereignty and, on the intellectual left, are resentful of the US.

Second, it makes no sense to say that the reforms were exogenously 'imposed' from Washington, whether the IMF and the World Bank or the US Treasury. The crisis in 1991 provided an opportunity to change course. Ever since Bhagwati and Desai (1970) provided in their book the agenda for reform that the post-1991 reforms would begin to implement in earnest, it was *domestic* thinking and writing, and the growing sense that Indian policy-makers had shot themselves and the economy in both feet with counterproductive policies, that had driven home the need for reforms. A significant part of the conditionality attached to the loans secured by India from the Bretton Woods institutions was simply underlining what we ourselves wanted to do. In fact, where the World Bank wanted to push further, such as a proper exit policy for the firms and de-licensing of consumer goods imports in the early 1990s (but we did not because of political constraints), were matters on which many of our own reform-minded economists had written for years earlier.

If there is still any doubt about this, just ask yourself: if this was unpalatable and imposed exogenously, why did India not revert to its bad old ways once the crisis was behind it? In fact, successive

12. The revolution in post-war theory of commercial policy has been described, and its main findings summarized by Jagdish Bhagwati (who led this revolution starting 1963) in his Stockholm Lectures, published as *Free Trade Today*, Princeton University Press: 2001. The contributions by the late V.K. Ramaswami and by T.N. Srinivasan also played a major role.

governments only reinforced the reforms, though with varying boldness and pace. One of us (Panagariya) was at the World Bank from 1989 to 1993 and knows first-hand that after the first structural adjustment loan of December 1991, which concluded in December 1992, the World Bank chose to lend to India not because the latter accepted its conditionality but because it wanted to stay involved in the country. It was the World Bank that needed India rather than the other way around.[13]

It is pertinent to quote the late prime minister, Narasimha Rao, on this subject since it was during his tenure that the reforms were launched. The reluctance of Rao to say almost anything about the reforms is well known. But when asked whether the reforms had been undertaken under pressure from the IMF and the World Bank, he is reported to have said:[14]

> The reforms initiated by my government were designed both as a measure to meet an immediate situation as well as a long-term strategy for the country in the changed world conditions.
>
> We thought that these reforms were necessary and this has now been confirmed and has acquired a national consensus cutting across political parties.
>
> However, to say that they were made at the behest of the World Bank and IMF is not correct.
>
> We have evolved a model which is suited to our conditions, which is being termed as the middle way and Market Plus.

---

13. Panagariya was a member of the World Bank mission for the trade and investment liberalization loan during its first visit to Delhi in late March 1993. Senior officials at the Bank had held the view that the loan would not proceed unless India agreed to abolish import licensing on consumer goods. When the mission was told, however, that this was not on the cards, the Bank leadership quickly changed its mind and proceeded with the loan anyway. As a post script, India liberalized consumer goods imports almost a decade later, on 1 April 2001. But the World Bank kept lending to India in the meantime, without so much as a hiccup!
14. See Ahmad (1995).

India's experience in launching reforms is no different from that of Russia and China. As Padma Desai, a leading economist expert on Russia, has observed, Gorbachev had decided that the Soviet Union could not go on with the old policy framework under which they were declining rapidly. Their reformers drew intellectual inspiration from several sources. What did the Washington Consensus have to do with it? In fact, when later our colleague Jeffrey Sachs sold shock therapy to Russia, he produced a disaster.[15]

Just as the Indian and Soviet reforms were therefore endogenously arrived at, so were those in China. The Washington Consensus had nothing to do with the reforms in these three major countries.

15. In economics, shock therapy refers to all liberalization in one go instead of several gradual steps that are phased out over a long period of time. For example, it might include freeing up trade, ending all capital controls, privatizing public sector enterprises and end to all price controls, subsidies and investment controls in a single stroke.

Part II

THE NEW CHALLENGES

Track I Reforms to Accelerate Growth and Make It Yet More Inclusive

7

Track I and Track II Reforms Distinguished

To achieve this ambitious target (of doubling India's per capita income in the next ten years), we have to undertake many important reforms in our economy. At the same time, we need to implement necessary reforms in our administration, our judiciary, in education and in other areas. Reforms are the need of the hour . . . To reform is to turn the inevitability of change in the direction of progress. To reform is to improve the life of every citizen. Take, for example, the reforms in the power sector that the Centre and various state governments are presently carrying out. These will reduce the losses of our electricity boards, stop the theft of power, and ensure adequate availability of power for increasing production and employment. Similarly, the reforms that we are implementing in the telecom sector will enable us to provide cheaper telephones, mobile phones, and Internet services in all parts of the country. There is no scope for either apprehension or fear about economic reforms. I remember that some people had expressed similar fears even during the Green Revolution. These fears later proved to be baseless.

The perspective of our economic reforms is based on our own concept. You know that almost all political parties have, at different times and in different ways at the Centre and in different states, been adopting the economic reforms programme. I urge our farmers, workers, other producers, industrialists, and our intelligentsia to contribute to building a consensus in favour of economic reforms.

—Prime Minister Atal Bihari Vajpayee in a speech in Hindi from the Red Fort on Independence Day, 15 August 2000.

In Part I, we emphasized that growth is necessary for poverty alleviation in a country that starts out poor, that growth reduces poverty directly by pulling the poor into gainful employment and that it facilitates additional poverty reduction by generating revenues that enable the financing of redistributive programmes principally aimed at the poor.[1] We also demonstrated that the growth-centred strategy for alleviating poverty, with these double-barrelled outcomes reinforcing each other, had worked once the reforms introduced significantly since 1991 turned India from a slow to a rapidly growing economy.

Therefore, the reforms that India has undertaken so far to accelerate growth and to additionally address the plight of the poor through the now-feasible redistributive anti-poverty programmes have gone some way towards pulling the country out of a state of hopelessness that prevailed until 1980.[2] Yet, the process of reforms remains a work in progress and a lot more must still be done.

---

1. In using the adjective 'redistributive', we do not necessarily imply that the enhanced revenues come from the rich and the expenditures go to the poor. In fact, one of the main worries that we address in Part III devoted to such redistributive programmes is that unless they are handled with care to ensure proper targeting and prevent massive leakage into political predation, they may fail to reach the poor.
2. Gary Fields (1980), one of the leading experts of his time on poverty, had expressed the gloom on India's poverty problem in 1980 in these words: 'India is a miserably poor country. Per capita yearly income is under $100. Of the Indian people, 45 per cent receive incomes below $50 per year and 90 per cent below $150. Of the total number of absolutely poor in the

(Contd....)

Recall that from the outset, the Indian planners and politicians had chosen to attack the problem of poverty through both growth and redistribution. Because the level of income at independence was extremely low and increased only by a small amount until at least the 1980s due to slow growth, the revenues available for redistribution remained meagre. However, with growth having accelerated, especially since 2003-04, more generous amounts of revenue have accrued to the government, making large-scale redistributive programmes such as the National Rural Employment Guarantee Scheme possible.

While this is good news, 300 million or more citizens still remain below the official poverty line. Moreover, since the official poverty line is itself set at the subsistence level, many among the officially non-poor are far from having a comfortable existence.

Therefore, the need for sustained and accelerated growth, which is progressively more inclusive in its impact, remains acute. Likewise, the redistributive programmes must be made more effective even as they expand with the intention of providing greater benefits to the poor.

This strategy calls for future reforms to proceed on two tracks:

- **Track I**: Reforms aimed at accelerating and sustaining growth while making it even more inclusive.

(…contd.)

world . . . more than half are Indian. During the 1960s, per capita private consumer expenditure grew by less than ½ per cent per annum. India's poverty problem is so acute and her resources so limited that it is debatable whether any internal policy change . . . might be expected to improve things substantially.' Fields did not seriously consider the possibility, however, that the reform of India's counterproductive economic-policy framework could accelerate growth sharply and produce a noticeable impact on poverty.

- **Track II**: Reforms to make redistributive programmes more effective as their scope widens.[3]

Past liberalization, which became systematic and systemic since 1991, has paid off handsomely. India grew at a striking 8.5 per cent annual rate during the eight years spanning 2003-04 to 2010-11. Therefore, at first blush, it may seem that the battle for Track I reforms has already been won and nothing more need be done.[4] This may even be the view of some within the current United Progressive Alliance (UPA) government, which appears to have chosen during its tenure to focus almost exclusively on the promotion of social programmes, which relate to Track II policies.

Yet, it would be wrong to think that Track I reforms can be put behind us. If truth be told, India is far from done on Track I reforms for two broad reasons. First, the potential for growth remains grossly underexploited. The economy remains subject to

---

3. These two tracks are, of course, not entirely independent. Growth directly impacts the volume of revenues and therefore determines the possible scale of the redistributive programmes. Symmetrically, education and health will generally create a more skilled and healthier workforce, which should help growth. Sometimes, a conflict between the two tracks may arise as well, though this is likely to be rare. Thus, for example, a macroeconomic crisis such as the one India faced in 1991 may necessitate large cuts in the fiscal deficit so that the economy is stabilized and returned to a rapid-growth trajectory. In turn, this may require cutting some of the social programmes in the short run. Symmetrically, a redistributive programme such as the National Rural Employment Guarantee Scheme, which progressively pulls the workforce out of the private economy for employment in public projects of unproven quality, can have an adverse effect on growth.
4. We concentrate on Track I reforms in Part II, leaving issues relating to Track II policies for Part III. We alert the reader that we do not try to be exhaustive but, instead, consider issues that are most critical in each area and require the government's urgent attention. For more detailed and leisurely treatment of a wider array of issues, the reader is invited to consult the recent book by Panagariya (2008a).

vast inefficiencies. Removing these inefficiencies not only offers the opportunity to arrest the recent decline in growth but to push the economy to a double-digit growth trajectory. Second, the poverty reduction that directly results from growth, in terms of enhanced wages and employment opportunities per percentage point of growth, can be increased: we can get a larger bang for the buck.

As regards the first issue, there are many indicators of the inefficiencies that constrict growth. For instance, according to a 2007 Government of India report, the high-productivity formal sector, generously defined to include all enterprises with ten or more workers, employed just 13.7 per cent of the workers in 2004-05. [5] And even within this sector, nearly half of the workers were employed on an informal basis with no employment or social security benefits. Besides, employees who are in the formal sector and also have formal status (that is, those with proper employment and social security benefits) are not just small in number but have hardly been growing.

We will develop in the rest of Part II support for these observations. In services, the evidence now shows that firms with four or less workers accounted for 73 per cent of the employment but only 35 per cent of the output in services in 2006-07.[6] Even more dramatically, 626 of the largest service sector enterprises produced 38 per cent of the output but employed only 2 per cent of the workers that same year. Larger firms also show dramatically higher growth: output grew at the annual rate of 28.2 per cent in

5. See the Government of India (2007).
6. See Dehejia and Panagariya (2010). The evidence is based on an NSSO survey that covered non-public enterprises in services other than construction, financial intermediation and wholesale and retail trade. The included sectors are hotels and restaurants; transport, storage and communications; real estate, renting and business activities; education; health and social work; and other community, social, and personal services.

firms with five or more workers but only 4.5 per cent in the smaller firms between 2001-02 and 2006-07.[7]

Manufacturing exhibits a similar pattern. An unusually large share of the workforce in India remains employed in very small enterprises in manufacturing. The point is best illustrated by comparing the employment patterns in apparel in India and China. In 2005, 90 per cent of apparel workers in India were employed in enterprises with eighteen or fewer workers. In comparison, only 2.5 per cent of the Chinese apparel workers were in such small enterprises the same year. At the other extreme, India employed 5.3 per cent of the apparel workers in enterprises with more than 200 workers compared with 56.6 per cent in China.[8]

Clearly, huge scope remains for improving efficiency and accelerating the growth rate through progressive expansion of formal employment in the formal sector. The productivity figures are per worker, of course, rather than for total factor productivity. But total factor productivity is certain to yield the same conclusion because the astonishingly small enterprises are characterized by inefficiencies that should translate into overall inefficiency in the sense that they get much less for the same inputs as the large enterprises.

Our second reason for continuing with additional Track I reforms is that they would make growth yet more inclusive than it already has been. While all evidence indicates that the acceleration in growth since the 1980s has helped reduce poverty,[9] this effect is far more muted in India than in countries such as South Korea and Taiwan in the 1960s and 1970s and in China more recently.

The key reason for this difference has been the nature of the growth. Whereas growth was driven by rapid expansion of labour-

7. See Dehejia and Panagariya (2010) for further details.
8. See Hasan and Jandoc (2012) for further details.
9. Recall our discussion in Chapters 4 and 5.

intensive industries such as apparel, footwear, toys and light consumer goods in these other countries, it has been propelled in India by capital-intensive and skilled labour-intensive industries such as automobiles, two- and three-wheelers, engineering goods, petroleum refining, telecommunications and software. While this difference resulted in a rapid movement of workers out of agriculture into gainful employment in manufacturing and services in South Korea and Taiwan in the 1960s and 1970s, and in China more recently, in India, the heavy dependence of workers on agriculture continued.

To put the matter concretely, South Korea grew at an annual rate of 8.3 per cent between 1965 and 1980. During this period, the proportion of the workforce employed in agriculture in the country fell by 25 percentage points from 59 per cent to 34 per cent. Simultaneously, the workforce employed in industry rose from 10 per cent to 23 per cent and in services from 31 per cent to 43 per cent. Alongside, real wages grew at 11 per cent per year.

In sharp contrast, the share of agriculture in employment in India fell by just 8 percentage points from 62 per cent to 54 per cent between 1993-94 and 2004-05. Worse yet, with the workforce rising rapidly, this small change in the share has not arrested the rise in the absolute number of workers in agriculture. On the other hand, with industry and services output growing far more rapidly than agricultural output, the share of agriculture in the GDP stood at 19 per cent in 2004-05. Thus, an extremely large proportion of the workforce depends on a very small proportion of income, and further Track I reforms are needed to provide a corrective.

It may be observed that these twin reasons for Track I reforms—accelerating growth and making it more inclusive—are mutually reinforcing. Productivity growth requires moving workers from low-productivity agriculture into high-productivity industry and services and from informal to formal sector within industry and services. These same processes would also make growth more inclusive.

We, therefore, address now in Part II the added policies we need in Track I reforms, leaving the analysis of Track II policies to Part III of the book. Specifically, we begin in the next chapter with a diagnosis of why Indian entrepreneurs have shied away from employing unskilled and low-skilled workers despite their vast numbers in the country and what corrective reforms are required.

8

A Multitude of Labour Laws and Their Reform

The time has come for all of us to seriously consider whether the present labour laws, and the machinery for their implementation, needs reforms to enable Indian exporters to tap the vast opportunities in the global market. It is my belief that the right kind of labour reforms will simultaneously protect the legitimate interests of the workers, create more employment, and sharpen the competitive edge of Indian exports.

—Prime Minister Atal Bihari Vajpayee in a speech accompanying the presentation of the National Export Awards, New Delhi, 21 January 1999.

Is it possible that our best intentions for labour are not actually met by laws that sound progressive on paper but end up hurting the very workers they are meant to protect?

—Prime Minister Manmohan Singh in a speech to trade unions, 23 November 2010.

Development of the Indian economy, which goes hand-in-hand with acceleration in growth as well as greater inclusion, will require three key transformations: first, movement of workers out of agriculture into industry and services; second, progressive shift of workers from informal to formal sector within industry and services; and third, more rapid urbanization. The last will follow from the shift of workers to formal sector manufacturing and services, which are likely to be in urban rather than rural areas. Even if the industry is located in or near rural areas, its growth will almost surely be accompanied by urbanization of the region. The most dramatic example of this is the Pearl River Delta in China, which was dominated by farms and villages until as recently as 1985 but has been transformed into a collection of mega urban centres by the industrialization that followed economic reforms. Prior to that, Singapore went through a similar transformation. Either way, industrialization and modernization go hand in hand with urbanization.

Recall that despite a significant decline in the output share, the employment share of agriculture in India has remained high and that employment in industry and services remains predominantly in small, informal firms characterized by low productivity.

It is equally noteworthy that urbanization has also proceeded very slowly in India. Based on the census conducted once every decade, the proportion increased from 17.3 per cent in 1951 to 18 per cent in 1961, 19.9 per cent in 1971, 23.3 per cent in 1981, 25.7 per cent in 1991, 27.8 per cent in 2001 and 31.1 per cent in 2011. These numbers show a 14-percentage points shift in sixty years, or a little above 2 percentage points per decade! The pace seems to have accelerated in the last decade with a 3.3-percentage points gain but this is hardly adequate to achieve rapid transformation.

Flight of the Indian Entrepreneur from Labour

At the heart of this slow progress along all three dimensions is the flight of Indian entrepreneurs in the formal sector from low-skilled labour. It is ironic that in a country with nearly 470 million workers, all evidence indicates extreme and even increasing reluctance of Indian entrepreneurs to employ unskilled workers. The number of workers in all private-sector establishments with ten or more workers rose from 7.7 million in 1990-91 to just 9.8 million in 2007-08. Employment in private-sector *manufacturing* establishments of ten workers or more, however, rose from 4.5 million to only 5 million over the same period.[1] This small change has taken place against the backdrop of a much larger number of more than 10 million workers joining the workforce every year. Three key factors are behind this dismal picture.

Slow Growth of Manufacturing

At the outset, recall that a common feature of the fast-growing low-income countries has been the rapid expansion of manufacturing, pulling unskilled workers from agriculture into gainful employment. Recall also that this pattern characterized the rapid growth in Taiwan and South Korea in the 1960s and 1970s and in China more recently. Today's industrial economies, such as the UK, Germany and the US, also exhibited a similar pattern when they transformed themselves from primarily agricultural to non-agricultural economies.

But this pattern has failed to emerge in India despite rapid growth. The share of manufacturing in GDP actually fell from 16.8 per cent in 1981-82 to 15.8 per cent in 2008-09. Insofar as manufacturing is often a major source of gainful employment in a

1. See *Economic Survey 2010-11*, Appendix Table 3.1, p. A52.

low-income but growing economy, its minimal growth has been behind the slow movement of the workforce out of agriculture.

Poor Performance of Labour-intensive Manufacturing

Even with a stagnant share of manufacturing, some impetus to gainful employment of the unskilled could have come from a shift in the output composition of organized-sector manufacturing in favour of unskilled labour-intensive and against capital- and skilled labour-intensive activities.[2] Unfortunately, this did not happen either.

In a recent study, Das, Wadhwa and Kalita (2009) analyse precisely this issue, using output and input usage data on ninety-six four-digit organized manufacturing industries from 1990-91 to 2003-04. They identify as labour-intensive thirty-one of these four-digit industries, such as food and beverages, apparel, textiles and furniture. These sectors accounted for only 12.94 per cent of the gross value added in organized manufacturing in 1990-91. Thus, the labour-intensive sectors were relatively unimportant in overall manufacturing, to begin with. But then they remained so: their share rose to 15.9 per cent in 2000-01 and fell back to 12.91 per cent in 2003-04. And, in all likelihood, this share has further declined since 2003-04. In fact, some of the fastest growing industries between 2003-04 and 2010-11 have been automobiles,

---

2. In India, the term organized sector, which principally relates to manufacturing activity, refers to the collection of manufacturing firms registered under the Factories Act, 1948. Firms with ten or more workers using electricity and those with twenty or more workers, even if not using electricity, are required to register under this Act. Because services firms are not required to register under the Factories Act, 1948, even large services firms such as WIPRO, Infosys and TCS are technically in the unorganized sector. This is the reason why we used the term 'formal sector' previously to include both manufacturing and services firms with ten or more workers.

two- and three-wheelers, petroleum refining, engineering goods, telecommunications, pharmaceuticals, finance and software. All these industries are either capital-intensive or skilled labour-intensive.

What about exports? The changes in the composition of merchandise exports of India corroborate the shift in production share towards capital-intensive goods. As Figure 8.1 shows, engineering goods, chemicals and related products, gems and jewellery and petroleum products, which are either capital-intensive or semi-skilled labour-intensive, accounted for 41 per cent of the total commodity exports of India in 1990-91. The share of these products had, however, come to account for 65 per cent of the total commodity exports by 2007-08. At the other extreme, readymade garments, which are among the most unskilled- or low skill-intensive products, saw their share decline from 12 to just 6 per cent during the same period. Engineering goods and petroleum products, both highly capital-intensive products, witnessed the largest expansion.

Clothing and accessories offer a telling example of the poor showing of India in the world markets for labour-intensive products.[3] These products represent an extremely large world market and formed China's leading exports in the 1980s and 1990s. Indeed, even though electrical and electronic products have emerged as its leading exports since the early 2000s, China continues to dominate the market for clothing and accessories. In contrast, India has scarcely been able to keep up with the much smaller Bangladesh.

3. Clothing and accessories refer to Category 84 in the UN SITC classification.

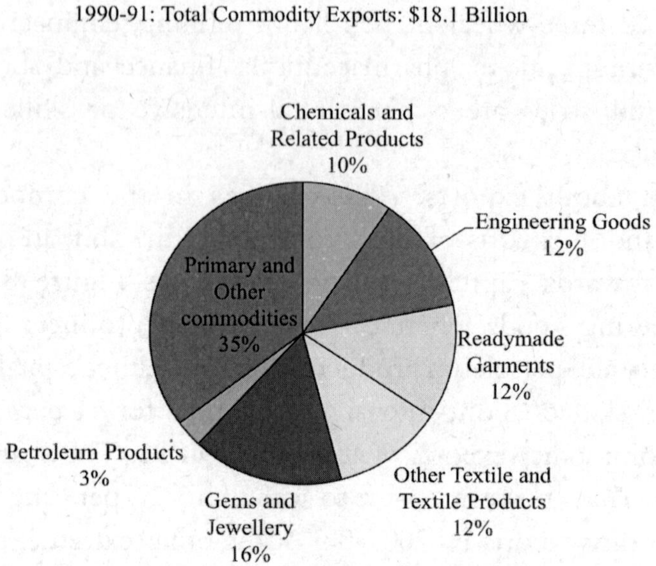

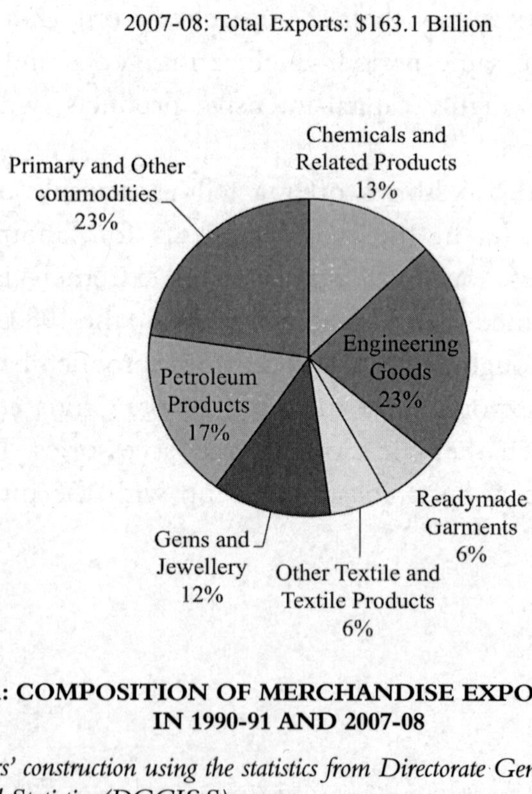

FIGURE 8.1: COMPOSITION OF MERCHANDISE EXPORTS BY INDIA IN 1990-91 AND 2007-08

Source: Authors' construction using the statistics from Directorate General of Commercial Intelligence and Statistics (DGCI&S).

TABLE 8.1: EXPORTS OF CLOTHING AND ACCESSORIES (SITC 84) BY INDIA AS PERCENTAGE OF THOSE BY BANGLADESH AND CHINA

	Bangladesh		*China*	
Year	USA	World	USA	World
2001	85.9	134.6	33.4	15.0
2002	95.0	143.0	32.1	14.1
2003	100.8	124.6	25.7	12.1
2004	98.8	110.0	23.9	11.2
2005	117.4	126.5	20.2	11.8
2006	107.4	115.0	18.5	10.0
2007	96.4	105.7	15.4	8.6
2008	N.A.	N.A.	15.3	9.1
2009	N.A.	N.A.	13.8	11.2

Source: Authors' calculations based on the United Nations commodity trade data.

This is evident from Table 8.1, which shows the exports of clothing and accessories by India as percentage of those by Bangladesh and China in the 2000s. The exports from India to the US were approximately the same as those by Bangladesh between 2001 and 2007. As regards the exports to the world as a whole, India had more than 40 per cent lead over Bangladesh in 2002. But it steadily lost ground with its exports exceeding those of Bangladesh by just 5.7 per cent in 2007.

When compared to China, India fares quite poorly in both the US and world markets. Even after the emergence of electronic products as its largest export, China's lead in clothing and accessories over India has considerably widened. In the US market, India's exports as a proportion of the Chinese exports fell from one-third to less than one-seventh between 2001 and 2009. The end to the multi-fibre arrangement under the Uruguay Round Agreement on Textiles and Clothing clearly exposed the inefficiency of the Indian industry vis-à-vis Bangladesh and China.

High and Rising Capital-intensity in Production

A final avenue to raising gainful employment of the unskilled could have been a shift towards labour-intensive technologies *within* each production sector while maintaining the same structure of production. But even here, the evidence points to movement away from, rather than towards, labour. Indian firms use more capital-intensive techniques in production in relation to the availability of these factors of prodcution to begin with; and technology has moved still further in this direction over the years.

Hasan, Mitra and Sundaram (2010) show that labour-capital ratios in the vast majority of manufacturing industries in India are lower than in other countries at a similar level of development and with similar factor endowments. Comparing India and China in nineteen manufacturing industries, for example, they show that the capital stock per worker in India is consistently higher in India than in China in the period 1980-2000. They also find that India's growth in capital stock per worker from 1980 to 2000 in these sectors is higher than that in China. It is not surprising then that whereas employment in these sectors shows steady growth in China, it has been stagnant in India.

In fact, the evidence in favour of a declining trend in the labour-capital ratio in Indian manufacturing generally is overwhelming. Thus, Rani and Unni (2004) find a sharply rising trend in the capital–labour ratios in both the organized and unorganized manufacturing sectors. Chaudhuri (2002) computes the labour–capital ratio in three-digit organized manufacturing sectors from 1990-91 to 1997-98 and also finds it to decline progressively. Again, Das, Wadhwa and Kalita (2009) find a sharply declining trend in the labour–capital ratio in thirty-one labour-intensive organized manufacturing industries between 1990–91 and 2003–04.

Link to Firm-size Distribution

Ultimately, the flight from unskilled labour that we have identified so far is intimately linked also to the firm-size distribution that our policies have produced. In particular, the contributions by Mazumdar (2003) and Mazumdar and Sarkar (2008) have drawn attention to the fact that employment in India is heavily concentrated in the small enterprises. While the large enterprises have some presence, the medium size enterprises are entirely missing.

More recently, Hasan and Jandoc (2012) have also analysed the firm-size distribution of some major sectors such as apparel and auto and auto parts that represent the highly labour- and capital-intensive sectors respectively. Their work sheds new light on the structure of Indian manufacturing that we have already sketched.

Pooling the data on the firms in the organized as well as unorganized manufacturing, Hasan and Jandoc (2010) first show that an astonishing 84 per cent of the workers in all manufacturing in India were employed in firms with forty-nine or less workers in 2005. Large firms, defined as those employing 200 or more workers, accounted for only 10.5 per cent of manufacturing workforce. In contrast, small- and large-scale firms employed 25 and 52 per cent of the workers respectively in China in the same year.

Upon disaggregation by sectors, Hasan and Jandoc find that the firm-size distribution is skewed towards even smaller enterprises in the labour-intensive sectors, with the large firms mostly concentrated in the capital-intensive sectors. Thus, workers in the highly labour-intensive apparel sector are concentrated almost entirely in small firms with 92.4 per cent workers in firms with forty-nine or less workers. This distribution contrasts sharply with that in China, where medium- and large-scale firms account for a gigantic 87.7 per cent of the apparel employment (see Figure 8.2). The firm-size distribution in apparel in India also contrasts sharply with the more capital-intensive auto and auto-parts sector within the country, in which large-scale firms employed 50.3 per cent of all workers in the sector in 2005 (see Figure 8.3).

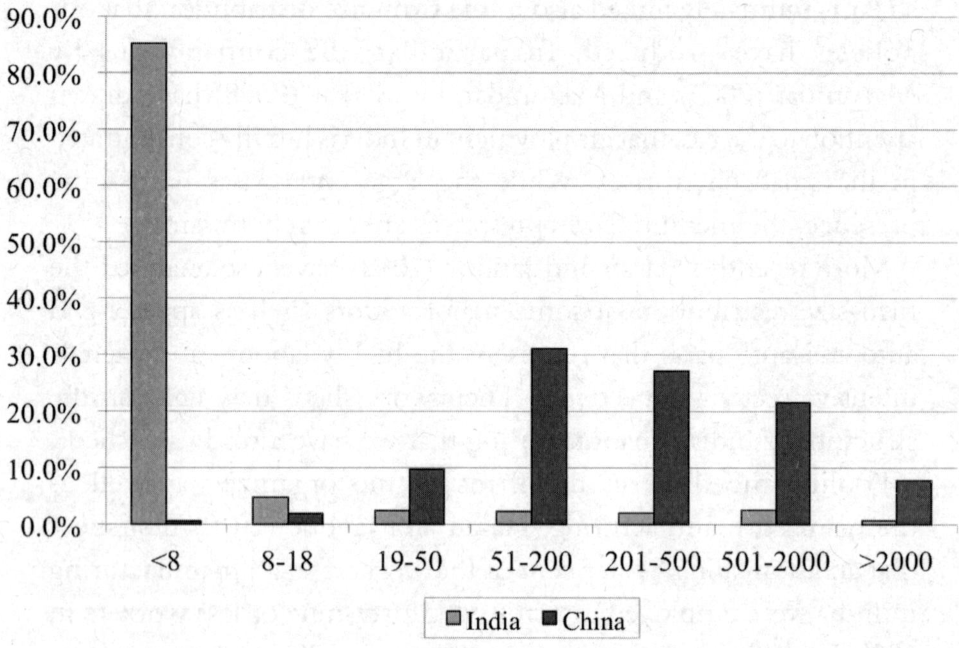

FIGURE 8.2: EMPLOYMENT SHARE BY FIRM SIZE IN CHINA AND INDIA, 2005

Source: Hasan and Jandoc (2010).

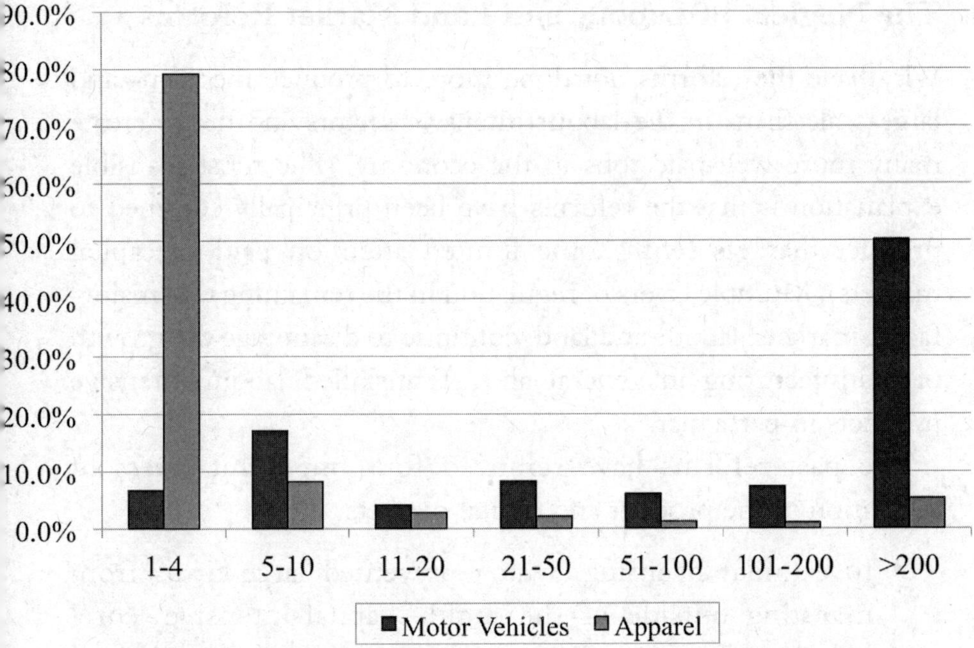

FIGURE 8.3: EMPLOYMENT SHARES BY FIRM SIZE IN APPAREL VERSUS MOTOR VEHICLES AND MOTOR PARTS, 2005

Source: Hasan and Jandoc (2010).

The near absence of medium and large firms in apparel, especially when compared with China, is clearly linked to the poor export performance of this sector. The inability to massively capture the export markets in this major sector with comparative advantage is in turn linked to the poor performance of labour-intensive manufacturing and, therefore, manufacturing in general. The ultimate reason why growth has not been as inclusive in India as in South Korea, Taiwan and China remains the absence of large-scale firms in the labour-intensive sectors in India.

The Neglect of Labour and Land Market Reforms

Why have the reforms not done more to produce medium- and large-scale firms in the labour-intensive sectors and hence create many more well-paid jobs in the economy? The most plausible explanation is that the reforms have been principally confined to product markets (with some limited attention paid to capital markets). Multiple layers of regulation in the remaining two major-factor markets, labour and land, continue to discourage the growth of manufacturing in general and of unskilled labour-intensive products in particular.

The past reforms have removed four important layers of regulation in the product and capital markets:

- Investment licensing, which prevented large firms from investing outside of the highly capital-intensive 'core' industries, has been eliminated;
- Protection, which had prevented firms from exploiting large world markets, has been substantially removed from industry and services though agriculture still remains heavily protected;
- The door to foreign firms with state-of-the-art know-how and with knowledge of and links to the world market has been opened; and
- Above all, the small-scale industries reservation policy, which reserved virtually all labour-intensive products for exclusive manufacture by small enterprises, has been effectively ended.[4]

Many analysts had expected that these reforms, especially the last one, would pave the way for the emergence of the large-scale firms

---

4. Although a handful of the products still remain subject to the reservation, a March 2000 executive order allows large-scale production of even these products by firms willing to export 50 per cent or more of their output. Therefore, for all practical purposes, the reservation is no longer binding.

in the labour-intensive sectors and lead to a boom in labour-intensive exports. But this did not happen. Why?

Initially, the lack of response in apparel, the labour-intensive sector with the largest world market, could have been attributed to the manner in which India had implemented the multi-fibre export quota. The Indian policy was to give the unused export quota not to existing users but to new applicants. This meant that the existing successful firms could not expand even though the small-scale industries reservation no longer applied and thus did not constrain them to stay small. But with the multi-fibre-arrangement quotas ending in 2005 as part of the successful closure of the Uruguay Round on multilateral trade negotiations, this explanation no longer holds.

The true explanation lies instead in the fact that additional layers of regulations and barriers remain to discourage the emergence of large-scale labour-intensive manufacturing in India. The dominant cause is a highly inflexible labour market, which makes the cost of labour in the formal sector excessively high.

In addition, there are three complementary factors impeding the emergence of large-scale labour-intensive manufacturing: the absence of bankruptcy laws permitting smooth exit in case of failure; a highly distorted land market; and poor infrastructure. Remarkably, despite the lapse of two decades since economic reforms began in earnest, there has been no attempt whatsoever to undertake the reforms of antiquated labour laws that affect all these issues, with new legislation being generally confined to giving yet more social protections to workers.

A Multitude of Labour Laws

Indian entrepreneurs face requirements laid out in a multitude of legislations from different sources. Under the Indian Constitution, labour is a 'concurrent' subject, meaning that both the Centre and the states can enact laws in this area. Neither has exactly been shy about exercising this right.

Thus the ministry of labour lists as many as fifty-two independent Central government Acts in the area of labour.[5] According to Amit Mitra, the former secretary general of the Federation of Indian Chambers of Commerce and Industry and now the finance minister in the new Mamata Banerjee government in West Bengal,[6] there exist another 150 state-level laws in India.[7] This count places the total number of labour laws in India at approximately 200. Compounding the confusion created by this multitude of laws is the fact that they are not entirely consistent with one another, leading a wit to remark that you cannot implement Indian labour laws 100 per cent without violating 20 per cent of them.[8]

To give an idea of the complexity of the laws and their rising burden as the size of the establishment in terms of workers employed rises, it is useful to describe some of them in greater detail. We initially provide the description with the sole objective to underline the complexity and burdensome nature of the regime without taking either a positive or negative view of any specific provision. We shall take up the issue of which specific provisions are on balance counterproductive despite appearing to protect the interests

5. See http://labour.nic.in/act/welcome.html (accessed on 29 October 2011). A report of the working group of the Planning Commission on 'Labour Laws and Other Labour Regulations' lists forty-three labour laws. See http://planningcommission.nic.in/aboutus/committee/wrkgrp11/wg11_rplabr.pdf (accessed on 29 October 2011).
6. Mamata Banerjee replaced the long-standing communist government in the 2011 state assembly elections.
7. Amit Mitra made this statement on the NDTV show 'Big Fight' at http://www.ndtv.com/convergence/ndtv/new/Ndtv-Show-Special.aspx?ID=289#VPlay (accessed on 29 October 2011).
8. Manish Sabharwal, CEO of TeamLease, made the remark on the NDTV 'Big Fight' episode on labour laws mentioned earlier (http://www.ndtv.com/convergence/ndtv/new/Ndtv-Show-Special.aspx?ID=289#Vplay) (accessed on 29 October 2011).

of the workers and, therefore, in need of reform after the discussion of various laws is complete.

At the outset, we may consider the Trade Unions Act, 1926. The Act requires that firms with seven or more workers should allow them to form a trade union.[9] This fact perhaps gives firms with six or fewer workers the most labour-market flexibility. The Act, for instance, empowers trade unions to strike and represent their members in labour courts in disputes with the employers. Because union officials can be outsiders, prospects for such disputes rise with the formation of unions. Firms can thus minimize labour-related problems as long as they are smaller than seven workers. The dominance of tiny firms in the apparel sector we saw earlier may well have something to do with this fact.

Again, factories engaged in manufacturing and employing ten or more workers, regardless of whether these factories use power, are subject to the Employees' State Insurance Act, 1948. State governments may also extend the provisions of the Act to other industrial, commercial or agricultural establishments. For employees hired at a wage up to Rs 10,000 a month, the Act provides benefits related to sickness, maternity, disability, dependents, old age medical care, funeral, employment injury and rehabilitation.

On the other hand, manufacturing units with ten workers using power and with twenty workers even if not using power are subject to yet another piece of legislation: the Factories Act, 1948. This Act limits the maximum hours of work per week to forty-eight; limits work without a day of rest to ten days; requires a paid holiday for each twenty days of work; prohibits the employment of children less than fifteen years of age; and bans the employment of women for more than nine hours per day and between 7 pm and 6 am.

---

9. More precisely, the Act says that seven or more workers in an establishment can form a trade union as long as they represent at least 10 per cent of the labour force. Alternatively, 100 workers in an establishment can form a trade union even if they are less than 10 per cent of the workforce.

In addition, the requirements extend to demands such as factory premises be kept clean, including whitewashing every fourteen months and repainting every five years. Proper disposal of waste is mandated; adequate and separate restrooms for men and women are required; and uninterrupted supply of drinking water has to be made available. The Act also makes extensive provisions for worker safety, including fencing of machines and moving parts of machines; the use of goggles to protect against excessive light and infra-red and ultra-violet radiation; precautions against fire; and limits on the weight permitted to be carried by women and young persons.

Moreover, the mandated requirements rise as the number of employees rises. For example, at 150 workers, lunchrooms must be provided; at 250 workers, a canteen must be available on factory premises; and if employing 30 women, a daycare centre must be made available.

Leave aside the fact that many of these regulations are costly to implement, and increase the cost of hiring more labour, the Factories Act also generates considerable paperwork. Thus, for instance, each factory must maintain registers of attendance, of adult workers hired, of the dates of lime washing and painting, of leaves granted with wages, provision of health care (in case of persons employed in occupations declared hazardous) and the incidence of accidents. It must also file information to appropriate authorities on half-yearly and annual returns.

Again, all establishments with twenty or more workers, whether in industry or services, are further subject to the Employees' Provident Fund and Miscellaneous Provisions Act, 1952. This Act provides three types of benefits: a contributory provident fund, pension benefits to the employees and his family members and insurance cover to the members of the provident fund.[10]

---

10. All employees earning Rs 6,500 per month or more have to join the provident fund scheme.

But we have hardly scratched the surface of the labour laws that suffocate Indian entrepreneurs. There are indeed several other legislations imposing a variety of requirements, some applying to all establishments and others to those with some threshold number of workers. Often the Central legislation gives the states the authority to extend the provision of the legislation to establishments not covered by it, which the states use unhesitatingly. Among the key Central legislations are the Maternity Benefit Act, 1961, applicable to all factories, establishments and shops depending on the state government; the Minimum Wages Act, 1948, which requires state governments to fix the minimum wage in specified employments; the Payment of Bonus Act, 1965, applicable to all firms registered under the Factories Act, 1948 and establishments with twenty or more workers; the Payment of Gratuity Act, 1972, applicable to all factories and establishments with ten or more workers; the Workmen's Compensation Act, 1923, which applies to all workers; and the Industrial Employment (Standing Order) Act, 1946, which applies to all industrial establishments with 100 (in some states fifty) or more workers.

Even if each of these and other Central and state legislations are poorly enforced, they imply considerable burden on the smaller firms in terms of paperwork and filing requirements. Indeed, many firms are not even aware of their precise obligations under the large number of Central and state legislations. Unwitting non-compliance in one or more areas is inevitable, especially for all but the exceptionally large firms, opening the door to corruption by labour department inspectors.

No discussion of labour laws would be complete, however, without inclusion of the Industrial Disputes Act (IDA), 1947. This is an important legislation that covers all industrial disputes regardless of the firm size. The disputes typically involve an employer and one or more workmen in his establishment. But the Act covers all other disputes as well, such as those arising between two or more workmen or between two or more employers. The Act lays down procedures and defines the institutional infrastructure for the resolution of disputes. It also states the conditions under which employers can alter the tasks assigned to workers, conditions under which they can be laid off or retrenched, and the rules regulating strikes. Key provisions that stack the deck disproportionately against employers, and must affect their willingness to hire regular as opposed to contract workers, need to be highlighted.

First, the IDA confers the power to regulate labour-employer relations on the labour department with jurisdiction over the firm, which is usually the labour department in the state in which the firm is located. The legislation defines an industrial dispute as *any* dismissal, discharge, termination or retrenchment of a worker in a firm of any size. The first step in settling a dispute is reconciliation, failing which it is referred to labour courts and tribunals that overwhelmingly rule in favour of workers on the theory that firms have deep pockets and workers do not. An attempt to reform the IDA for its anti-employer bias through alternative legislation in 1950 failed and no subsequent attempt has been made.

Second, Section 9A of the IDA requires that the employer give three weeks' notice to workers of any change in their working conditions in all industrial establishments with fifty or more workers. These changes may relate to shift work; grade classification; rules of discipline; technological changes impacting the demand for labour; and employment, occupation, process or department. The workers have a right to object to these changes, which may culminate in an industrial dispute.

Third, and most importantly, Chapter V-B of the IDA effectively makes it impossible for an industrial establishment with 100 or more workers to lay off or to retrench workers even if it is unprofitable and is, therefore, forced to close the unit. This chapter was first introduced in 1976 and initially applied to industrial establishments with 300 or more workers. Later, a 1982 amendment, which became effective beginning 1984, reduced the threshold from 300 to 100 workers. Establishments subject to the regulation have to seek permission from the labour department with jurisdiction over the firm for any layoffs and retrenchment. Concerned labour departments rarely give such permission even when the unit is unprofitable and must be shut down. The owner is effectively required to pay the workers from profits in other operations in case of closure.

The final labour legislation of importance is the Contract Labour (Regulation and Abolition) Act, 1970. Contract workers are indirect employees of an establishment: they are hired, supervised and paid by a contractor who has in turn contracted with the establishment to deliver certain services in return for a specified compensation. The establishment has no direct responsibility to contract workers; indeed, he need not even know who these workers are. Typically, the contractor hires the contract workers for specified tasks and duration. While economic factors justify use of contract workers under many conditions, factories and establishments also prefer contract workers to avoid the burden imposed on them by the onerous labour laws.

The Contract Labour (Regulation and Abolition) Act, 1970, attempts to limit this erosion of legislative requirements. It aims to regulate the employment of contract labour in certain establishments and to provide for its abolition under certain circumstances. The Act applies to establishments employing twenty or more workers and to contractors employing the same number of workers. Several of the provisions in the Act are aimed at protecting the interests of the contract worker. But a key provision gives the government the power to prohibit an establishment from using contract labour for work of perennial nature or work that is central to the manufacturing process. The government is also empowered to deny the use of contract labour for a task if other similar establishments use regular workers for that same task. Many states have used this provision to ban the use of contract labour in entire sectors.

Why Sceptics of the Adverse Impact of Labour Laws Are Wrong

The burdensome labour laws explain why entrepreneurs in sectors such as apparel, in which labour costs account for more than 80 per cent of the total costs, choose to stay tiny. The costs due to labour legislations rise progressively in discrete steps at seven, ten, twenty, fifty and 100 workers. As the firm size rises from six regular workers towards 100, at no point between these two thresholds is the saving in manufacturing costs sufficiently large to pay for the extra costs of satisfying the laws. It may well be that only at a very large scale will the cost saving become big enough to pay for the costs of labour laws. Under such circumstances, we will end up with either tiny or very large firms with the middle missing, as has been the case in India. But when it comes to the labour-intensive sectors, very few firms seem to find it attractive to operate at any scale other than the tiny.

Economist Ajay Shah of the National Institute of Public Finance and Policy tells an interesting story highlighting the dilemma of Indian entrepreneurs considering entry into labour-intensive sectors.[11] Some years ago, he asked a leading Indian industrialist the following question, 'You're a smart guy, you saw the (multi-fibre arrangement or MFA) quota regime going away, why did you not make a big play for it, given that you were already in yarn and cloth?' The industrialist replied that with the low profit margins in apparel, this would be worth his while only if he operated on the scale of 100,000 workers. But this would not be practical in view of India's restrictive labour laws, he added.

11. Shah told this story at a conference in New Delhi several years ago and recently confirmed it in email correspondence with Panagariya.

Nonetheless, some analysts remain sceptical of the argument that labour-market rigidities are at the heart of the absence of mid- and large-size firms in labour-intensive sectors. These analysts offer seven alternative arguments in support of their position.

First, they blame a lack of adequate literacy among potential workers. According to them, even the so-called 'unskilled' tasks such as cutting, sewing, stitching and packaging garments require a level of literacy that is lacking in India. This claim is false. For one thing, tailors currently employed in smaller establishments, of which we have aplenty, fulfil multiple tasks. They are surely capable of repeatedly performing one or more of these same tasks in a factory setting. Equally, the Indiawide gross enrolment ratios in education decisively contradict the claims of insufficient literacy. In 2007-08, the gross enrolment ratios in classes XI and XII were 36.3 per cent for boys, 30.4 per cent for girls and 33.5 per cent overall.[12] The ratios for students in classes IX and X were much higher: 62.6 per cent for boys, 53.2 per cent for girls and 58.2 per cent overall. In 2007-08 alone, a total of 28.2 million boys and girls were enrolled in classes IX and X and another 16.3 million in classes XI and XII. It is wrong, therefore, to suggest that potential Indian workers lack the basic education necessary for gainful employment in factories.

The second counterargument relies on the observation that female workers have predominantly populated the large-scale factories in labour-intensive sectors in countries such as China. According to

---

12. The gross enrolment ratio for a class (or classes) equals the number of students enrolled in that class as a proportion of the population in the age group that normally attends that class. For example, eighteen-year-olds normally attend the twelfth grade. Therefore, the gross enrolment ratio for the twelfth grade is the number of students (of any age) enrolled in the twelfth grade as a proportion of the population of eighteen-year-olds. Because students older or younger than eighteen years can also be in the twelfth grade, the gross enrolment ratio can exceed 100 per cent.

this argument, social attitudes and the legal framework in India do not support the employment of women in large factories.[13] Thus, the reasoning goes, families are reluctant to send womenfolk to work in factories, and laws such as the 1948 Factories Act prohibit the employment of women in night shifts that last from 7 pm to 6 am. Once again, the basic premises behind this argument are faulty. There is no reason why men could not be employed in apparel, footwear and toy factories. As regards the employment of women, while it is desirable to amend the Factories Act to permit them to work night shifts, even under the current law, they could be employed during the day shift with men assigned to night shifts.[14]

Third, some argue that labour-intensive products, most notably apparel, require just-in-time delivery to export destinations such as the US and Europe. The argument goes like this: There is seasonality in demand for clothing and accessories and bulk buyers such as Walmart require delivery according to very tight schedules. Such delivery in turn requires first-rate infrastructure. Any delays due to unreliable links between factory and the port, for example, can result in a loss of the order. Indian infrastructure is simply too unreliable to fulfil such just-in-time delivery. While there is some truth in this argument, infrastructure is not a binding constraint everywhere in India.

Gujarat has put in place excellent infrastructure, including ports that handle loading and unloading of goods proficiently and expeditiously. While poor infrastructure in some states may be a contributory factor, it cannot explain by itself the absence of large-scale labour-intensive manufacturing in every state.

---

13. Economist Yasheng Huang of the Sloan School at MIT had made this argument to one of us (Panagariya) some years ago.
14. A bill amending the Factories Act, 1948 to allow women in night shifts has been before Parliament since at least 2008.

Fourth, some argue that growing beyond the small size requires access to credit, which most firms aspiring to grow big lack. But this argument is also falsified by the fact that both medium- and large-size firms account for a much larger employment in the capital-intensive sectors such as motor vehicles and motor parts than in the labour-intensive sectors such as apparel (see Figure 8.3). Unless something else, such as the labour laws, have made apparel a riskier business than motor vehicles and vehicle parts, there is no obvious reason why the banks would discriminate in favour of the latter in a labour-abundant country.

Fifth, it is argued that when interviewed for business environment surveys, firms rarely point to labour-market rigidities as the key problem. But this phenomenon is wholly misleading; it is the result of what economists call a 'selection' problem in the sample of firms surveyed. Mid-size and large firms in the labour-intensive sectors, which are likely to complain about the onerous labour laws, simply do not exist and are therefore not represented in the sample. Large firms in the sample surveys also typically come from either the service sectors or the capital-intensive manufacturing sectors. Services firms are not subject to some of the most constraining labour laws such as chapter V-B of the Industrial Disputes Act, 1947 and, therefore, are unlikely to point the finger at them. Indeed, many of their employees probably do not even qualify as 'workmen' under the Industrial Disputes Act, 1947. As regards the large firms in the capital-intensive sectors, their labour costs are less than 10 per cent of the total costs and they have high profits per worker, making it worthwhile to bear the costs of labour-market rigidities. They can handle even the problems of layoffs through voluntary retirement in return for golden parachutes. Large firms in the labour-intensive sectors, in which labour costs are 80 per cent of the total costs and profits per worker are low, do not have this option.

Sixth, some argue that while labour laws may be onerous on

paper, they are not enforced or that the firms are able to get around them. However, the fact that large firms have chosen not to enter labour-intensive sectors in India while they routinely do so in other comparable countries suggests they are not able to get around labour laws in a cost-effective manner. Being able to get around does not mean getting around at low cost. After all, the firms had also learned to get around the import and investment licensing and high trade barriers before reforms began in earnest in 1991. But we now recognize that they did so at a huge cost, that only a few of them were able to do it, and that the country paid dearly for the regulations in terms of low growth for four decades.

An example of how rigid laws, combined with an overburdened judiciary, can be highly costly even to large firms in the capital-intensive sectors is provided by the infamous Uttam Nakate case. The following succinct summary of the case from Sanjeev Sanyal (2006, p. 9) is instructive:

> In August 1983, Nakate was found at 11:40 am sleeping soundly on an iron plate in the factory in Pune where he worked. He had committed three previous misdemeanours but had been let off lightly. This time his employer Bharat Forge began disciplinary proceedings against him, and after five months of hearings, he was found guilty and sacked. But Nakate went to a labour court and pleaded that he was a victim of an unfair trade practice. The court agreed and forced the factory to take him back and pay him 50 per cent of his lost wages. Both parties appealed against this judgement (Natake wanted more money). The case dragged on through the judicial system for another decade and in 1995 another court awarded Nakate more money because he was now too old to be rehired. Bharat Forge eventually had to approach the Supreme Court and in May 2005—more than two decades after the original incident—the apex court finally awarded the employer the right to fire a worker who had been repeatedly caught sleeping on the job.

Surely, this 'getting around' was a costly affair for Bharat Forge!

A final counterargument offered is that labour-market rigidities apply to only a tiny section of the labour force. In this view, the fact that more than 90 per cent of the labour force is in the informal sector or employed informally in the formal sector implies that the bulk of the labour market is highly flexible despite the ill-designed labour laws. However, this is a rather disingenuous argument. After all, the entire debate is about the smallness of Indian firms and, in particular, the absence of medium- and large-size firms in labour-intensive sectors. The question this argument begs is why such a small part of the labour force has found formal employment in India. Should it not be our objective to bring more of the labour force into such employment?

In conclusion, we may cite some positive evidence on how differences in state-level labour laws affect the firm size in the labour-intensive sectors differently. In their search for the causes of the near-absence of large-scale firms in the labour-intensive sectors, Hasan and Jandoc turn to state-level differences in policies and outcomes. They first compare the firm-size distributions of all manufacturing between states with flexible labour regulations and those with inflexible ones and find almost no cross-state differences. However, when they restrict the sample to apparel, large-scale firms exhibit proportionately significantly larger shares of employees and small-scale firms significantly smaller share in states with flexible labour regulations (Figure 8.4). Given the fact that labour laws remain highly restrictive even in the states classified as relatively more flexible, and thus hinder the emergence of medium- and large-scale firms in greater proportion, the existence of these state-level differences is particularly significant.

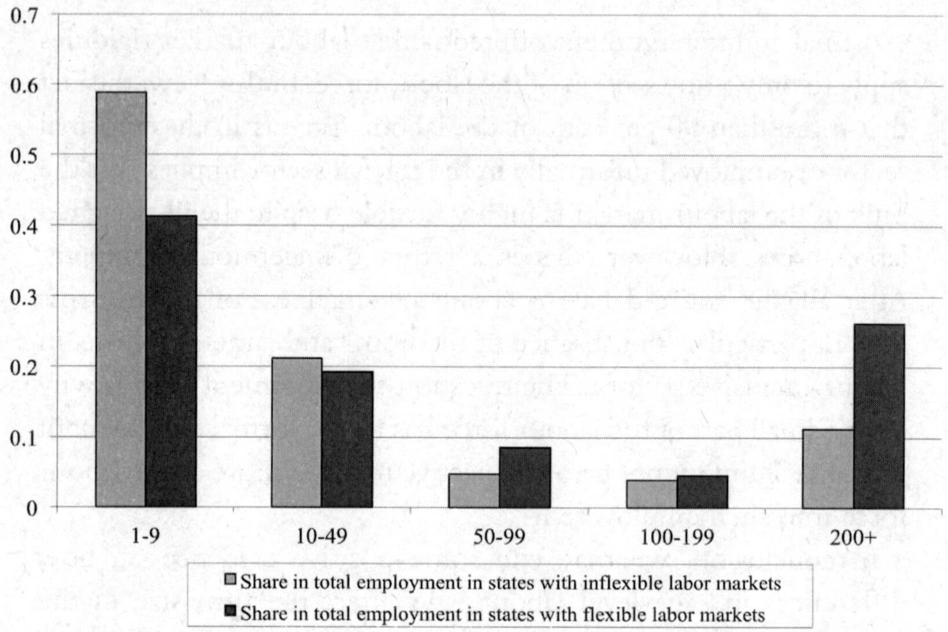

FIGURE 8.4: FIRM-SIZE DISTRIBUTION IN APPAREL IN STATES WITH FLEXIBLE VERSUS INFLEXIBLE LABOUR LAWS

To be sure that other factors are not behind the state-level differences, Hasan and Jandoc also do a comparison between states with and without good infrastructure. But this comparison yields no real differences in the employment shares of large and small firms across states.

Labour Laws: What Must Be Done?

Nearly all labour laws in India are more than four decades old, with the Contract Labour (Regulation and Abolition) Act, 1970, being the last major labour legislation passed by Parliament. At the time, these laws perhaps had some rationale in terms of redistribution in favour of the worker. Investment and import licensing gave guaranteed profits to the domestic firms that were lucky enough to get the licences. Therefore, forcing them to share those profits with the workers through ultra-high protection to the latter was defensible.

But with the investment and import licensing abolished and trade opened up, domestic firms are subject to intense competition. The same ultra-high protection to workers in certain dimensions under these circumstances has only prevented the economy from specializing in the goods in which India enjoys comparative advantage. If we are to move the economy towards specialization in labour-intensive products, which is essential to the creation of more formal-sector jobs, and therefore for making growth more inclusive, reform of the labour laws is urgent.

Ideally, India needs to reform the labour laws wholesale. But labour legislation is one of the toughest to manage politically. So reform may well have to be focused first on the most damaging laws on the book. Evidently, the law in the most urgent need of reform is the 1947 Industrial Disputes Act. This legislation is stacked too heavily against the employers to leave sufficient incentive for a massive expansion of employment-intensive sectors. With the wages in China reaching levels at which it is likely to be forced out of these sectors, India is well-positioned to become the manufacturing hub of the world. But if the costs of employment remain what they currently are, that opportunity is likely to be seized by a large number of smaller countries such as Vietnam, Cambodia, Bangladesh, Sri Lanka, and even some African countries.

Several changes in the IDA would be enormously helpful. First, the definition of retrenchment for purposes of industrial disputes (in firms of all sizes) needs to be tightened. The IDA defines retrenchment as 'the termination by the employer of the service of a workman for any reason whatsoever' other than a punishment inflicted by way of disciplinary action; voluntary retirement; retirement upon reaching the age stipulated in the contract; and termination due to non-renewal of a contract on its expiry or failure of the worker to meet conditions stipulated in the contract.

Under this definition, even a discharge of employees due to declining sales or unanticipated change in technology would be interpreted as retrenchment. Debroy (2001) laments that under this definition, Indian courts have even gone on to interpret as retrenchment the discharge of an employee on probation and non-confirmation of an employee failing a test required for confirmation. The provision has naturally resulted in the multiplication of industrial disputes as well as in a disincentive to hire workers. A tighter definition of retrenchment for purposes of industrial disputes would clearly bring down the number of such disputes and encourage more hiring of workers.[15]

Second, the IDA allows every single industrial dispute to go to the labour courts and tribunals. This practice should be replaced by one under which an independent authority is empowered to deliver a time-bound and final verdict in a designated class of cases. At least in cases in which the basis of retrenchment is not in dispute (as in the Nakate case), the independent authority can be authorized to give a final verdict within the rules under which retrenchment is permitted.

Third, Section 9A of the IDA, which imposes a heavy burden on an employer wishing to reassign a worker to an alternative task,

15. Debroy (2001) quotes a Supreme Court judge from the Excel Wear vs. Union of India case of 1978, who wrote, 'Gradually, the net was cast too wide and the freedom of the employer tightened to such an extent by introduction of the impugned provisions that it has come to a breaking point from the point of view of the employers . . . It is not quite correct to say that because compensation is not a substitute for the remedy of prevention of unemployment, the latter remedy must be the only one. If it were so, then in no case closure can be or should be allowed . . . But, so long as the private ownership of an industry is recognized and governed on an overwhelmingly large proportion of our economic structure, is it possible to say that principles of socialism and social justice can be pushed to such an extreme so as to ignore completely, or to a very large extent, the interest of another section of the public, viz. the private owners of the undertakings?'

needs to be replaced by one that gives the employer greater flexibility. Minimally, the employer should be permitted to reassign the worker to a set of pre-specified tasks upon short notice and without challenge. For example, if a change in technology renders the task of an existing employee redundant, the employer should have a clear right to assign him or her to an alternative task for which he or she fulfils the qualifications. More broadly, the employer should be given the right to reassign the workers within a broad set of pre-specified tasks.

Fourth, while the IDA prohibits strikes by public utility services without notice, no such restrictions apply to strikes in other industrial establishments except during the time that conciliation or arbitration proceedings are under way. Nor does the law require a secret ballot by trade union members before a strike is called. This state of affairs encourages wildcat strikes that can be very harmful to the health of the establishment. Change in the IDA in this regard is necessary.

Fifth, chapter V-B of the IDA, 1947, which makes it nearly impossible for an employer of a factory with 100 or more workers to lay off workers under any circumstances, needs to be repealed. Interestingly, this chapter was added only in 1976, so that the IDA had existed for twenty-nine years without it. We need to return to the pre-1976 IDA along this dimension. With careful steering, this may be politically doable. For example, the government could begin the process by changing the law for a handful of labour-intensive sectors in which there are only a few large firms in the first place. For instance, if the apparel distributions shown in Figures 8.2 and 8.3 are still valid, repeal of chapter V-B in this sector will impact only a small number of employees. If even this is politically difficult, the initial change could start with exemption for apparel factories with 100 to 500 workers, which account for a tiny proportion of the employment in the sector, making it even easier to exempt the existing employees from Chapter V-B provisions of the IDA.

Among other labour laws, the 1948 Factories Act should be revisited to see if it contains provisions that are too onerous for firms with ten or even twenty workers. Our own reading of the Act is that small firms are unlikely to have the staff and expertise to understand and ensure fulfilment of the myriad regulations in the Act. If this reading is correct, there is need for an alternative set of fewer and more manageable regulations applicable to firms that employ less than fifty workers. Successful large firms often emerge from smaller firms and a case is to be made for giving greater leeway to the latter.

The 1926 Trade Unions Act also needs to be modified. It has led to a proliferation of trade unions in larger firms. Originally, this law allowed any seven workers to form a trade union. A 2001 amendment introduced the qualification that those forming the trade unions should minimally include 10 per cent of the workforce or 100 workers. But even this amendment leaves room for a large number of trade unions in larger firms. As a result, we find that the Neyveli Lignite Corporation Limited has as many as fifty trade unions and associations.[16] This organizational feature makes the collective bargaining process highly problematic since an agreement reached with one union does not automatically apply to another. There needs to be further reform of the Act that would limit the number of trade unions to a manageable level.

Is there any way to provide minimal social protections to the myriad workers in the informal sector, often consisting of establishments of less than ten workers? Such protection seems impractical in view of their extremely large number. In our view, the solution has to be indirect and lies in the labour-market reforms we have proposed, which should accelerate the growth in formal-

16. See http://www.nlcindia.com/news/news_awardficci.pdf (accessed 4 November 2011).

sector employment; investment in skill creation that will make workers employable in better-paid jobs; and strengthening of the Track II redistributive programmes (discussed in depth in Part III of this book) made possible by enhanced growth from Track I reforms.

9

Land Acquisition

Like labour, land represents yet another factor of production whose market has remained largely untouched by the post-1991 reforms. The antiquated and dysfunctional state of regulations concerning land acquisition creates serious economic inefficiencies.

The Land Acquisition Act, 1894, which lays out key regulations, is more than a century old. Though the Act has been amended several times, with the last major amendment carried out in 1984, its basic provisions remain intact and the process of land acquisition continues to be archaic.

There are at least two issues which need to be addressed in the matter of land acquisition. First, if land is to be acquired from a private party, the government must define the 'social purpose' for which it can be so acquired. Second, the price at which the owner is to be compensated must be calculated.

The definition of 'social purpose' to acquire land is not an exclusively economic issue. In the US, the Supreme Court recently allowed 'taking' private property for social purpose to include building a mall, on the ground that without the mall, the town would not be able to raise enough revenue to survive. The judgement had the support of liberal (that is, progressive) judges such as Justice Stephen Breyer. Yet, there was a hue and cry in several states, and legislation was advanced to overturn the judgment.

Ultimately, the decision on what is legitimate social purpose for acquiring land has to be democratically determined. The Indian experience has been disruptive because the government has acquired privately owned land at below-market prices and handed it over to industrialists in Special Economic Zones and for housing and large-scale industrial projects by private players. Violence erupted in the case of the Tata Nano project in Singur in West Bengal, which had to be eventually moved to Gujarat, and in the case of the Orissa Steel project proposed by the Korean firm POSCO.

It must be emphasized that the original intention behind compulsory land acquisition was to prevent a few holdouts from holding up a 'socially necessary' project like the building of a highway or a railroad. No such acquisition was to be undertaken on a massive scale at less-than-market-value prices, which amounts to a levy on the private owners whose land was being acquired. This original purpose needs to be restored. Any significant acquisition of land cannot be at less than market prices, especially since this also amounts to a regressive tax whose proceeds will be typically shared between the government and the beneficiaries, who are typically substantial private parties.

In fact, the current legislation enables a cooperative rip-off of private landowners by unscrupulous state governments and big industrialists who offer to bring their projects to these states. For example, as Panagariya (2008b) has recounted, the conflict in Singur, West Bengal, surrounding the Nano car project of Tata Motors had its origins in a secret tripartite agreement between the latter on the one hand and the West Bengal government and West Bengal Industrial Development Corporation (WBIDC) on the other in March 2007. While floating its plans for this small-car project, Tata Motors had pitted the states of Uttarakhand, Himachal Pradesh and West Bengal against one another in a bidding war. In the end, West Bengal won the contest by promising the company prime land at a throwaway price in Singur, a town just 48 kilometres northwest of Calcutta, and very substantial other subsidies at the cost of the general taxpayer.

The WBIDC did not finance the extraordinarily cheap land by a subsidy. Instead it forcibly acquired the land for a pittance in the most opaque manner, asking farmers to transfer their land even before it told them the price! The mobilization of farmers by the opposition politician Mamata Banerjee against the heavy-handed tactics of the government and the meagre compensation it offered for the land eventually forced Tata Motors out of Singur.[1]

There is much to be said, therefore, for the purchase of land to be undertaken at market prices. Is there still a rationale, underlying the origin of the forced acquisition legislation, for the government to intervene if private owners hold out in order to extract exorbitant prices? The representatives of business interests as well as landowners have argued that the government must remain involved to resolve this 'holdout' problem. But to our knowledge, this is an infrequent, even rare, possibility in practice. In states such as Gujarat, Punjab and Karnataka, land acquisition for numerous projects has been smoothly accomplished through direct negotiations between private parties. With land costs being a tiny proportion of the total costs, industrialists have been in a good

1. A wrinkle in this episode was the firing by the police against the demonstrators, which inflamed them hugely. Such tactics have long been given up in India and their use by the West Bengal government was perhaps attributable to the fact that the communists were in charge of the government and they do not accept dissent without tough countermeasures. In fact, the West Bengal government had till then been the only state government that had not been thrown out by the electorate once they got in, unlike most other states which have experienced turnover. A reason often cited is that they simply exterminated opposition in the countryside.

position to make the deal attractive to the sellers.[2]

A slightly different version of this argument is that farmers simply do not want to sell their land. Therefore, no acquisition is possible unless the government is involved in the process. This is a specious argument, as numerous acquisitions in the states of Gujarat, Haryana, Punjab, Tamil Nadu and Karnataka testify. More interestingly, Sukumaran and Bisoi (2011) report the interesting case in which the chief minister of Karnataka issued a statement on 27 July 2011 stating that no land acquisition was possible for the POSCO steel project in his state. Soon after, several farmers petitioned the chief minister to reconsider his decision. The petitioning farmers were aware that industrial developers in Karnataka, including the public sector company NTPC, had paid lucrative prices for the land they had acquired, and they did not want to be deprived of the same. Within two days, on 29 July 2011, the chief minister reversed his decision.

Advocates of the rights of landowners argue that the exclusion of government from land acquisition for private projects would result in the exploitation of landowners by industrialists. They argue that many small farmers do not know the value of their land or the laws governing their rights, leaving them vulnerable. While no one would deny that it is important to protect the rights of the small farmers in land transactions, if recent agitations surrounding the government's own forced acquisition at below-market prices is any guide, landowners do have a keen sense of the value of their land. When the acquisition is done at below-market prices, NGOs in India are quick to get into the act on behalf of the owners. Moreover, mandatory advertisements of the prevailing prices by the buyer of large tracts of land offer a better solution to the imperfect information problem. The problem can also be alleviated through

---

2. See Sukumaran and Bisoi (2011).

public posting of guidance prices by the relevant revenue departments in the state.

Two arguments have been made against any acquisition or purchase of farmland for non-farm purposes, whether public or private. First, some advocates of farmer interests argue that nothing can compensate the farmers for the loss of their livelihood if their farms are sold. But it is surely possible to invest the proceeds from the sale of land in an annuity that guarantees the farmer a stream equivalent to what he or she would have generated on average by working the land.[3]

Second, some food-security advocates contend that the deployment of farmland into alternative uses would undermine India's food security. But the impression that non-agricultural users of land have been diverting much of the land in India from agriculture is false. Based on the latest available data, which relate to the year 2006-07, non-agricultural uses of land such as housing, establishments for industry and services, roads, railways, ports and airports together account for only 8.4 per cent of India's land area. In contrast, the net area under cultivation accounts for 45.8 per cent of the total area. The area under forest is 22.8 per cent. The remainder 23 per cent is barren, fallow or uncultivated. Thus, the impression that many vociferous NGOs in India convey, that land acquisition for industrialization will somehow lead to the extinction of farming or farmers, has no foundation whatsoever in facts.

Instead, food security depends on raising agricultural productivity (with food prices increasing on a trend basis worldwide as incomes rise and the poor rising above the poverty line demand more food).

---

3. If the farmer has no knowledge about how to do this, owing to illiteracy or unfamiliarity, there is a role for the government to ensure that these farmers are given the necessary guidance to do this. NGOs can also play this role. This is surely better than denying these farmers the ability to profit from the sale of their land at better prices.

It requires a number of other policy measures such as the successful introduction of the new BT and GM seeds, which can be the second Green Revolution. It also depends on providing against volatility in supplies due to temporary shortfalls, through the building up of buffer stocks.

10

Infrastructure

The need for building twenty-first century infrastructure—multilane highways, all-weather rural roads, railway lines, airports, ports, telecommunications, well-functioning cities and electricity—is well recognized. In fact, the theme of infrastructure enhancement characterizes even the US today, where the difference among politicians is over stimulus spending but not over whether it ought to be on infrastructure, which is widely considered to be in need of repair: 'London Bridge is Falling Down' is more like a dirge than a nursery rhyme.

India also is not afflicted by the 'infrastructure curse', which often arises when infrastructure is built ahead of the growth that would require it. Roads, for example, do not mean that commerce will develop along them. It is often forgotten, especially in some African countries where aid agencies and recipient governments wish to spend monies on building roads and ports, that simply building infrastructure will not automatically generate the growth that would then generate the necessary demand for it. In such cases, we are putting the cart before the horse. Fortunately, growth has occurred in India, leading to demand by common consent for infrastructure that needs to be built.[1]

Given this consensus on the need for improved and increased provision of infrastructure along various dimensions, the issues before the Track I reformers, therefore, have mostly to do with 'how to manage and deliver'. With the possible exception of telecommunications, infrastructure in different sectors and areas will require the public sector to take the lead, even as it seeks the participation of the private sector through public-private partnerships.

The issues are manifold but here we focus only on those that have a bearing on the task of intensifying Track I reforms.[2]

Air Transport

Regarding air transport, progress has been notable in the construction of modern airports in New Delhi, Mumbai, Hyderabad, Ahmedabad, Bangalore and even some smaller towns such as Jaipur. At the same time, satisfactory progress has been made in building associated air-transport infrastructure.

The key pending reform in this area concerns Air India, which absorbed more than $10 billion in subsidies in 2010-11 alone.[3] The government must give serious consideration to its privatization. Jet

---

1. It is common therefore to see trucks carrying produce overturned on the congested roads, making road travel hazardous. Once one of us (Bhagwati) was in the Lufthansa lounge in New Delhi and a German couple entered. The man had a collar around his neck and the woman's arm was in a sling. It turned out that they had run into a truck on the road from Agra to Delhi.
2. A more comprehensive treatment of the issues can be found in Panagariya (2008a, Chapters 17 and 18).
3. This airline ran up losses for several reasons such as the issuance of automatic upgrades to politicians (a practice which has now been curtailed) as distinct from customers who show loyalty and offer more custom later; and the award of free lifetime travel to persons chosen by the government

(Contd....)

Airways, which runs a superb international service, provides an excellent model.

Highway Construction

In the construction of highways, while there have been issues of financing, an equally important bottleneck has been the lack of coordination among various arms of the government. Under the National Democratic Alliance (NDA) government, which originally launched, in December 2000, the ambitious National Highway Development Programme (NHDP) to convert the Golden Quadrilateral highway into four lanes, the process of issuing of contracts to completion under Phase I of NHDP was substantially accomplished within just four years.

Despite this excellent beginning, the highway construction programme languished under the United Progressive Alliance (UPA) government. The Planning Commission practically banned the National Highway Authority of India from issuing new contracts from early 2005 to at least the end of 2006 on the ground that the contract the NDA had used was flawed and a new Model Concession Agreement was required.[4] Even after the Planning Commission came out with a new Model Concession Agreement in late 2006, the contracting process could not move forward smoothly.

The situation has subsequently improved only marginally. As late as July 2010, the then minister for road transport, Kamal Nath,

---

(contd....)

where the ministers making such awards act like Evita Peron and have no accountability because the losses they entail get absorbed in the yawning deficit which plagues the airline anyway! Perhaps the way to get at this type of depredation on Air India is to insist on transparency so that the airline has to make public who have been the beneficiaries, and how often, of such expensive largesse so that opprobrium attaches to them.

4. See Panagariya (2009b).

who had wanted to accelerate highway building to 20 kilometres per day, stated at a seminar on highways, 'When I joined this ministry, everyone told me that the Planning Commission will never let you do it.' He went on to describe the commission as 'an armchair adviser', noting that the commission was unfamiliar with the ground reality. He elaborated: 'Building a road in Kerala is different from building a road in Madhya Pradesh. We must have a concept that is flexible. Public-private partnership for Kerala has to be different from Madhya Pradesh.'[5]

Statements such as these clearly illustrate the detrimental effect of a lack of coordination among various arms of the government. As the swift progress on the Golden Quadrilateral under the NDA and in Delhi under the dynamic Congress chief minister Sheila Dixit shows, there is nothing inherently difficult about building roads and bridges. The prime minister should take steps to coordinate the various arms of the government to ensure that the country works coherently to accelerate the road-building programme.[6]

Power

Perhaps the infrastructure problem that needs most urgent and concerted attention is power. Power shortage is a critical handicap when India has an ambition to sustain 8-9 per cent annual growth. Low-cost electricity is required to keep labour-intensive products competitive due to generally low profit margins in the latter. This would make growth more inclusive, as we demonstrated earlier.

---

5. See 'Kamal Nath, Ahluwalia Spar over Roadblocks,' *The Economic Times*, 5 July 2010 at http://articles.economictimes.indiatimes.com/2010-07-05/news/27569574_1_kamal-nath-planning-commission-plan-panel (accessed 7 November 2011).
6. According to a newspaper report, there has been acceleration in road construction recently to 11 kilometres per day but it remains to be seen whether even this pace will be sustained. See, '11 km added per day, highways back on track,' *The Economic Times*, 17 October 2011.

But power is also necessary because we must bring electricity to those living in rural areas. The provision of electricity in rural areas is not only important for making day-to-day existence more comfortable but also for stimulating entrepreneurial activity locally.

Although the NDA government had initiated a major reform in the power sector through the Electricity Act, 2003, the process appears to have come unfortunately to a near standstill, with even a reversal (with the end to cross-subsidy in electricity tariffs) under the UPA government. More importantly, per capita consumption of electricity is very low and rising at an extremely slow pace. Figure 10.1, which makes some pertinent cross-country comparisons, illustrates this sharply.

The figure shows that both Brazil and China have much higher consumption of electricity in per capita terms than India. Besides, the gap between them and India has steadily widened since 1990. From approximately one half of China's consumption per capita in 1990, India dropped to less than a quarter of it in 2008. What is even more disappointing is that Vietnam, which consumed a little more than one-third of India in 1990, had reached almost one-and-a-half times India's level by 2008.

Urban Infrastructure

Finally, India also needs to make a concerted effort to build its urban infrastructure. Urbanization is an integral part of modernization and requires well-functioning cities. With the possible exception of New Delhi (and many will dispute even that), few Indian cities function well today. Traffic jams, potholed roads and the absence of a mass rapid-transit system characterize major Indian cities such as Bangalore and Mumbai. Slow movement in and out of cities in turn contributes to the phenomenon of workers having to find living space within the city, fuelling in turn the growth of slums.

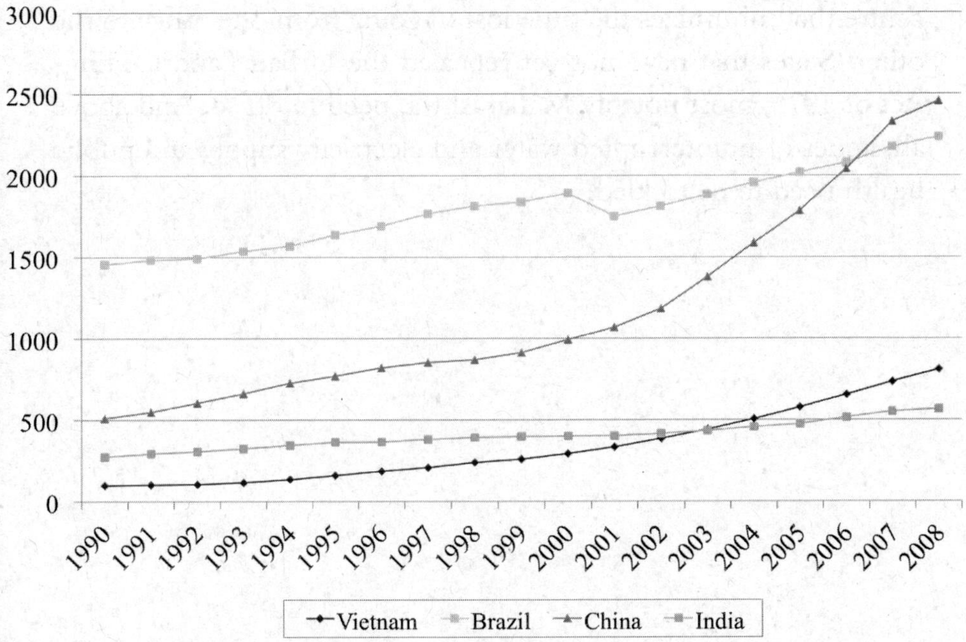

FIGURE 10.1: PER CAPITA ANNUAL ELECTRICITY CONSUMPTION IN KILOWATT HOURS

An important source of the problem in Indian cities has been their horizontal nature, a phenomenon reinforced by tight restrictions on the floor-space index, which specifies the maximum floor space that can be created on a plot of given size.[7] Relaxing the floor space index, and thus allowing taller buildings, can release valuable space for widening the roads and building mass rapid transit systems above ground. It can also help build a vibrant city

7. The floor space index, usually fixed by the urban authorities, equals the maximum floor space allowed to be built on a given size plot. In the central business district of Mumbai, this index has been fixed at 1.3 since the early 1990s. This means that only 1300 square metres of floor space can be built on a plot of 1000 square metres. The restriction has resulted in buildings with one or two floors in areas where land is extremely scarce and, therefore, expensive.

centre that minimizes the time lost in going from one office to the other. States that have not yet repealed the Urban Land Ceilings Act of 1976, most notably Maharashtra, need to do so. And above all, issues of uninterrupted water and electricity supply and public health need to be tackled.

11

Higher Education

In contrast to elementary education, which is also a predominantly social objective and for that reason belongs to the Track II policy agenda, discussed in Chapter 17 in Part III, higher education belongs to the Track I agenda.

Higher education reforms are necessary in a fast-growing economy, which requires an increasing volume of skilled workers, a steady stream of innovation of new products and processes and the progressive adaptation of technologies already available from past research in other countries. But they also offer a double dividend because, by improving the educational access of millions of those who aspire to partake of the opportunities opened up by the growth-enhancing post-1991 reforms, they increase the inclusiveness of the growth.

It would be an understatement to say that the higher education system in India is in a crisis. Except for a handful of institutions, the poor quality of instruction in the classroom is a well-known handicap afflicting India, whether we consider public or private institutions. True, universities and colleges have an adequate curriculum and, recognizing the high returns to good college performance, better students manage to do well by mastering this curriculum. But the quality of instruction in the classroom is far from satisfactory; indeed, it is poor.

International rankings of universities reflect this situation as well. In the latest QS World University Rankings, released in September 2011, no Indian university, including the celebrated Indian Institutes of Technology, found a place among even the top 200 institutions. In contrast, universities from several other Asian countries, such as China, Japan, Hong Kong, Singapore and Taiwan managed to be represented among the top 100 institutions in this ranking.

Perhaps even more important, the enrolment ratio in higher education in India is low and rising at a snail's pace. The gross enrolment ratio, which measures the proportion of those in college to college-age population, was 8 per cent in China and 10 per cent in India in 2000. By 2007, the ratio had shot up to 23 per cent in China but crept up to only 13 per cent in India. Apparently, many students are unable to proceed to higher education, not just due to lack of finance but also due to shortage of space in colleges and universities.

The comparison with China on both quality and quantity dimensions is especially disturbing since Chairman Mao Zedong had almost entirely decimated China's higher education system during the Cultural Revolution of 1966-68. In contrast, India has had an uninterrupted history of modern universities for more than 150 years. The universities of Calcutta, Bombay and Madras had been founded as early as 1857. While the university system in India was considerably strengthened in the early post-independence era, it has languished during the last three decades, precisely the period during which the Chinese have rebuilt their system.

The problems with India's higher education are many. However, a central problem is an antiquated administrative structure that imparts virtual monopoly to the University Grants Commission (UGC), a statutory body since 1956 at the apex of the system. The UGC determines curriculums at various levels, degrees to be awarded and fees and (indirectly) faculty salaries. Most important of all, it acts as the gatekeeper for the emergence of all universities. Without its approval, no new university can be started.

There are only two ways that new universities can be started in India: either the UGC deems an existing academic institution, such as a college or research institute, to be a university or the Central or a state government passes legislation to establish a new university provided the UGC gives it approval.

Private colleges are allowed to exist but they must affiliate themselves to a public university in order to award degrees. Entry of private universities is very difficult and, when they do manage to enter, they must remain unitary: they cannot affiliate colleges to award degrees. Nor are they allowed to open satellite campuses in other states without UGC approval, which involves complex procedures.

This tight control has been maintained in the name of ensuring high standards of education, notwithstanding the fact that the quality of education in public universities leaves much to be desired and is continuously declining.

In contrast, in areas of management and chartered accountancy, which fall outside the purview of the UGC since they do not award degrees, private institutions have thrived and served the students and the country well. Even in undergraduate engineering institutions, where private entry has been relatively liberal, private institutions have broadly managed to maintain the flow of engineers of adequate quality in sufficiently large numbers to keep India's growth going. It is anybody's guess as to what would have happened to Indian growth had the private engineering colleges and management institutes not expanded at the rapid pace they did to supply the market with qualified engineers and managers.

The same expansion has failed to take place in medical education except in a handful of states such as Karnataka and Maharashtra, due to the tight control by the Medical Council of India, a powerful institution that threatens to shut down, at the drop of a hat, colleges that have existed for decades. The monopolistic working of the MCI, which has an interest in reducing the supply of new doctors,[1] is predictable: the same phenomenon has characterized the American Medical Association, which has long been understood as practising entry-prevention tactics in several ways. These medical associations can literally get away with murder, no pun intended, because they can always pretend that if they are not allowed to restrict entry of new doctors through tight regulations, the patients will suffer serious consequences. But a developing country like India can ill afford to indulge the MCI.

These issues are particularly salient at the moment in India because, with a demographic transition under way, massive numbers of young Indians are expected to pass though college-going age in the next two decades. The United Nations Population Division estimates that between 2010 and 2025 alone, the population in the age group 20 to 49 years would rise by 131 million in India. The government is short of financial resources to expand universities and colleges at the pace necessary to accommodate this burgeoning young population. Therefore, while it should do as much as it can to expand public sector higher education, it needs to drop the pretence that it can serve the country's young men and women well without massive participation of the private sector.

The only educational policy choice before the government,

---

1. It is likely that corruption has also played a role in the slow growth of medical education in India. Some of the MCI members allegedly demand bribes in return for the approval of new colleges and letting the existing colleges stay open. These factors deter entry of new colleges and the smooth functioning of the ones that exist.

therefore, is for it to end the de facto licence-permit raj in this sector and let both for-profit and non-profit institutions of domestic as well as foreign origin enter the market with ease. The UGC may lay down a set of criteria that private institutions must satisfy; but beyond this, its current gatekeeper role must be ended.

Again, under the current system, another important problem arises because a committee headed by a retired high court judge determines the tuition fees even in the private institutions that are allowed to operate. The committee presumably arrives at the fee through cost estimates that include the assumption that the teachers will be given salaries prevailing in other similar institutions. Such a fee naturally limits the financial capacity of the institution to pay teacher salaries that would be required to attract the best teachers. In effect, the cap on the fees set by the committee also caps the salary the institution can pay its teachers, thereby limiting its ability to get the best teachers. Given the current scarcity of good teachers, it is important that private colleges and universities have the flexibility to attract talented young Indians getting education abroad. But this is not feasible without flexibility in the salaries they are able to pay. Lifting its control over tuition fees in both public and private universities seems, therefore, to be a policy change that the UGC must consider.

The argument commonly made that high fees would increase the gap between haves and have-nots is a non sequitur. Good education yields high private returns to the recipient and, unlike primary education, has no obvious externalities. Therefore, there is a good efficiency-based economic case for market-based tuition fees. The equity issue should be separately dealt with through the provision of loans for those qualified for admission to any given institution.

In this regard, excellent analysis and policy proposals worthy of India's attention can be found in the recent report by the independent panel on higher education appointed by Great Britain under the chairmanship of Lord Browne.[2] Although Britain had abolished its University Grants Committee (after which India's UGC was partially modelled) in 1989, its universities have continued to decline in relation to the US universities. Aware of this fact, the country has been actively reforming its higher education system over the last fifteen years. The panel headed by Browne was the latest step in this direction. Its charge was to come up with recommendations to increase investment in education, ensure that the quality of teaching was world class and make higher education accessible to anyone with the talent for it.

The Browne report recommended that Britain eliminate the existing tuition fee cap of £3,000 altogether, with two key provisions to ensure access. First, students should have to pay no upfront fees, with the government paying it to the university up to £6,000 per student. Institutions charging more than £6,000 should be required to pay a progressively rising tax on the margin. The tax should then be used to finance grants to students from low-income background to meet the living expenses. Second, after graduation, students should be required to begin paying back the costs paid by the government once their income reaches a threshold recommended to be £21,000.

The Browne report argues, correctly in our view, that this package will force greater competition among universities since they can expect higher fees for better education. At the same time, with no fees to pay upfront, it will also give students greater choice and access. The proposed system would give them freedom to join the institution at which they expect the highest net returns. It would also stimulate much-needed investment in higher education.

Consider next the role of foreign universities in raising the quality and supply of higher education in India. The ongoing efforts by the minister of human resource development, Kapil

---

2. For more extensive analysis of the Browne report, see Panagariya (2010b).

Sibal, to grant entry to foreign universities are to be applauded even as they have led to controversies.[3] A popular objection to the proposal to let in foreign universities into India is that with their deeper pockets, foreign universities will drain distinguished Indian institutions such as the Indian Institutes of Technology and Indian Institutes of Management of their best faculty. This is, however, not a persuasive objection.

First, the best researchers want other best researchers around them. Therefore, moving the faculty from established institutions of excellence is not going to be a cakewalk for foreign universities. This is illustrated by the experience of the Indian School of Business (ISB), an institution that comes the closest to being a world-class foreign educational institution in India. Only four out of approximately thirty of its resident faculty members came from the well-established Indian Institutes of Management.

Second, the key source of faculty for foreign universities will surely be Indian scholars abroad. Of the thirty resident faculty members at the ISB, approximately twenty are recent foreign graduates. An impressive 71,000 Indian graduate students were enrolled during the academic year 2009-10 in the US alone and could be potentially tapped to fill faculty positions in India. Likewise, modest incentives can bring many existing senior faculty members at universities abroad to teach on Indian campuses on a part-time basis. The ISB and Indian Institutes of Technology (IITs) list several world-class Indian scholars abroad among their non-resident faculty.

Third, even if some faculty members leave Indian institutions of excellence to join a foreign university located in India, does it constitute a net loss? After all, they will still be serving Indian students. And the competition that such movement will generate might, on balance, benefit rather than harm the country as a whole.

---

3. See Panagariya (2010c) for details.

Also, the notion that the loss of some will undermine the productivity of the rest reflects the earlier 'brain drain' model: today, faculty mostly work with faculty of similar specialization in other institutions by e-mail, telephone, and occasional visits and conferences where personal interaction is important. As the economist Frances Cairncross wrote some time ago, we are witnessing the 'death of distance'; or, since working in the same area has been called 'geography' by the economist Paul Krugman, one of us (Bhagwati) has remarked: 'Geography is history now.'

Besides, it is highly unlikely that the proposed Foreign Universities Bill will lead to a flood of foreign universities in India. With the large number of safeguards contained in the bill, many are likely to find entry unattractive. For instance, one of the provisions would limit foreign universities to the same fee regulations as domestic unaided private universities. This would automatically limit their ability to pay high faculty salaries, for instance. In all likelihood, the present bill, even if passed without changes, will not bring very many foreign universities to Indian shores and will eventually require amendment.

12

Other Track I Reforms

Our discussion has been confined to several of the most important areas where measures must still be undertaken to broaden and deepen the Track I reforms that were systematically begun in 1991. But there are still other areas where further reforms would have a payoff. Among them are reforms in international trade, foreign investment and agriculture.[1]

Trade liberalization in India, while on course in a slow but sure process, has come to a standstill since the UPA government came to power. Although India is now largely quite open to trade in industrial goods and services, further scope for liberalization in these areas remains. The top industrial tariff rate, not counting a number of peak tariffs, remains 10 per cent. Because of several

1. Panagariya (2008a) addresses Track I reforms in yet other areas such as Indian bankruptcy law, civil service, subsidies, privatization, land titles and financial sector policies. In fact, the full agenda of reforms that we could usefully implement is so large, because of the counterproductive nature of our policy framework prior to 1991, that the task before our reformers is akin to cleaning up after a tsunami.

rather high peak tariffs, however, the simple average of industrial tariffs is approximately 12 per cent. This is still high by today's standards; there clearly remains scope for bringing these tariffs down further.

Turning to services, the recent opening of multi-brand retail to Foreign Direct Investment (FDI) is a welcome step. Given that the domestic companies have been active in this sector for more than five years, we have seen that the feared injury to small 'mom-and-pop' shops is minuscule: the small and large happily coexist because they supply different needs. At the same time, the upside potential in terms of developing supply chains and the expansion of exports through foreign retailers such as Walmart and Pepsico is high.[2]

Agriculture in India also remains highly protected. Fears that opening to trade might hurt our farmers are grossly exaggerated, as was the case prior to 1991 with respect to manufactures. Just as liberalization in manufactures strengthened rather than weakened them, India should benefit from progressive liberalization in agriculture.

But India also needs to move ahead with reforms in agriculture more generally. This is necessary both to bring prosperity sooner to the many who continue to be employed in agriculture and to speed up the outward movement of the population into industry and services. Key reforms need highlighting.

First, it is essential to introduce much greater competition in the market for agricultural produce than currently exists. Somewhat surprisingly, while product market reforms have gone a long way in manufacturing and services, progress in agriculture has been limited. Under the original Agricultural Produce Marketing Committees (APMC) Act, the government has had monopoly over the produce of the farmer, which it buys from them and sells

2. See, in particular, the comprehensive analysis in Kohli and Bhagwati (2012) and a more abbreviated discussion in Bhagwati and Kohli (2011).

to wholesalers and retailers. This has proved to be highly inefficient and detrimental to the interests of the farmers. The reform of the APMC Act has been under way since the days of the National Democratic Alliance government but progress has been slow and uneven across states. In particular, some major states such as Uttar Pradesh and West Bengal have yet to introduce it and others such as Punjab, Haryana and Delhi have introduced only partial reforms. A full-fledged reform would allow farmers to sell their produce directly to whomsoever they please, including consumers; allow private firms to purchase produce from farmers; and permit farmers to contract to sell their produce directly to contract farming sponsors. If India is to take full advantage of the eventual entry of multiproduct foreign retailers and facilitate the growth of modern agricultural produce supply chains, the APMC reform is essential.

Second, India must finally remove all restrictions on interstate movement of grain, which currently prevent the country from functioning as a single market. This will require the repeal of the Essential Commodities Act of 1955, which gives states wide powers to impose restrictions on storage, transport, price, distribution, and processing of agricultural produce.

Third, the Food Corporation of India (FCI), which oversees the public distribution system in India, has turned into a white elephant with 400,000 employees and a highly inefficient network of storage and distribution. Rotting and washing off in rain of vast quantities of food grain and leakages through the distribution system are endemic. While we will consider the policy in this area in greater detail in Part III, we may note here that the FCI needs to be greatly downsized with a large number of activities undertaken by it transferred to the private sector through various policy initiatives.

Finally, various measures aimed at increasing agricultural productivity are required. These include giving land titles to farmers and simplifying the laws relating to renting and sales of land. Public investment in extension services to support investment in new seeds and methods of cultivation is required. Without such support, it will be impossible to obtain the productivity gains that GM and BT seeds promise.

PART III

THE NEW CHALLENGES

Track II Reforms to Make Redistribution More Effective and Inclusive

13

Track II Reforms: What Are the Issues?

Much of the focus of economic reforms in the past decade has been on reducing the role of the government in controlling the private sector; controls that hampered entrepreneurial dynamism and often bred corruption. This was necessary. Yet there are many areas, critical areas, that directly affect the quality of life of every citizen, where the government has a role. These include provision of social and physical infrastructure for development, the provision of elementary education and public health, providing drinking water and sanitation.

—Prime Minister Manmohan Singh
(Address to the nation, New Delhi, 24 June 2004).

Recall that the eradication of poverty and the provision of minimum levels of nutrition, health and education for all are the fundamental objectives that India sought to promote from the beginning of its post-independence history.

In principle, growth through Track I reforms, appropriately

improved and intensified in ways we just discussed in Part II, will also reduce poverty. The reduction in poverty, in turn, can also be confidently expected to result in improved clothing, shelter and other expenditures that an improved standard of living implies. Whether this also translates necessarily into adequate improvements in education, nutrition and health outcomes is less plausible, however, since nothing guarantees that the added expenditures will be devoted to improved nutrition, health and education.

For instance, nutrition may worsen rather than improve if higher incomes lead to fast food consumption, with the result that malnourishment from underconsumption is replaced by malnourishment from the wrong kind of consumption. Take the illegal immigrants from across Rio Grande in Mexico to the US with children who are malnourished because of sparse diets back home, consisting of a burrito (similar to the Indian 'chapatti') with onions and chili to spice it up. They may now buy doughnuts, hamburgers and French fries, which they can afford even at their low US wages (which exceed greatly the Mexican wages they left behind), leading to obesity and associated nutritional damage. Poorly informed parents think, like in any poor community worldwide, that fatter children are better than thinner ones.

So, the answer to this problem is not just more income but also information and education. 'Nudging' the poor to spend more virtuously is surely an important part of the overall policy framework if improvements in nutrition and health care are to be assured as poverty declines.[1] Equally, Indian planners from the outset have supplemented poverty-reducing policies with a clear statement of

1. These issues and policy proposals to address them were discussed at length twenty-five years ago by Bhagwati (1988), drawing on much economic research, in the Vikram Sarabhai Lecture in 1987 in Ahmedabad on 'Poverty and Public Policy.'

improved nutrition, health care and education as independent objectives.

We discussed in Part II how Track I reforms can increase the incomes of the poor through improved prospects of well-paid jobs. These higher incomes, and hence expenditures, can be further boosted by redirecting to the poor the additional revenues produced by the reforms. The policies that affect such redistribution are what we have called Track II policies and are the subject of Part III.

Like Track I policies, Track II policies raise issues of design. We shall discuss them at length in the context of specific social objectives in the following chapters. But it is useful here to briefly touch on them in broad terms.

Direct Transfer Versus Wage Employment

With increased revenues available for spending to remove poverty, other than by more growth through Track I policies as discussed in Part II, there is one important policy option: the addition to the purchasing power of the poor.

Here, there are two options to choose from. Either direct transfer can be made to the poor or employment at above-market wages can be increased through public works.[2] In the former case, the transfer is unilateral; in the latter case, the beneficiary must work if he is to get the payment.[3] The latter option also raises the issue as to how the workers' labour is to be allocated to various activities and what implications this allocation would have on the labour market. These are complex issues and we shall consider them in detail in Chapter 14.

2. The wages paid in such public works have important implications, as discussed below.
3. Note here that whether the payment is provided in cash or kind is a separate issue that we consider below. In principle, both the transfer and wage can be provided in cash or kind.

Transfers in Cash Versus Kind

While the purpose of employment schemes and some transfers is to merely transfer minimal purchasing power to the beneficiary, the government may sometimes want to use the transfers to influence the consumption pattern of the beneficiary. For example, it may want the beneficiary to exclude certain socially undesirable goods and services such as alcohol and prostitution from his consumption basket. Alternatively, it may want him to include certain socially desirable goods and services such as nutritious foods, education and health services in it.

In-kind transfers through free distribution or sales at below-market prices of specific commodities are often seen as the instruments of achieving this objective.[4] A moment's reflection should make clear, however, that as long as a private market exists in the commodity in which the transfer is made, the government would in general fail to alter the expenditure pattern of the recipient through the in-kind transfer. Thus, for example, suppose the government makes the transfer by selling a specified quantity of rice at below-market price to the beneficiaries. As long as the price of rice in the private market exceeds the subsidized price, such subsidy will fail to influence the beneficiary's consumption basket. He has the option to sell the subsidized rice at the higher market price and convert the transfer into cash. Cash and in-kind transfers are equivalent in this situation; indeed, cash transfers may have certain advantages over in-kind transfers in terms of administrative costs.[5]

---

4. For example, the Food Security Bill that is currently under consideration proposes to encourage increased consumption of rice and wheat by offering these grains at highly subsidized prices through the public distribution system.
5. The only way the government can eliminate the possibility of turning in-kind transfer into cash is by offering subsidy on unlimited quantity. In this case, the market price will drop down to the subsidized price, making it impossible to turn in-kind subsidy into cash. In this case, the lower effective price of rice will also lead to increased consumption of it.

This objection is weakened when in-kind transfer involves a service. For example, if the transfer is available only through a school voucher that bears the name of a specific child, it cannot be readily turned into cash because by definition there is no private market for the purchase and sale of such vouchers. The same can be said of vouchers bearing the names of specific beneficiaries for health care services.

But even this argument works only if the government has the ability to transparently enforce the use of the vouchers by the beneficiaries. In the absence of such ability, beneficiaries may still be able to turn the in-kind benefit into cash. For instance, in the case of the education voucher, the parent of a child may make a deal with a school whereby he provides the latter the voucher in return for, say, half of its face value in cash, without availing of the school benefit. The school may in turn get full value of the voucher from the government without having to incur the cost of educating the child. Similar deals may be struck between patients and doctors with regard to health care vouchers.

Public Versus Private Provision

One way the government can successfully alter the consumption pattern at least in the case of services is through their direct provision at subsidized prices, possibly even free of charge. Offering free education in public schools and low-price health care in public hospitals, dispensaries and primary health care centres are ways to ensure that the beneficiaries consume what the government deems socially desirable.

This is clearly a viable alternative but often runs into difficulty as governments are unduly inefficient at the provision of the services. As we shall see, this has been the case in education and health sectors in India, with the result that potential beneficiaries have chosen to seek private sources of supply even though the latter may charge a higher price.

The issue of government provision, of course, also arises in the context of goods. The most notable example of this in India is the public distribution system of food grains, whereby the government procures large volumes of grain each year that it, in turn, sells at subsidized prices to the poor. As we will see, this public provision has been highly inefficient with massive leakages, rampant corruption and very limited delivery of the subsidy to the intended beneficiaries.

Conditional Versus Unconditional Transfers

An alternative route to influencing the spending patterns of the beneficiaries while still making transfers in cash is to ask them to produce a proof of having consumed certain goods and services. This approach is not much different from in-kind transfers and is subject to the same abuse as the latter. If enforcement is weak and corruption endemic, as is the case in India, fake invoices can be obtained at a small price as proof of having met the conditionality. Like in-kind transfers, conditional transfers are also likely to succeed in altering the beneficiary expenditure pattern only if the government is substantially able to enforce the laws.

Universal Versus Targeted Transfers

A final choice one must make with respect to Track II reforms is whether the intended transfers are targeted to the poor and socially disadvantaged or made universal. The main argument the advocates of universal transfers make is that this is the only way to ensure that the poor and disadvantaged groups are not shortchanged and receive the benefits. The human rights groups that strongly favour the rights approach to every social goal also join these advocates.

We have seen no empirical evidence showing that universal transfers are either necessary or sufficient to ensure that all those in need receive the intended benefits. For a long time, the public distribution system for food grains in India was universal. But dissatisfaction with its reach to the poor led to a switch to the current, more targeted system. It is simply not clear why reverting to a universal system will now work better. More importantly, if the objective is to bring food security, health and education to the poor, at the current state of economic development, revenues are grossly inadequate to run universal programmes that could then make substantial contribution per individual. We could either bring marginal benefits to all or substantial benefits to the bottom 30 or 40 per cent of the population. The argument that the poor are not easily identified is also no longer valid. For example, the National Rural Employment Guarantee Scheme has surely identified the rural poor.

Our Preferred Strategy

In the light of these considerations of the different choices in regard to designing Track II policies, what is our preferred menu? We may stress that there is general agreement on the objectives of social policy. All analysts favour speedy delivery of basic needs with respect to food, clothing, shelter, education and health to the poor and the socially disadvantaged. The differences relate to the approach to be taken to achieve this goal.

Our preferred policy mix consists of unconditional cash transfers that are targeted so as to minimally exclude those clearly identifiable as non-poor, with the beneficiary having the option to choose between private and public providers of food, education, health care and other necessities of life. This broad preference for cash transfers may be tempered by two exceptions: vouchers in the case of education and insurance in the case of major illnesses. Let us briefly explain why.

In principle, an approach that assigns a prominent role to the government could deliver on the desired goal as stated in the previous paragraph. The government could offer employment in the public works programmes at a pre-specified wage to combat poverty and provide the socially desirable goods such as food, health care, education, and even shelter, free of charge or at subsidized prices to the beneficiaries. It could bear not only the financial burden associated with the employment programme and provision of food, education and health but also take on the responsibility of their delivery.

But the success of this approach is predicated on the ability of the government to run public works programmes efficiently and to deliver the goods and services efficiently. In our discussions in the following chapters, we will repeatedly see that the government's track record in delivery has been extremely poor. The task is especially compounded by the existence of endemic corruption at all levels of the government administration. Therefore, we will repeatedly lean in favour of an approach that minimizes the role of the government, or at least requires it to compete with the private sector providers on equal terms. In turn, this choice translates in a heavy reliance on cash transfers that place the purchasing power directly in the hands of the people.

We also favour targeted instead of universal programmes. The concern that targeting may exclude many among the poor and disadvantaged from accessing the benefits is readily addressed by applying the exclusion rather than inclusion criteria to identify the beneficiaries. That is to say, unless identified as ineligible according to certain criteria, each individual may be considered eligible for the benefits. Exclusion criteria may include the ownership of a motorcycle, scooter, car, a specified amount of land or other similar assets. This might result in a larger proportion of beneficiaries than what would be suggested by a reasonable set of inclusion criteria but would ensure that all the poor and disadvantaged are included. At the same time, a substantial exclusion will prevent the social expenditures from being spread too thinly and thus diluted.

Finally, it will be best to make the transfers unconditional. Given the limited administrative ability of our government at all levels, adding conditions to the transfers will only result in corruption without delivering the desired outcome. The objective of influencing the consumption basket should, instead, be pursued through alternative instruments. For example, nutrition improvement can be achieved through requirements of fortification of key foods. Likewise, education and health goals can be promoted through advertising campaigns.

14

Attacking Poverty by Guaranteeing Employment

The principal instrument of direct attack on poverty in India has been schemes providing employment to the poor in the rural areas. While the Central and state governments have sponsored a variety of these schemes over the past decades, the Central government-sponsored scheme launched under the National Rural Employment Guarantee (NREGA) Act of 2005 eclipses them all in magnitude and scope.[1] Implemented over the entire country, this scheme is the principal vehicle for placing minimum purchasing power in the hands of the rural households today. Therefore, it is imperative to examine the weaknesses in its design and functioning, leading to suggestions for reforms that would achieve the scheme's objective at lower cost and with greater effectiveness.

1. NREGA has recently been renamed as the Mahatma Gandhi National Rural Employment Guarantee Act scheme. But we shall continue to refer to it by its original acronym in this volume.

The Progress So Far

The NREGA has been implemented in three distinct phases. Under Phase I, which began on 2 February 2006, it was implemented in the 200 poorest districts. Under Phase II, another 130 districts were covered beginning on 1 April 2007. The remaining 274 districts came under the scheme as a part of Phase III implemented with effect from 1 April 2008. Therefore, the scheme has now been in operation over the entire country for four full financial years (ending on 31 March 2012).

The broad contours of the NREGA are easily defined. The programme guarantees one member of every rural household, whether poor or not, 100 days' worth of unskilled manual employment at a wage no less than that specified by the Central government. Originally specified at 60 rupees per day, the wage was revised to 100 rupees per day in January 2009. Beginning 1 January 2011, it has been linked to the consumer price index at the level of the states and Union territories.[2]

If an applicant is not provided employment within fifteen days of seeking it, the state is obliged to compensate him or her at a rate no less than one-fourth of the specified wage rate for the first thirty days and at no less than half of the wage rate for the rest of the period. The state is required to bear the burden of this compensation. At least one-third of the beneficiaries are required to be women who have registered and requested for work.

Labour hired as a part of the programme is to be employed in public works and other activities specified in the legislation, such as water conservation and water harvesting; drought proofing, including forestation and tree planting; irrigation canals; land development; flood control and rural connectivity. The cost of material component of projects and skilled and semi-skilled workers

2. Consequently, the specified wage rose from 17 per cent in Meghalaya to 79 per cent in Haryana from 1 January 2011.

is capped at 40 per cent of the total cost. The Central government covers only 75 per cent of the material cost, with the state having to fund the remaining 25 per cent. The legislation makes very detailed provisions for the creation of the implementation machinery at the Central, state, district, block and village levels.

TABLE 14.1: KEY ACHIEVEMENTS OF THE NREGA AS OFFICIALLY REPORTED

Item	*2006-07*	*2007-08*	*2008-09*	*2009-10*	*2010-11*
Financial					
Total amount spent (billion nominal rupees)	88.2	158.6	272.5	379.1	393.8
Of which wages (billion nominal rupees)	58.4	107.4	182	255.8	256.9
Per cent share of wages in the total	66.2	67.7	66.8	67.5	65.2
Physical					
Households receiving employment (million)	21	33.9	45.5	52.5	55
Person days of work done (billion)	0.91	1.44	2.16	2.84	2.57
Per cent share of Scheduled Castes and Tribes	61	57	53.7	51.2	51.5
Per cent share of women in the work done	41	43	47.9	48.1	47.7
Average person days per household employed	43.3	42.5	47.5	54.1	46.7

Source: For years 2006-07 and 2007-08, see http://www.nrega.net/csd/Forest/field-initiatives/Sustainable%20Developemnt.pdf (accessed on 18 November 2011) and for the last three years, see 'DMU Report' at http://nrega.nic.in/netnrega/home.aspx (accessed on 18 November 2011).

Table 14.1 reports the key achievements of the NREGA in terms of financial and physical indicators, as officially reported. Beginning with the total expenditure of 88.2 billion rupees ($1.9 billion) in 2006-07, the programme spent a total of 393.8 billion rupees ($ 8.6 billion) in 2010-11. Of this, approximately two-thirds was spent on wages and the rest on materials.[3] The number of households benefiting from the programme rose from 21 million to 55 million over the same period. Having peaked in 2009-10, the total person days and person days per household declined slightly to 2.57 billion and 46.7 days respectively in 2010-11. Clearly, the average person days per household receiving employment under the programme is well below the maximum 100 days offered under the programme.

Going by just the wages paid, the NREGA programme placed 4,671 rupees per household on average in 2010-11 in the hands of the households covered by the programme. But this average masks one key implication of Table 14.1: the Scheduled Castes and Scheduled Tribes benefited disproportionately from the programme. According to the 2001 census, the Scheduled Castes and Tribes account for 24.4 per cent of the Indian population. But their share in the days they worked in 2010-11, shown in Table 14.1, was 51.5 per cent. If we assume that the distribution of households by caste in the beneficiary population mirrors that in the general population, we would conclude that the SC and ST households received 2.2 times the average sum, or approximately 10,275 rupees per household, in 2010-11. Of course, to the extent that the SC and ST households were proportionately more numerous among the beneficiaries than they are in the general population, this figure would be lower. Whatever one assumes, the

3. The dollar conversion is done using the average dollar-rupee exchange rate for the fiscal year reported in the RBI Handbook of Statistics on Indian Economy, 2011.

data do seem to point to a proportionately larger part of the benefit going to the SC and ST households that also happen to have a higher incidence of poverty.

Pitfalls of the NREGA Scheme and the Superiority of Cash Transfers

Proponents of the NREGA scheme often defend it against the counterfactual, in which there is no other scheme. Few critics of the scheme would consider the scheme so counterproductive as to advocate its elimination, even if no other anti-poverty scheme replaces it. Indeed, most would agree that the NREGA has done more to transfer purchasing power to the poor than almost all existing redistribution programmes, including subsidies on food, fertilizer, water and electricity, and even education and health expenditures. Even accepting that the NREGA is subject to significant leakages as the money flows from the Centre all the way down to the actual beneficiary, and that it has contributed to larger fiscal deficits and inflation and has adversely impacted economic activity by distorting the labour market, it is to be viewed positively vis-à-vis a situation without NREGA insofar as it has placed a significant sum of money in the hands of the poor households, at least going by the official statistics reported in Table 14.1.

But the picture looks much bleaker if we compare the situation with the NREGA to one in which it is replaced by an alternative policy of making direct transfers to the poor households. Proponents of universal schemes such as the NREGA often argue that a targeted scheme runs the risk of excluding some of the poor due to identification problems. But they exaggerate since one can readily minimize the exclusion error by including all who are not proven non-poor according to a set of carefully chosen criteria. For example, households with a scooter or motorcycle, more than 2 hectares of land, a 'pucca' house or a modern toilet could be excluded. This will still include some non-poor among the recipients of the benefit but will nevertheless allow significant savings over the inclusion of all households.

Advantages of such a transfer scheme over the NREGA are many and it has virtually no disadvantages. First and foremost, transfers will virtually eliminate the leakages. The volume of leakages under the NREGA is not known with precision but even the proponents of the scheme do not deny that it is significant. A study by Sharma (2009), jointly sponsored by the National Council of Applied Economic Research and the Public-Interest Foundation, observed that leakages in Jharkhand, Orissa and Uttar Pradesh went up to 'one-third to half of the stipulated wages', adding that since the leakages were disguised through the addition of fictitious names to the muster rolls, employment generation was also overstated. Sharma (2009 footnote 7, p. 128) states, 'All three states have what is referred to as the PC or "percentage" system in which bribes have to be paid according to fixed percentages to the whole hierarchy of staff up to the block level, and sometimes going higher.' For Orissa, Sharma is able to provide more precise estimates. He notes (footnote 8, p. 129), 'The study estimates that only 58 per cent of wages disbursed in sample works during the first two years of the programme reached workers listed in the muster rolls, the proportion being only 26 per cent in KBK (Kalahandi, Bolangir, Koraput) region.'

Cash transfers should substantially eliminate these leakages. Advances in technology now allow an official in New Delhi to deposit money into the bank account of the beneficiaries held in a distant village with just a few keystrokes. Lest one doubts it, consider the only careful study available of a small experience with officially sanctioned cash transfers in India. The states of Rajasthan and Karnataka have recently experimented with cash transfers to the elderly and widows with strikingly positive results. Summarizing their study of these experiences, 'Small but effective: India's targeted unconditional cash transfers,' Dutta, Howe and Murgai (2010) note:

> India's approach to social security stresses the provision of subsidized food and public works. Targeted, unconditional cash transfers are little used, and have been hardly evaluated. An evaluation of cash transfers for the elderly and widows, based on the national household survey data and surveys on social pension utilization in two states, Karnataka and Rajasthan, reveals that these social pension schemes work reasonably well. Levels of leakage are low, funds flow disproportionately to poorer rather than richer households, and there is strong evidence that the funds reach vulnerable individuals. A comparison with the public distribution system reveals that the main strength of the social pensions scheme is its relatively low level of leakage.

The authors are careful to note that the study is not decisive since it relates to programmes that are small in scale. Nevertheless, it greatly strengthens the case for giving cash transfers a further play rather than acquiescing to knee-jerk assertions by critics that these are not feasible or that these too will be subject to equal corruption. The Central government, which has repeatedly shied away from carrying out proper pilot projects, needs to evaluate the feasibility of the cash transfers on a larger scale.

Second, even assuming equal volume of leakages as under the NREGA, which is highly implausible, cash transfers will place a greater volume of purchasing power in the hands of the poor for other reasons. Thus, while NREGA gives the beneficiary a wage that is higher than what would prevail in the market in the absence of this scheme, it takes away his or her labour in return. Under a cash transfer, the beneficiary will receive the equivalent amount of public money and will also get to keep his labour, for which he can earn additional wage in the market. Moreover, NREGA ends up spending 35 per cent of the expenditures on construction material. Under cash transfers, these funds will be available for distribution to the poor.

Furthermore, cash transfers will not suffer from an important regressive feature plaguing the NREGA. The NREGA provides that the labour of a worker can be used in the 'provision of irrigation facility, horticulture plantation and land development facilities to land owned by households belonging to the Scheduled Castes and the Scheduled Tribes or below poverty line families or to the beneficiaries of land reforms or to the beneficiaries under the Indira Awas Yojana of the Government of India or that of the small farmers or marginal farmers as defined in the Agriculture Debt Waiver and Debt Relief Scheme, 2008'.[4] Surely, most workers offering their labour under the programme are poorer than many of the entities entitled to their free labour under this provision. In contrast, under a cash transfer, the workers would retain the right to sell their labour at the market wage.

Then again, NREGA has also led to severe distortions in the labour market that cash transfers would prevent. Three such distortions are worth emphasizing. One, by diverting a fraction of the labour force from its productive private sector deployment to public works projects, it has replaced genuine value addition to the national income by projects likely to be of dubious value. Because NREGA funds can only be accessed for pre-specified activities considered to serve public interest, local authorities have an incentive to come up with projects fitting this list even when the social return on them is low, possibly even minuscule. Normally, it is the social return that drives the search for resources to finance a project. But NREGA reverses this process: the availability of the funds drives the search for projects.

Unsurprisingly, therefore, available studies have recorded projects of zero or even negative social value being undertaken under the scheme. Reporting on the quality of assets created, Sharma (2009, p. 125) states, 'It is difficult to argue emphatically about the quality of assets that have been created because very little information is

4. See Government of India (2009b).

available on them, but a few examples provided here underscore the problems in terms of the quality of these assets. Ponds were dug in a drought-prone area with scanty rainfall, soil was sandy and had no water retention power and others were without water (Haryana). But, some had become like swimming pools due to heavy expenditure incurred on material and masonry works.' He goes on to add, 'A lot of money was spent on digging ponds without conceptualizing factors like catchment area, sources of recharging, technical sanctions, and preparation of detailed estimates. Assets created in Karnataka were not according to specification and quantities executed were not as per the technical sanction.' He notes similar problems in road projects in Orissa, Tripura, West Bengal and other states.

The second form of distortion created by the NREGA has worked through the effect it has had on the wages. Just as high effective labour costs of operating in the formal economy have led the firms to opt for capital-intensive products and technologies, a NREGA-induced hike in rural wages will lead to a premature shift in favour of capital-intensive farm products and techniques. While the current empirical evidence on this is limited to press reports, it is only a matter of time before more systematic corroborative evidence would emerge.

Finally, there is likely to be another detrimental long-term impact of NREGA on economic development. Given that the primary purpose of public works is to generate employment and the creation of an asset is largely incidental, the work effort demanded by them is likely to be leisurely.[5] In turn, this would have an adverse impact

5. One might argue that setting wages at piece rates, as provided by the law, would solve this problem. But this is unlikely since the piece rate must be sufficiently high to give the worker the minimum daily wage that the legislation sets. Moreover, enforcement of work as per the piece rate is likely to be lax in public works programmes, especially since the primary purpose of such programmes is to create employment in the first place.

on the work culture. Eventually, work effort is likely to decline even in private employments paying the same wage as the public works.[6]

In a similar vein, since the public projects discourage the use of any machinery save simple implements such as shovels and exclusively offer manual and unskilled work, they offer the workers no scope for skill creation. A yet more detrimental developmental impact is likely to be added disincentive for migration. Because public works under NREGA are confined to rural areas, they require presence in the rural areas and slow down a process of income-improving outmigration that is already moving at snail's pace. A cash transfer that the household can receive even as one of its members migrates to work elsewhere does not suffer from this pitfall.

6. Indeed, one of us (Panagariya) has found this to be the case in his informal conversations with businessmen from Bhilwara district in Rajasthan, who told him that workers now refuse to work at wages similar to NREGA wages, arguing that the latter are available to them for limited effort while employment in the private sector requires a lot more effort.

15

Adult Nutrition and Food Security

There are serious questions over policy initiatives required currently to secure nutritional improvement. Unlike the concern with the poor alone, this issue is seen as cutting across all classes of the population. In particular, with adult nutrition in mind, many civil society groups now demand an expansion of the public distribution system through a right-to-food legislation that would guarantee an adequate quantity of food grains at highly subsidized prices to all citizens of the country.

Questioning the Decline in Calorie Consumption as an Indication of Increased Hunger

The concern for adult nutrition has originated primarily in the steady decline recorded in per capita calorie consumption (though a decline in protein intake is also an issue). A 1996 report on nutrition by the National Sample Survey Organization (NSSO) provides some of the early documentation of this trend.[1] Additional

1. See National Sample Survey Organization (1996).

data appear in similar follow-up reports.[2] The long-term trend is one of declining calorie consumption in both rural and urban areas though the trend is steadier in rural rather than urban areas. Protein intake has shown similar patterns in rural and urban areas, though the intake of fats has steadily climbed up. Figures 15.1 and 15.2 depict these movements graphically.

The trends in calorie consumption and protein and fat intake reflect a shift away from cereals (Deaton and Dreze, 2008, Table 4) to other lower-calorie, lower-protein, more fatty and sugary foods. Such a shift in diet due to increased income is likely— finer grains, white flour, rice, fruits and oily foods replace coarse grains and whole-wheat flour. Consumption of fruits, fried products and desserts has seen a steady rise in the last few decades.

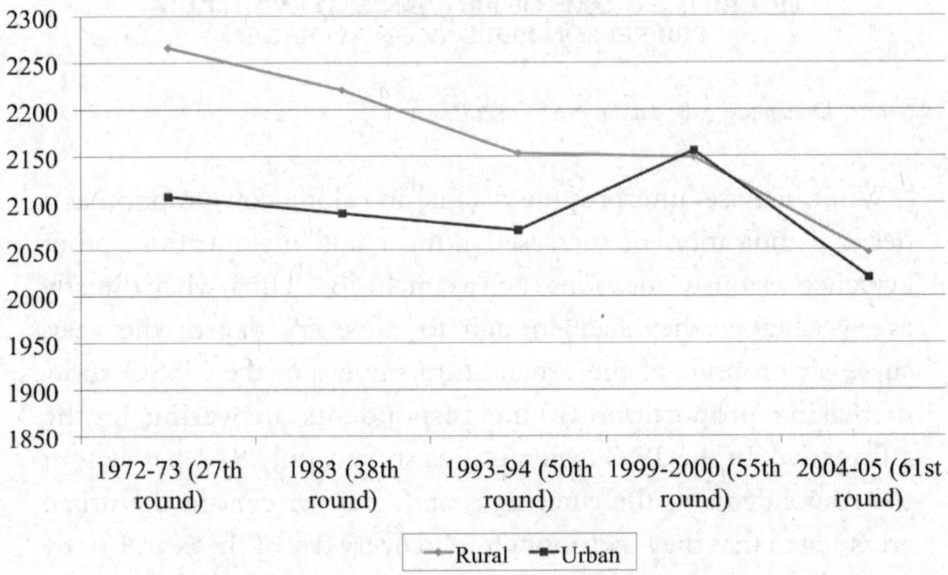

FIGURE 15.1: AVERAGE CALORIE INTAKE PER PERSON PER DAY

Source: Drawn using the data in NSSO (2007a, p. v).

---

2. See National Sample Survey Organization (2001a and 2007a).

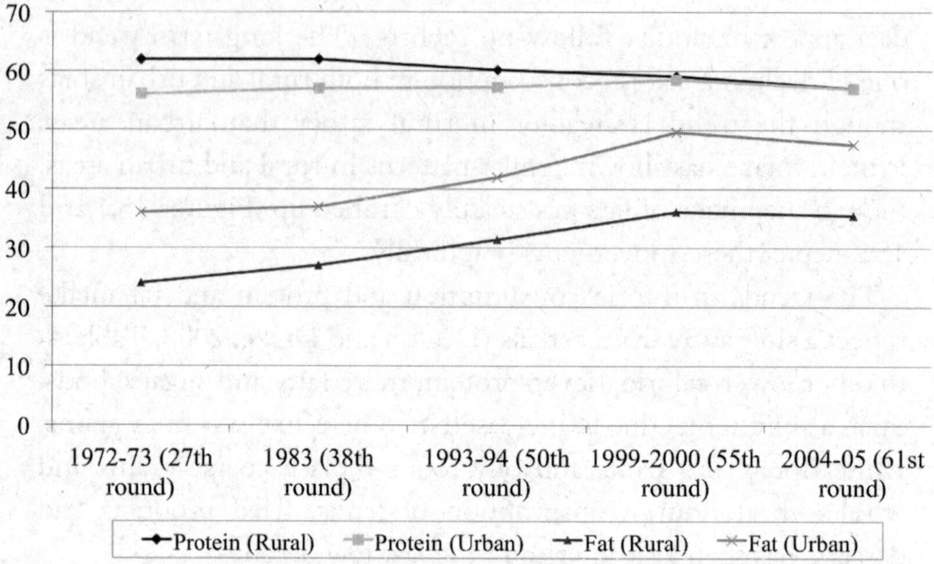

FIGURE 15.2: GRAMS OF PROTEIN AND FAT INTAKE PER PERSON PER DAY ON AVERAGE

Source: Drawn using the data in NSSO (2007a, p. v).

While activists interpret the decline in calorie consumption as a decisive indication of increased hunger and malnutrition, other evidence seriously questions such a conclusion. Thus, when directly asked whether they had enough to eat every day of the year, successive rounds of the expenditure surveys of the NSSO show increasing proportions of the respondents answering in the affirmative. In the 1983 expenditures survey, only 81.1 per cent of the respondents in the rural areas and 93.3 per cent in the urban areas stated that they had enough food every day of the year. But by 2004-05, these percentages had risen to 97.4 and 99.4 per cent, respectively.[3] Figure 15.3 depicts these trends in rural and urban India.

3. Data on the first three surveys are from the National Sample Survey Organization (2001b) and for the last one from National Sample Survey Organization (2007b).

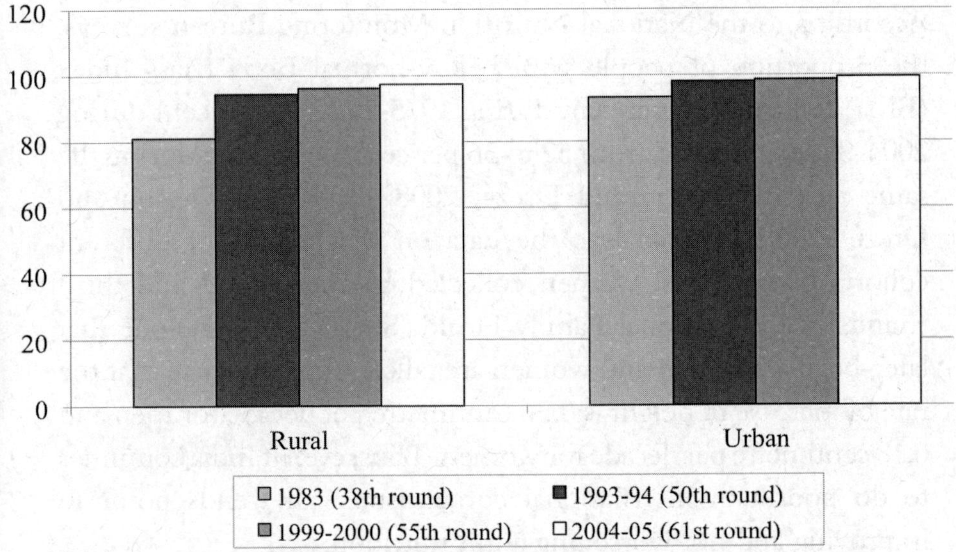

FIGURE 15.3: PER CENT OF RESPONDENTS STATING THEY HAD ENOUGH TO EAT ON ALL DAYS OF THE YEAR

Source: NSSO (2001b and 2007b).

Conceptually, the rising trend in the proportion of the population stating that it had enough to eat throughout the year can be reconciled with the declining trend in calorie consumption once we recognize the factors that explain why there may be a decline in the need for calorie consumption. For example, greater mechanization in agriculture, improved means of transportation and a shift away from traditional physically challenging jobs may have reduced the need for physical activity. Likewise, better absorption of food made possible by improved epidemiological environment (better child and adult health and better access to safe drinking water) may have lowered the needed calorie consumption to produce a given amount of energy.

Hence, the inference that declining calorie consumption implies increasing malnourishment is not warranted. Indeed, the inference is also contradicted by the weight and height trends of adults.

According to the National Nutrition Monitoring Bureau surveys, the proportion of people with below-normal Body Mass Index (BMI) fell from 56 per cent during 1975-79 to 33 per cent during 2004-05 for men and from 52 to 36 per cent for women during the same period (Deaton and Dreze, 2008, Table 10). Deaton and Dreze (2008) also analyse the data on the heights of different cohorts of men and women collected by the second and third rounds of the National Family Health Survey and conclude that later-born adult men and women are taller. They calculate that the rate of increase of height is 0.56 centimetre per decade for men and 0.18 centimetre per decade for women. Thus, even if India continues to do poorly in international comparisons, all trends point to improving and not worsening adult nutrition.

Parenthetically, we note here our puzzlement at the implicit endorsement by Deaton and Dreze (2008, p. 45) of the argument that the declining calorie consumption represents rising poverty.[4] While the declining trends in both calorie consumption and protein intake can be sources of concern, surely poverty is not to be measured by the ex post calorie consumption. It must be measured, instead, by how many calories the individuals are able to afford ex ante. The policy response greatly depends on which measure of poverty we choose.

---

4. To quote the authors (Deaton and Dreze 2008, p. 45), 'As has been suggested by several authors, including Palmer-Jones and Sen (2001) and Ray and Lancaster (2005), we could take the calorie intakes associated with the original lines as fixed poverty norms and compute the fraction of the population living in households whose per capita calorie consumption falls beneath 2,400 calories in the rural sector and beneath 2,100 calories in the urban sector. Such calculations are shown in Table 5. Because the distribution of per capita calories is moving to the left over time, these numbers show *rising* poverty rates, from two-thirds of the rural population in 1983 to four-fifths in 2004-05, and from 65 per cent to more than 75 per cent in India as a whole.'

If we measured poverty by the ex post calorie consumption, we would be tempted to offer free food to Bollywood actresses trying to stay slim on low-calorie diets! If, however, we measured poverty, correctly in our view, by the amount of calories the individual is able to afford *ex ante*, we would be spared the obvious policy mistakes. Thus, if the decline in calorie consumption turns out to be the result of lack of affordability, the solution would be to improve the purchasing power of the citizenry through growth and redistribution. If, instead, the decline took place in spite of sufficient purchasing power and, therefore, due to ill-informed decision-making, we would want to supply better information, undertake persuasive advertising to 'nudge' people into healthy eating and pass laws requiring fortification of major foods by necessary nutrients.

Regrettably, the dominant view today, aggressively pushed by activists in India and around the world and by influential international organizations such as the World Health Organization, the Food and Agricultural Organization and the World Bank, is that the decline in calorie consumption represents increased poverty and therefore increased hunger. The fact that more and more people in India are able to afford increased rather than reduced food purchases over time and that the decline in calorie consumption has occurred across all individuals, whether they be rich or poor and whether they be residents in rural or urban areas (Deaton and Dreze 2008, pp. 45-47 and Figures 1 and 2), would suggest, however, that something other than purchasing power—that is, reduced need for calorie consumption due to the various factors detailed here—is behind the change. But the increased poverty school has conveniently ignored this inconvenient truth.

Pitfalls of the Right-to-Food Bill

This diagnosis of malnutrition, that it is due not to poverty and hunger but rather due to unhealthy consumption, also implies that the current reliance on the right-to-food legislation, and implementation of further expansion of public distribution of food grains, is misguided.

A bill to this effect has just been approved by the Cabinet and is soon to be tabled in the Parliament. The bill proposes to provide subsidized grain through the public distribution system to 75 per cent of the rural and 50 per cent of the urban population. Specified exclusion criteria exclude 25 per cent of rural and 50 per cent of urban population from receiving subsidized food. A minimum of 46 per cent of the households in the rural and 28 per cent in the urban areas are priority (that is, poor) households. The remaining households not falling under the exclusion criteria are designated 'general' households. Under the bill, the government would supply 7 kilograms of millet, wheat or rice per person per month at the prices of 1, 2 and 3 rupees per kilogram, respectively, to priority households. With five persons per household, the quantity of subsidized grain would amount to 35 kilograms per household. The bill also proposes to give a minimum of 3 kilograms of millet, wheat or rice per person per month at prices not exceeding 50 per cent of the respective support prices to general households.

In the case of many beneficiaries who may already be consuming adequate grains—with malnutrition reflecting a lack of balanced diet, as we have argued—such an objective itself is questionable. But even accepting that the increase in grains consumption is a desirable goal, it is unlikely that the proposed programme would accomplish it. Given that a private market for food grains offers significantly higher prices than the subsidized prices under the bill, beneficiaries will have the option to buy grains at the low prices from the public distribution system and sell it in the private market for cash at a profit.[5] There is no guarantee, therefore, that the

---

5. In principle, there is one qualification. Earlier work by Bhagwati and Balbir Sihag (1980) showed that the offtake of the rations at lower prices in the

(Contd....)

programme will encourage increased consumption of food grains if the beneficiaries do not see the need for it. Indeed, non-priority beneficiaries (the general households in terms of the definition used in the bill), who would receive only partial supplies from the public distribution system, are likely to cut their purchases kilogram-for-kilogram from the private market. This argument is reinforced by the fact that the ongoing decline in the consumption of calories from cereals has taken place in the presence of an extensive public distribution system providing subsidized wheat and rice.

Indeed, the subsidy structure in the bill makes it unviable at the implementation level.[6] Recognizing that the absolute subsidy per kilogram is the largest in rice, the eligible households would stand to maximize the implicit transfer to them by buying rice and no other grain from the public distribution system. By reselling this rice in the private market, they would be able to convert this maximized in-kind subsidy into cash. They would then be free to spend the proceeds as they wish. Of course, with all eligible households buying rice for their entire permitted quotas, the government distribution system will simply fail to procure enough rice. Thus, there is a clear mismatch in the bill between the objective of pushing calorie consumption and the instrument chosen.

When we add to these considerations the high delivery costs of the public distribution system, the Right-to-Food Bill makes even less sense. Wastage, leakage and theft in the public distribution

---

(...contd.)

public distribution system was less, the lower the differential between these prices and the higher free-market prices. The reason, they argued, was that there is an opportunity cost attached to lining up to get the ration. But the difference between the current market prices and the subsidized prices in the proposed bill is too large to be offset by such opportunity costs for most poor households.

6. See Panagariya (2011f) for additional details.

system have been widely documented. The system lacks adequate warehouse facilities with vast volumes of grain stored in the open. Rains frequently wash away large proportions of these stocks. Parts of stock go unused for sufficiently long to rot. Pests and rats take their share as well. Finally, there are significant leakages as grain moves from procurement by the Centre to distribution to the states, districts, villages and eventually, the actual beneficiaries.

A recent study by Jha and Ramaswami (2011) estimates that in 2004-05, 70 per cent of the poor received no grain through the public distribution system (exclusion error) while 70 per cent of those who did receive it were non-poor (inclusion error). They also estimate that as much as 55 per cent of the grain supplied through the public distribution system leaked out along the distribution chain, with only 45 per cent actually sold to beneficiaries through fair-price shops. The share of food subsidy received by the poor turned out to be an astonishingly low 10.5 per cent.

Many proponents of the Right-to-Food Bill say that ensuring inclusion of all poor is the key justification for universal or nearly universal coverage (Drèze and Khera 2010, and Himanshu and Sen 2011). They base this argument on the evidence of large exclusions of the poor from the current targeted rather than universal public distribution system. But even this justification for yet further expansion of an already broken system fails to stand up to close scrutiny. In his excellent analysis, Svedberg (2012) makes this point forcefully and it is worthwhile to quote him at some length:

> The evidence in support of universality as an efficient method for eliminating, or even notably reducing, exclusion errors, is not altogether convincing. Before 1997, the PDS was in principle universal, but large proportions of poor households were either effectively excluded, or purchased very small amounts of subsidized grains. On the basis of 1993-94 NSS data, Dutta and Ramaswami (2001) found that the poorest household quintile, on average, managed to purchase about 10 per cent and 20 per cent of the PDS

(Public Distribution System) grains allowed in Maharashtra and Andhra Pradesh, respectively. Other evaluations of the pre-1997 PDS also report blunt de facto targeting of poor households (Jha 1992; Ahluwalia 1993; Howes and Jha 1992, 1994; Dev and Suryanarayana 1991; Parikh 1994).

One may also gauge the extent to which universality reduces exclusion errors by consulting more recent estimates from Tamil Nadu, the only state that opted for a universal PDS after 1997. In 2004-05, about 80 per cent of the households in the three lowest MPCE (Monthly Per Capita Expenditure) deciles in Tamil Nadu reported consumption of PDS rice, but practically no wheat. This share is more than twice as high as the all-India figure (National Sample Survey Organization 2007c), but it still reflects substantial exclusion of poor households. To have a right to purchase subsidized grains is obviously not sufficient for eliminating exclusion; the system has to be known, attractive and accessible as well, and ensuring this entails costs.

To conclude: the Right-to-Food Bill can be expected to neither boost grain consumption nor target the poor significantly better than the current system. It may result in some transfer of purchasing power to some of the poor but only at a huge cost in relation to the benefit accrued. Add to this the fact that for the vast proportion of the population, calorie consumption may not even be the main factor accounting for poor nutrition. Instead, the key deficiency is most likely a lack of proper balance in diet: for example, the malnourished families should be shifting their diet to more milk and fruits rather than consuming additional quantities of grain on which the Right-to-Food Bill has focused.

What Must Be Done

It needs to be emphasized again, in the present context as earlier, that significant gains in efficiency can be achieved by replacing the public distribution system by cash transfers. The argument against such transfers, that the beneficiaries might spend the money on something other than grains, is spurious. As argued above, such an outcome is also readily achievable under in-kind transfers by selling the grain in the open market. The advantage of cash transfers is that they would greatly minimize the leakage along the distribution chain and also eliminate the huge wastage that characterizes the public distribution system. It is ironic that many activists insist on in-kind transfers while simultaneously advocating the rural employment guarantee scheme, which, after all, pays the participants wages in cash. If they think that they not only know what the right pattern of expenditure to ensure proper nutrition is and can also regulate the expenditures to achieve this pattern through in-kind transfers, surely they should also insist on paying the wages under the rural employment guarantee scheme in kind rather than in cash. But we know of no significant activist movement favouring in-kind payment of wages under NREGA!

Once the issues of transfer of purchasing power and the right basket of consumption are separated, the focus of policy can shift to ensuring that consumers make the right consumption choices. This would require two sets of measures. One set would inform and then 'nudge' the public in several ways towards a more nourishing diet. The second set, which is more likely to produce results, would aim at getting wholesalers and retailers to fortify various foods with necessary nutrients. The Food Safety and Standards Authority of India can play an important role in the implementation of this set of measures.

Of course, even though demand can be shifted towards dairy products, fruits, vegetables, fish and meat, policy must also be directed to ensure increased availability of these items. Here Track I and Track II reforms come squarely together. The availability of products needed to promote good nutrition depends on both domestic production and imports. It is surprising, however, that discussions on food security, which focus on enhancing the availability of various food items over time, rarely mention imports.[7] This omission has often resulted in India failing to fully exploit the benefits of imports. For example, in the last three years, the key component of 'food inflation' has been milk. Clearly, easing the imports through a reduced tariff on powdered milk could have greatly alleviated the shortage of this critical item. But the government did not take advantage of this channel.

As for domestic production, there is, in fact, a critical need for raising productivity on the farm as well as along the supply chain, for nearly every agricultural commodity. Per-hectare yields in India are lower than in most of the comparable countries in most crops. Likewise, vast volumes of fruits and vegetables perish in transit as the produce makes its way from the farm to the final consumer. The agricultural economist Ashok Gulati reminds us that water tables in the original Green Revolution states of Punjab, Haryana and western Uttar Pradesh have been falling at rates of almost a foot per year.[8] Therefore, the effort to enhance yields has to move to the eastern part of the country, where abundant water supply exists. Gulati cites the successful Chinese experience with hybrid rice varieties, noting that it produces almost 200 million tons of paddy from 29 million hectares compared to India's 150 million tons from 44 million hectares.

A key element in improving productivity is to reform the laws with respect to sales and rentals of agricultural land. Over the years, land-holdings have shrunk in size, with the result that today more than 80 per cent of the land-holdings are less than two

---

7. For example, a recent article even by the leading agricultural economist Ashok Gulati in a *Wall Street Journal* blog (http://blogs.wsj.com/indiarealtime/2011/03/17/india-journal-how-to-achieve-food-security/), which discussed at length possible measures to engineer a second Green Revolution to improve food security, made no mention whatsoever of the role imports can play in enhancing food supply.
8. See blog http://blogs.wsj.com/indiarealtime/2011/03/17/india-journal-how-to-achieve-food-security/ (accessed on 5 December 2011).

hectares and more than 60 per cent holdings less than one hectare. Only 6.5 per cent of the holdings are four hectares or larger. Ease of sales and rentals will help in the consolidation of holdings. Flexible rental laws, that allow the owner and the tiller to negotiate and sign formal agreements, will provide better security to the tiller and provide the necessary incentive for making productivity enhancing investments in land.

Improvements in the supply chain also require the development of contract farming, infrastructure and organized retail. Contract farming can establish a direct link between the farmer and the processor of the produce, thereby cutting all intermediaries and minimizing waste. It can also ensure a good price to the farmer. Infrastructure development includes the provision of uninterrupted supply of electricity at reasonable prices and road and railway transport. The former allows the development of cold storage while the latter rapid movement of produce from the producer to the consumer. Moreover, organized retail has the capacity to develop efficient supply chains.

Finally, agricultural productivity increases today depend additionally on a new Green Revolution. The old Green Revolution was based on the new seeds invented under the leadership of Dr Norman Borlaug and spread in India under the scientific leadership of Dr Swaminathan. Today, they depend on the adoption and absorption of the GM (genetically modified) and BT (Bacillus Thuringiensis or natural insecticide) seeds and agricultural crops like cotton and brinjal. Some NGOs have objected to these as Frankenstein foods, though scientific evidence does not support such fears. The environment ministry has handled this issue ineptly, going back on the GM and BT innovations after going to these NGOs in public meetings but not with scientists who can respond to these fears. We cannot afford to forego the new Second Green Revolution in this way. Else, we will have also replaced the highly improbable Frankenstein by the certain Grim Reaper as scarcity overtakes plenitude in the production of food grains and crops!

16

Reforming Health Care

We argued in Part II that contrary to common assertions, India has made definite, if inadequate, progress in areas such as life expectancy, infant mortality and maternal mortality compared to countries with similar levels of income. The common impression of India's failure in this area results from the low levels with which India started. But as far as improvements are concerned, steady progress has been made. Moreover, when health indicators, such as those relating to child nutrition, show below-average progress, the scientific foundation of such indicators turns out to be shaky.

Of course, being still a poor country, India has hardly won the battle against ill health. There remains vast scope for improvement along all dimensions of health. Therefore, in this chapter, we discuss possible reforms in the health sector, especially those belonging to Track II. Reforms are necessary in five key areas: public health, routine health care, care involving hospitalization or outpatient surgeries, human resources and oversight of the health system.

Preventive Public Health

Public health services, which constitute a classic case of public good, fall into two categories: *population-wide* environmental services that reduce exposure to and spread of disease; and *clinical* services such as screening and vaccination that prevent the spread of diseases from one individual to another.[1] Because the benefits of public health services are spread over a wide population, and once provided, the services become available to all at no additional cost, the market typically fails to supply them in adequate volume.

For example, the cost of disinfecting a swamp to prevent the spread of vector-borne disease such as malaria, dengue fever or chikungunya may be minuscule in relation to the combined benefit to households living around the swamp but no single household will find it attractive to undertake this cost. This is because each household will count on the other households taking the action and on 'free riding' its benefits. If the group involved is small, its members may be able to solve the 'collective action' problem by coming together and making small contributions to cover the cost. But typically, even within small groups, some refuse to join in the hope that others will take the action anyway.

1. Economists distinguish between private and public goods. Public goods have two properties, non-rivalry in consumption and non-exclusion. Non-rivalry means that the consumption of the good by one individual does not reduce its availability to others. Non-exclusion means that once a good is made available, individuals cannot be excluded from its consumption even if they did not pay for its provision. Defence is the commonest example of a public good. Its availability to one citizen does not reduce the availability to others and once provided, no citizen can be excluded from benefiting from it. Private goods exhibit rivalry and exclusion. If an individual drinks a bottle of Coca-Cola, it is no longer available to another individual (rivalry in consumption). Moreover, once she buys the bottle, they can exclude others from drinking it (exclusion). Usually, the market would adequately supply private goods but not public goods. In the latter case, government intervention is required.

Intervention is also likely to be required when the benefits of an action to an individual are large but still fall short of the total benefits to the society as a whole, as is the case with vaccination. Because vaccination of one individual lowers the chances of others around him or her contracting the same disease, fewer people will take vaccines on their own than is socially desirable. For example, a schoolchild without tuberculosis vaccine who thus runs the risk of contracting the disease also places other students in the school at risk. Yet, since the vaccine itself is not costless, many students (or their parents) may opt out of it, thereby placing other students at risk.

Nonetheless, the Central, state and local governments in India have done a very poor job of supplying public health services. Drainage systems, the supply of drinking water and general standards of hygiene in public places in India remain extremely poor. A bout of monsoon rains is often enough to create conditions conducive to quick spread of communicable diseases. While the governments have run some effective campaigns against specific communicable diseases such as smallpox, polio and Guinea worm disease, its record in the provision of day-to-day public health services has been disappointing.

In part, the undersupply of public health services may reflect inadequate public expenditures on health in general. But the problem has been exacerbated by political-economy factors. These factors have biased the allocation of health expenditures in favour of medical services rather than public health.

Thus Das Gupta et al. (2009), who have carefully analysed this problem, note that Sri Lanka has been able to provide public health services at a satisfactory level by spending only 0.2 per cent of its GDP. They attribute the neglect of public health services in India to an organizational change immediately following independence. Following the recommendation of the 1946 Bhore Committee Report, the Central government and all states, except Tamil Nadu, merged the medical and public health services into a single department. Later, as per the Jungalwalla Committee report of 1967, they also combined the medical and public health cadres of services into a single service. The combined effect of these changes was the neglect of public health services in favour of medical services, whose proponents, the well-organized doctors' lobby, have more prestige with the public and carry much greater clout.

According to Das Gupta et al. (2009), Tamil Nadu, which retained public health services under a separate department, has been more successful in improving health outcomes than other states. But the evidence in this regard is mixed. Tamil Nadu does come right on top in terms of vaccination. But its performance along other indicators, while generally among the top five out of the fifteen larger states, is less compelling. Nevertheless, there is some merit in the argument Das Gupta et al. make. In principle, establishment of a separate agency entrusted with public health services with its own separate budget should help boost the provision of these services.

Two additional public health measures are worth implementing. First, governments at all levels must carry out regular campaigns to inform the public of the benefits of a healthy local environment.[2] When people end up living in neighbourhoods with unhygienic conditions for several years, even decades, they become so used to the unhealthy conditions that they do not even notice them. Some demonstration that cleaner conditions are possible, and that they are both healthier and nicer, may go some distance towards generating beneficial public action at the individual level.

2. It is arguable whether India also needs campaigns to emphasize personal hygiene. As the economist Padma Desai has written, middle-class Indians, devoted to personal hygiene and a clean home, will typically collect garbage at home but will then dump it in the street outside. Nonetheless, many households could use advice on other health-related matters such as the health effects of traditional cooking stoves and the dangers of wearing rayon and nylon saris close to the fire when cooking.

Second, it is important to make the Food Safety and Standards Authority of India (FSSAI), established under the Food Safety and Standards Act, 2006, more effective. The authority is mandated to lay down science-based standards for articles of food and to regulate their manufacture, storage, distribution, sale and imports. But achieving this objective effectively requires the consolidation of food supply chains. In the end, it is not possible for any administrative unit to monitor the supplies from innumerable and unknown sources and distributed by as many retailers spread over a vast territory. Consolidation of food-supply chains through participation of local and foreign retail chains is essential. In this respect, the recent decision to open multi-brand retail to foreign investors is a step in the right direction.

Routine Health Care

Let us next turn to health care, which we shall divide into two categories: routine health care and major illnesses. The former involves ailments such as cold, cough, fever and minor injuries. These ailments afflict nearly all, often several times a year, and are not hugely expensive to treat per episode. In many cases, even home remedies and rest may suffice. In contrast, major illnesses include those requiring prolonged treatment at home, surgeries on an outpatient basis and hospitalization.[3] These illnesses, discussed later, afflict an individual at most a few times during his life, occur with unpredictable frequency and are costly per episode.

3. In its surveys, the National Sample Survey Organization distinguishes between non-hospitalized and hospitalized treatments. These can be approximately identified with what we call routine health care and major illnesses, respectively, in this chapter but the correspondence is not exact. In particular, the surveys most likely include treatment at home of prolonged illnesses and outpatient surgeries in 'non-hospitalized' treatment whereas we include them in major illnesses category.

Setting aside considerations of poverty for the moment, the case for free public provision of, or subsidy on, routine health care is extremely weak. The recipient mostly internalizes the benefits of routine health care service so that externality-related arguments discussed in the context of public health services do not have decisive force here.

An argument for government provision is, however, made by some on the alternative grounds of asymmetric information. These analysts argue that since the patient is unable to assess the quality of the service in relation to the price, private providers may dupe the patient into paying high prices for worthless service. Government provision of the service can overcome this problem.

But this argument has at best limited force when it comes to routine health care since repeated interactions with the provider and conversations with other patients provide the patient an opportunity to observe and assess the quality and price of the service. Moreover, even if one accepts the information asymmetry as being a serious issue, it is far from clear that the Government of India has the ability to deliver high-quality routine care at a reasonable price. According to a National Sample Survey Organization (2006, p. H-2) survey conducted during January-June 2004—the latest such survey available—81 per cent of urban and 78 per cent of rural patients in India sought private providers for non-hospitalized care in preference to the government sub-centres and primary health care centres in rural areas and government dispensaries and hospitals in urban areas.

In their important work, Das and Hammer (2007) provide even more direct evidence questioning the ability of the public sector to provide quality service. They show that though the public sector employs well-qualified doctors and pays them relatively high salaries, this hardly translates into quality care. The benefits of better qualifications of these doctors over those in the private sector are offset by a lack of effort on their part to fully apply their knowledge to the provision of patient care. The government may be able to use its access to public money to hire better doctors but it is not able to make them deliver better service.

A different case for government intervention is sometimes made on the ground that better health service improves the ability of individuals to work and therefore helps produce a healthier workforce. But once again, this increase in productivity should generate private benefits to the recipients of the service in terms of higher wages. Therefore, this argument also falls short of providing a persuasive case for intervention by the government.

In the ultimate analysis, the principal plausible justification for government intervention in the provision of routine outpatient care is poverty. A large chunk of the population at the bottom of the income distribution in India is too poor to afford even a minimum socially acceptable level of health care. To the extent that financial resources permit it, a modern welfare state must strive to provide a minimum level of health care to those unable to afford it. This view is reflected in the aim to provide access to 'comprehensive primary health care' in the National Rural Health Mission (NRHM), launched in 2005.

The key policy question, however, is whether such care is provided through the government *provision* of outpatient care or by other means. We noted in Part I that India had begun to build up the primary health care infrastructure as early as the 1960s following the recommendations of the Health Survey and Planning Committee (Mudaliar Committee 1961). But nearly fifty years of efforts in building this infrastructure have not led to the provision of effective health care in rural India. As just noted, no more than one-fifth of the rural patients seek routine outpatient care at public health facilities. The remaining three-quarters of the patients go to rural medical providers (RMPs), who are largely unqualified providers of routine health care in rural India.

Given the inability of the government to deliver the service after half a century of effort, alternative models must now be given a chance. In our view, the best course is to place the financial power to buy health services in the hands of the patients: give cash transfers to the poor to meet their routine health care expenses. The government can continue to provide services but its facilities must compete against the private providers and meet all their costs from the revenues they earn by charging the patients. Once the poor are given the financial resources, public health care facilities will be justified to charge for their services. They should then be able to recover their costs by selling their services. This will force market discipline on the government facilities while giving patients greater choice of providers.

An important question in this context is whether the transfers should be conditional on meeting certain requirements or given unconditionally. According to the bulk of the empirical evidence from Latin America, requirements such as regular medical check-ups are useful devices to ensure that the financial transfer is used for the intended purpose. Nevertheless, the benefits of the conditional approach must be weighed against the corruption they are likely to engender in Indian conditions. Given the extreme shortage of doctors, certification of regular check-ups could itself turn into a business. Doctors would extract a part of the transfer from patients just for providing certification. Therefore, it is our view that the best course is to make transfers to the poor without conditions, perhaps to the seniormost female member of the household. This way, households may even be encouraged to maintain a healthy lifestyle to avoid visits to the doctor, thereby releasing the funds for expenditures on items such as milk and fruits that improve the natural immunity of the body.

It is easy to see that if the government were to opt for cash transfers, it could accomplish its objectives well within the current fiscal constraints. Make the generous assumption that the transfers will be given to the entire bottom half of the population, that is, to approximately 600 million individuals. Assume further a cash transfer of 500 rupees per individual. These figures imply 300 billion rupees at 2010-11 prices in total expenditure. With a GDP of 78,779.47 billion rupees at market prices in 2010-11, the transfer amounts to 0.38 per cent of the GDP. Even doubling the transfer to 1000 rupees can be accomplished for less than 0.8 per cent of the GDP.

Major Illnesses

Major illnesses, in which we include childbirth and maternity care as well as prolonged illnesses even when they are treated at home, differ from routine health care in two important respects: their frequency is much lower but the cost per episode is high, and their frequency as well as the magnitude of the associated expense at the level of the individual are unpredictable.[4]

These characteristics make the market for the care of major illnesses a perfect candidate for insurance. In common with other insurance markets, we face the adverse selection problem here: those already hit by an illness or suffering from a prolonged illness would seek insurance while those in good health would avoid it. The common solution to the problem is group insurance. Since many of the poor in India would not have the means to pay the premium, government subsidy to cover them would be required.

A beginning in this direction has been made in recent years.

---

4. Most, though not all, major illnesses require hospitalization. Therefore, we can get at least some rough idea of the incidence of major illnesses at the aggregate level from the data gathered by the National Sample Survey Organization (2006) mentioned earlier. According to it, during January-June 2004, the average rate of hospitalization was 2.3 per 100 individuals in rural and 3.1 per 100 individuals in urban areas. The associated average expenditure per hospitalization was 5695 rupees in rural and 8851 rupees in urban areas in current rupees. In comparison, the average expenditure on non-hospitalized care per ailing person in a fifteen-day period was 257 rupees in rural and 306 rupees in urban areas.

Stimulated by the opening of insurance to the private sector, including 26 per cent foreign direct investment in 2001, a nascent private market for insurance has been emerging. Within this context, the government has also tried to address the needs of the poor by requiring private entrants to issue a specific proportion of their policies to the rural populations. This provision has led some private insurers to team up with self-help groups such as SEWA to insure entire groups in rural regions. One scheme along these lines, the Yeshasvini Cooperative Farmers Health Scheme in Karnataka, was launched in 2003 and covered approximately three million farmers against the risk of expensive surgeries. The scheme is funded partially by premiums and partially by government subsidy. Members receive medical services for listed procedures at approved public and private hospitals and nursing homes, which numbered 462 in 2010-11.[5]

A far more ambitious scheme aimed at the poor is the Rashtriya Swasthya Bima Yojana (RSBY), launched by the Government of India on 1 April 2008. The scheme is funded in a 3:1 ratio by the Central and state governments and is available to households below the poverty line. Under the scheme, the government pays the premium for five members of each covered poor household and issues it a smart card that can be used to access empanelled public and private hospitals. A long list of illnesses requiring hospitalization is covered up to a maximum expenditure of 30,000 rupees per year for a family of five. As of 8 December 2011, 25.6 million smart cards were in circulation across twenty-three states.[6] State governments have introduced similar schemes; these include Arogyasri in Andhra Pradesh, the Vajpayee scheme in Karnataka and the Kalainger scheme in Tamil Nadu.

5. See http://sahakara.kar.gov.in/Yashasivini.html (accessed 10 December 2011) for details.
6. See http://www.rsby.gov.in/overview.aspx and http://www.rsby.gov.in/about_rsby.aspx (both accessed 10 December 2011) for further details.

In our view, these schemes are on the right track. They target the poor, cover major illnesses, carry significant but fiscally manageable coverage and allow private and public providers to compete for the patients. They also seem scalable. The operation of several schemes rather than a single national one allows for experimentation according to local needs as well.

The eventual fiscal costs would depend on who is covered and the benefit provided. As an example, suppose we make the generous assumption that half of the population in India is poor. This implies coverage to 600 million individuals at the expense of the state. Making a further generous assumption that 5 per cent of the individuals require hospitalization in any year, which is higher than the current rates, insurance will have to pay for 30 million hospitalizations per year. Assuming the cost of hospitalization on average is 10,000 rupees at 2010-11 prices, the total expense would be 300 billion rupees. With a GDP of 78,779.47 billion, this represents 0.38 per cent of the GDP. Assuming five members per household, it is thus possible to provide 50,000 rupees per household coverage for less than 0.4 per cent of the GDP.

Before we move on to a discussion of human resources and oversight of a reformed health system, it is pertinent at this stage to say a few words about the provision of *universal* health coverage by the state. This has been proposed by civil society groups, which have now captured not just the National Advisory Council headed by the Congress president Sonia Gandhi, but also the Planning Commission. Thus, a report by a high-level expert group appointed by the Planning Commission (2011), consisting of relatively few economists and chaired by a medical doctor- turned-activist, recommends a national health package accessible to all Indian citizens and free of charge by 2022.[7] It is our view that before

7. K. Srinath Reddy, the president of the Public health Foundation of India, chaired the group.

jumping on this 'right-to-health' bandwagon, the government must take a hard look at the rationale behind it and, more importantly, at its ability to provide universal coverage.

Astonishingly, the expert group report provides no satisfactory rationale for its proposals for a package equally available to all. Nor does it document how it proposes to transform the public health infrastructure from its current debilitated state to a level that would attract rather than repel patients from seeking hospitalized as well as non-hospitalized care in the rural as well as urban areas. We find ourselves largely agreeing with the scathing critique of the report by Rao (2012), who pointedly comments: 'The HLEG (High Level Expert Group) report neither recognizes the problems, constraints and compulsions of the departments of health at the national, state and district levels, nor offers any solutions on how to deal with them.'

Finally, insofar as universal coverage is being increasingly connected to the recognition of the associated social goal as a legal right, the government must take a cautious view of such proposals. When universal coverage is close to reality as, for example, in elementary education (see the next chapter), its recognition as a right may be a useful instrument of solidifying access to all. But when it is a distant goal, such recognition can be costly and counterproductive.

Human Resources

India faces critical shortage of health-related human resources, including doctors, nurse practitioners, nurses, midwives, pharmacists and other health workers. Unqualified providers currently dominate the private sector, especially in rural areas. Improvements in access to health care, growth in population and growth in personal incomes can be expected to further expand the demand for these personnel. On the supply side, shortages of medical personnel in the rest of the world due to aging of populations are likely to accelerate the exit of the personnel from India. Therefore, in the absence of a major push to expand the supply, India will face massive shortages of medical personnel. Unfortunately, the problem seems not even on the radar screen of the policymakers.

The need for rapid expansion in two particular areas is particularly acute. First, rural medical providers (RMPs) serve much of rural India. These practitioners have picked up some rudimentary skills either as employees in hospitals or while working as assistants to doctors, but lack true qualifications for the job they do. Replacing the RMPs with proper doctors with MBBS degrees in a short period is an unrealistic goal even if it is desirable to do so in the long run. Therefore, what is needed is the creation of a cadre equivalent to what are called 'nurse practitioners' in the US. Even a one-year training programme for the current RMPs may lead to a significant improvement in service and reduce risk to the patients.

Second, the expansion of the number of qualified MBBS doctors must begin right away. Recall that the Medical Council of India has treated medical education as its fiefdom. Some of its members are alleged to have extracted large bribes for authorization of new medical colleges and for letting the existing colleges stay open.

The result of this tight control and associated corruption has been an overall shortage of doctors with an MBBS degree. Often politically powerful and well-connected entrepreneurs are the ones successful in getting approval for the opening of medical colleges in a handful of states. Table 16.1 graphically brings out this point. Maharashtra and the four southern states currently account for 54 per cent of medical colleges and 57 per cent of MBBS seats in the whole of India. To dramatize the contrast, there is one MBBS seat per 157,280 people in Bihar compared with 10,868 people in Karnataka.

India clearly needs to loosen the stranglehold of the Medical Council of India on the expansion of medical colleges.

TABLE 16.1: MEDICAL COLLEGES AND MBBS SEATS WITH STATES ARRANGED IN ASCENDING ORDER OF POPULATION PER MBBS SEAT

State	*Number of medical colleges*	*Number of seats*	*Population per seat*
Karnataka	41	5625	10,868
Kerala	23	2800	11,924
Tamil Nadu	40	4815	14,982
Andhra Pradesh	37	4850	17,457
Maharashtra	41	4860	23,122
Punjab	10	1145	24,196
Gujarat	19	2380	25,371
Haryana	5	600	42,255
West Bengal	14	1850	49,377
Rajasthan	10	1300	52,785
Madhya Pradesh	12	1370	52,991
Orissa	6	750	55,930
Assam	4	526	59,257
Uttar Pradesh	25	2899	68,845
Bihar	10	660	157,280
India	335	40,335	30,004

Note: Population in the last column is taken from Census 2011.
Source: Medical Council of India, http://www.mciindia.org/, accessed 8 August 2011.

Oversight of the Health System

During the six decades since independence, health services in India have operated under a largely regulation-free environment. This has allowed health services to grow rapidly with competition keeping the prices of not just everyday outpatient care but also surgical procedures relatively low. Absence of medical malpractice suits has kept the costs of most services low. Likewise, the provision of only process and not product patent on medicines until 2005 has greatly facilitated the growth of a low-cost medicine industry.

This absence of regulation is by no means without cost. Reports of sales of fake medicines and their use by private providers as well as government-run hospitals are commonplace. RMPs and many providers in urban areas lack the required qualifications. Many hospitals and nursing homes are known to operate without licence or registration. Likewise, many diagnostic facilities exhibit poor standards.

Should India turn to regulation to combat these deficiencies? Our view is that a move towards systematic and substantial regulation at this point is premature. Once introduced, regulation in India has a way of quickly turning into a licence-permit raj. Therefore, there is need for moving cautiously in this direction. For now it may be best to go after egregious cases of malpractice and rely on informal oversight by NGOs and committees consisting of medical professionals and representatives of citizens at village, block, district and city levels. Regulation may be introduced gradually as medical services expand in the organized sector. But even then, initially, such regulation is best left to local jurisdictions, so that it is designed taking the local conditions and constraints into account. Only after a sizeable organized sector emerges nationwide should full-fledged national-level regulation be considered.

17

Elementary Education

Because higher education is critical to growth even while contributing to inclusion, its discussion belongs to Track I policies and was therefore taken up in Part II. In contrast, elementary education, though helpful in promoting and sustaining growth, is an important social objective in itself. Therefore, we consider it here as a part of Track II reforms.

Elementary education consists of primary (grades I to V) and middle (grades VI-VIII) school education. In the following, we first offer a brief review of progress towards universalizing it and the effectiveness of private relative to public schools. We then follow up on the key policy issues for which the recent Right to Education Act of 2009 provides the context.

Progress So Far

The Indian Constitution, which came into effect on 26 January 1950, stated in one of its directive principles of state policy: 'The State shall endeavour to provide, within a period of ten years from the commencement of this Constitution, for free and compulsory education for all children until they complete the age of fourteen years.' But this goal proved to be overly ambitious in view of the country's meagre financial and physical resources and the target date was repeatedly deferred first to 1970 and then to 1980, 1990 and 2000.[1] It was not until the 86th Constitution (86th Amendment) Act of 2002 that education for children between ages six and fourteen was promoted from a directive principle of policy to a fundamental right. Even then, the lack of financial resources held up the implementing legislation.

In the end, the Right of Children to Free and Compulsory Education Act of 2009 (or Right to Education Act for short) was passed in August 2009 and brought into force on 1 April 2010. Provisions of this Act have been highly controversial and we will devote the bulk of this chapter to a critical examination of its salient features.

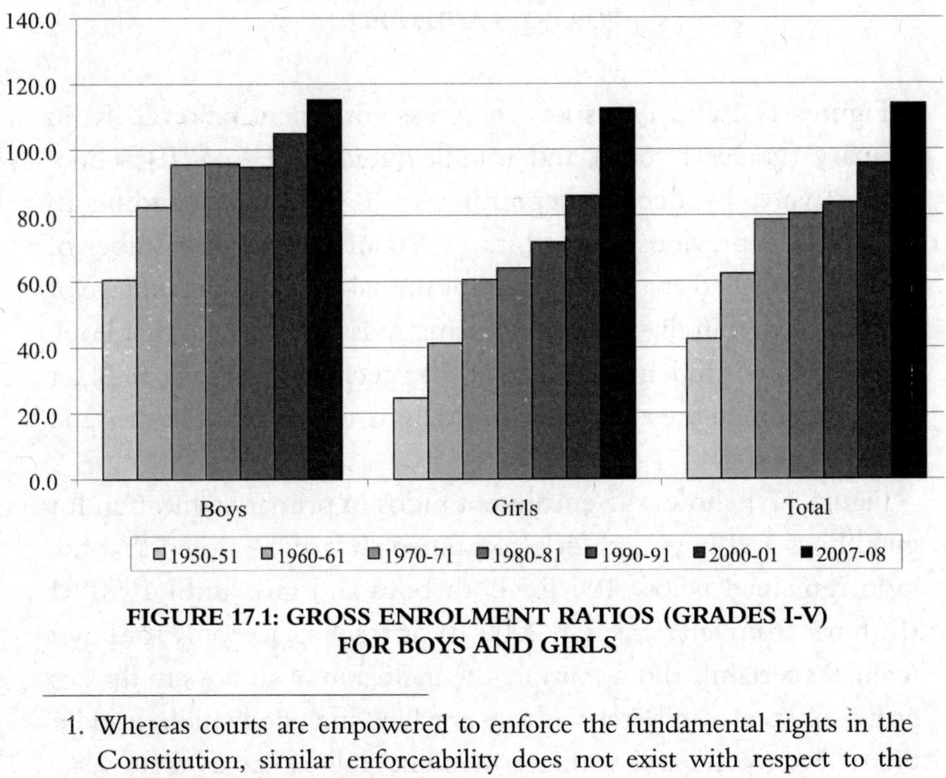

FIGURE 17.1: GROSS ENROLMENT RATIOS (GRADES I-V) FOR BOYS AND GIRLS

1. Whereas courts are empowered to enforce the fundamental rights in the Constitution, similar enforceability does not exist with respect to the directive principles of the state policy.

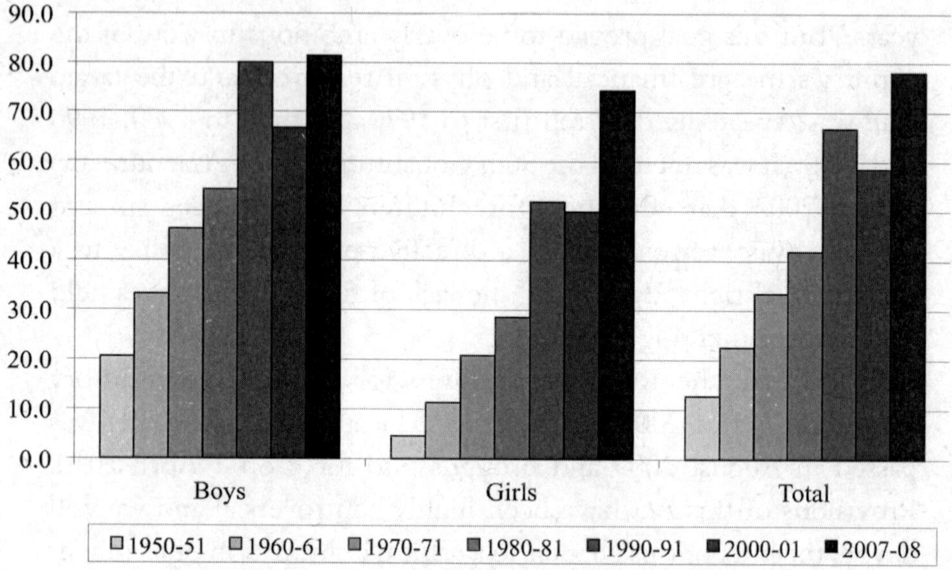

FIGURE 17.2: GROSS ENROLMENT RATIOS (GRADES V-VIII) FOR BOYS AND GIRLS

Figures 17.1 and 17.2 show the gross enrolment ratio (GER) in primary (grades I to V) and middle (grades VI to VIII) school respectively, by decade beginning in 1950-51 and ending in 2007-08. As previously noted, the GER measures the number of students enrolled at a particular educational level as a percentage of the population in the age group normally associated with that level. Because some students enrolled at the specified level may be older or younger than the age group normally associated with it, the ratio can exceed 100.

Figure 17.1 shows the enrolment ratios in primary education for girls, boys and boys and girls combined. It may be noted that the ratio remained below 100 for both boys and girls until 1990-91 (fifth bar from left). Even in 2000-01, it reached 100 only for boys; it almost certainly did not imply the inclusion of all boys in the age group six to eleven because those enrolled included children older than eleven years and younger than six. Till as late as forty years following the original deadline in the Constitution, the government lacked the resources to achieve universal education even at the primary level.

Enrolment ratios in the middle school have been consistently below those at the primary level and well below 100 even in 2007-08, the latest year for which we have the official data (Figure 17.2). Of course, this feature partially reflects the fact that many children in the eleven-to-fourteen-year age group are enrolled in primary school. This inference is supported by the enrolment ratios for grades I to VIII combined, shown in Figure 17.3.

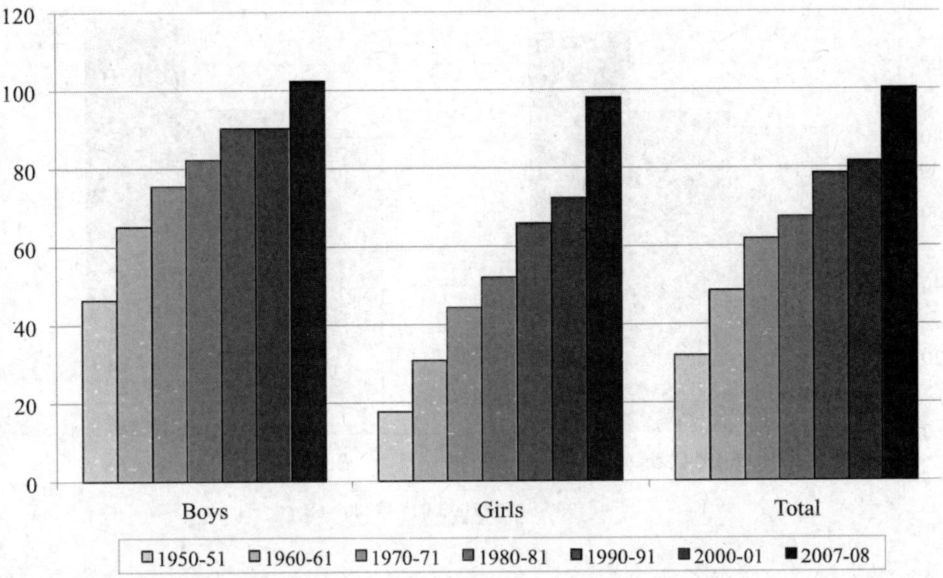

FIGURE 17.3: GROSS ENROLMENT RATIO (GRADES I-VIII)

Progress has been made across all social groups, including the Scheduled Castes and Scheduled Tribes. We show the enrolment ratios for boys and girls combined in these groups for grades I to VIII as a whole in Figure 17.4. For both the Scheduled Castes and Tribes, the ratios had crossed the mark of 100 per cent in 2007-08.

Thus progress in achieving improved outcomes has taken place across the board.

That most children aged six to fourteen years are now in school is further corroborated by the annual surveys conducted in the rural areas by the NGO Pratham. According to its latest survey, summarized in the report Aser 2010, the percentage of children aged six to fourteen years not enrolled in school fell from 6.6 per cent in 2005 to 3.5 in 2010 in rural India. The proportion of girls not enrolled fell from 11.2 to 5.9 per cent over the same period.

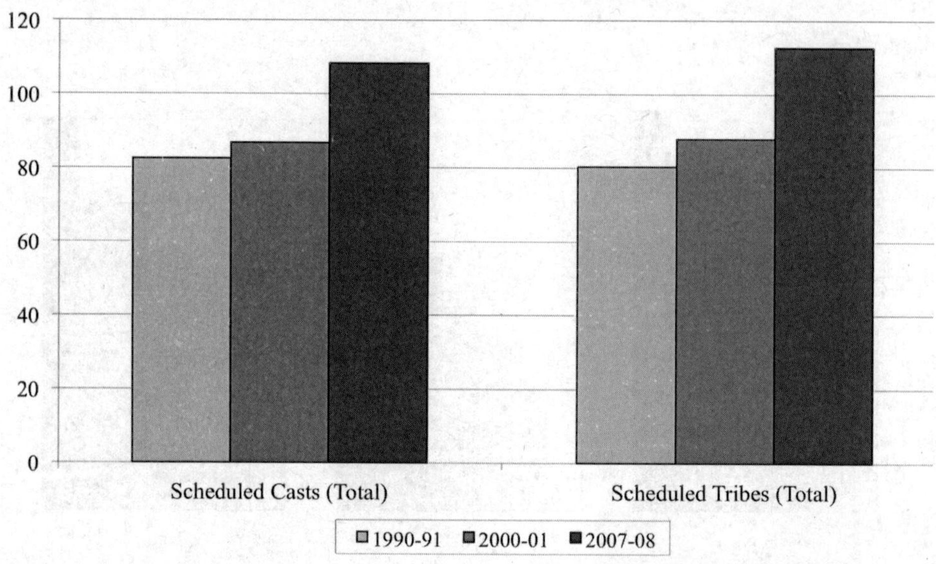

FIGURE 17.4: GROSS ENROLMENT RATIOS FOR SCHEDULED CASTES AND TRIBES, BOYS AND GIRLS

Source data for Figures 17.1 to 17.4: http://www.educationforallinindia.com/ses.html (accessed on 12 December 2011).

These trends show the power of growth—directly and through enhanced revenues—to support social goals. Given the increasing role private schools have played in the provision of elementary education, the direct role of growth in its spread cannot be denied.[2] At the same time, the government has been able to expand public schools more rapidly, thanks to enhanced revenues. The government effort became particularly intense after the launch of the Sarva Shiksha Abhiyan (SSA) (universal education movement) in November 2000. It is on the strength of this expansion in both private and public sectors that the Government of India was able to adopt free and compulsory elementary education as a fundamental right beginning on 1 April 2010.

Public Versus Private Schools

It is important to discuss the effectiveness of private schools, which have become an increasingly important part of India's elementary education landscape, in relation to public schools. These schools represent a wide range in terms of physical infrastructure and other resources, formal training of teachers and tuition.

At one extreme, we have a small proportion of select government-recognized schools, which offer excellent infrastructure, trained teachers, low student-teacher ratios and very high tuition fees. This set of schools attracts talented students from elite families and produces outcomes superior to those by public schools. At the other extreme, we have a large number of 'unrecognized' schools with relatively poor infrastructure, untrained teachers and low tuition fees. These schools exist in both rural areas and in poor neighbourhoods and slums in the cities. The number of private schools now ranges in hundreds of thousands across India.

---

2. According to Aser 2010, enrolment of children aged six to fourteen years in private schools as a percentage of the total enrolment rose from 16.3 per cent in 2005 to 24.3 per cent in 2010. In the four southern states, where growth has been more robust and which also happen to be relatively rich, the ratio rose from 29.7 per cent to 36.1 per cent in just one year between 2009 and 2010.

According to available evidence, even the low-end unrecognized schools have produced outcomes superior to those by their public counterparts operating in the same geographical area. They have done this while paying salaries to teachers that are a small fraction of public-school salaries. Compared to the latter, they are also generally poorly equipped in terms of playgrounds, classroom space and libraries. The single most important key to their success has been the accountability of teachers. Public schoolteachers are state employees and are almost entirely immune from layoffs under any circumstances. Therefore, unless they feel morally obligated to teach their pupils, they have no incentive to carry out their assigned duties with any degree of sincerity. Teachers in private school do not enjoy such immunity and can be shown the door if they fail to deliver minimum outcomes. The result has been far greater incidence in the public schools of teacher absenteeism and poor performance by the teachers when present in the classroom.

Muralidharan and Kremer (2006), who have collected a nationally representative sample from rural India in 2003, estimate that 28 per cent of the rural children in India had access to fee-charging private primary schools in the village where they lived that year. They show that children in these schools exhibited higher attendance rates and test scores than in government schools even after controlling for family and school characteristics. Private schoolteachers were 2 to 8 percentage points less likely to be absent and 6 to 9 percentage points more likely to be teaching when present than government schoolteachers. Muralidharan and Kremer also report that private schoolteachers received salaries that were typically one-fifth and sometimes as low as one-tenth of those received by government schoolteachers.

The authors point to the ability of the head teacher to discipline the teachers under him as the key reason for lower absenteeism in private schools. They note that out of 3000 government schools they surveyed, only one head teacher had dismissed a teacher for repeated absences. In the private sector, they found thirty-five such cases in just 600 schools surveyed.

Tooley and Dixon (undated) who undertook a census of primary and secondary schools in one of the poorer areas of Delhi, Shahdara, in 2004-05 report very similar findings. They found a total of 275 schools in the area, of which 27 per cent were government-owned; 7 per cent private but government-aided; 38 per cent private, unaided and recognized; and 28 per cent private, unaided and unrecognized. The last two categories, accounting for 66 per cent of the total number of schools, represented entirely private schools.

Tooley and Dixon state that upon unannounced visits, their researchers found 38 per cent teachers teaching in government schools against 70 per cent in private schools. They tested 3,500 students and found that compared to their government school counterparts, students in unrecognized private schools scored on average 72 per cent higher in mathematics, 83 per cent higher in Hindi and 246 per cent higher in English. Students in the recognized private schools did even better. The private school advantage was maintained after controlling for background variables.

Tooley and Dixon further report that the government teachers earned seven times as much as teachers in private unrecognized schools. Though class sizes were larger in the government schools, the salary per pupil in them remained two-and-a-half times that in private unrecognized schools. Yet, surprisingly, the teachers in unaided schools reported that they were no less satisfied than their counterparts in government schools in terms of salaries, holidays or social standing.[3]

Against this background, we may examine the current elementary

3. The findings by Muralidharan and Kremer (2006) and Tooley and Dixon (undated) mirror those documented earlier in the comprehensive report by the Probe Team (1999) and Kingdon (2005).

education policy of the Government of India. The key features of this policy are now enshrined in the Right to Education (RTE) Act, 2009, and the model rules that elaborate upon several of the provisions in the Act. We provide the salient features of the RTE Act in Appendix 3. Here we limit ourselves to a critical examination of this Act.

Problems with the Right to Education Act of 2009

At one level, the RTE Act is quite pernicious. Potentially, it can do to elementary education what we found the Industrial Disputes Act of 1947 to have done to manufacturing: enforce standards of protection that end up hurting the very population it is intended to protect while bringing significant benefits to the lucky few. On one hand, the IDA has provided ultra-high protection to workers lucky enough to land a handful of the jobs in the organized sector. On the other hand, it has been destructive of organized sector labour-intensive manufacturing and, therefore, well-paid manufacturing jobs. As our discussion suggests below, if implemented as provided, the RTE Act would similarly end the access of millions of poor children to decent private elementary education while giving a select few access to the country's best private schools.

The RTE Act provides that every child between six and fourteen years of age has the right to free and compulsory elementary education. The 'right' is given to the child while the burden of 'compulsion' falls on the state government (or the Central government in the case of the Union territories) and on the local government such as the municipal corporation in the city and panchayat in the village.

Given that universal elementary education is now within India's grasp, this provision is clearly a welcome one. Yet, the simultaneous requirement that local governments proactively pursue every child in their jurisdiction to place him or her in school is quite unrealistic.[4] For one thing, state and local governments in India lack the capacity to enforce such a requirement. And besides, given the high levels of poverty, there are bound to be cases, especially in rural areas and among the tribes, where families are so poor that they need children to work to help them get two square meals a day.

The RTE Act further requires all unaided private schools to reserve 25 per cent of the seats in grade I for children from weaker sections and disadvantaged groups in the neighbourhood. The Act requires the government to reimburse the school at per-student rate that it spends in public schools.

It should be obvious that this provision does not advance in any way the right to education since it crowds out one-for-one the students from other sections of the society in favour of the students admitted from weaker and socially disadvantaged families. Therefore, it is purely a redistribution measure that gives the children from weak and disadvantaged families access to high-quality private schools. While this is a worthy objective, its promotion as a right-to-education measure is misleading and for this and other reasons it was challenged in the Supreme Court, though unsuccessfully.

There are other downsides of the provision. It essentially amounts to a cross-subsidy. Reimbursement by the government at the rate of per student expenditure in public education will fall short of the

---

4. The provisions of the RTE Act legally bind the local government to seek out and enrol every single child within its jurisdiction in an elementary school. The model rules accompanying the RTE Act require the local government to conduct household surveys to identify all children within its jurisdiction and to maintain records on them from birth to fourteen years of age. The record, which is to be in public domain, must include information on name, sex, date and place of birth, parents' names and occupation, pre-school of the child, disability, if any, and whether the child belongs to a weaker section or disadvantaged group.

actual expenditure incurred by the high-quality private schools. This will raise the cost to fee-paying students and will discourage the entry of new high-quality private schools on the margin. A more efficient instrument would have been for the government to offer to cover the entire fee of the selected students and provide for the expense from the general budget. Alternatively, it could offer the children vouchers worth the per capita expenditure in public schools and then have them find the private school of their choice willing to admit them in return for the voucher. This would have encouraged rather than discouraged the emergence of private schools.

The government's approach to promote equality in the manner it has chosen raises other questions. The poor and the disadvantaged who are nevertheless lucky enough to live in areas where quality private schools exist will gain access to such schools. But the poorest among the poor, who live in poor neighbourhoods and remote villages where quality private schools do not exist, get nothing at all. Indeed, as we discuss below, another provision in the RTE positively hurts them. Thus, the Act effectively divides the underprivileged themselves into beneficiaries and victims.

Finally, there is a real danger that implementation of the provision will lead to wholesale interference in the admission process by influential politicians and bureaucrats. The government must first devise the means to identify the weak and disadvantaged families. It must then match the children from these families with the schools. Given that no admission tests are permitted under the Act (see Appendix 3), there would seem to be no obvious alternative transparent mechanism for this matching other than by lottery. But one-and-a-half years into the implementation phase, the mechanisms are far from clear.

The most pernicious provision of the Act involves setting of minimum norms and standards for all schools. These norms and standards take the form not of outcomes such as achievements of children in reading, writing and problem solving but instead physical amenities in the school. They include a student-teacher ratio of thirty for primary and thirty-five for middle-level education; an all-weather building with one classroom per teacher, kitchen for midday meals and a playground; a well-equipped library; games and sports equipment; and more. All schools are required to achieve these norms by 31 March 2013.

At the fee they charge, the vast majority of the low-end unrecognized schools will not be able to meet these norms and standards.[5] At the same time, the poor families whom they serve cannot pay significantly higher fees. Therefore, if implemented, the impact of this provision will almost surely be a closure of many of these schools. Alternatively, it will create a large-scale 'inspector raj' in elementary education whereby government inspectors will falsely certify that the school meets the prescribed norms and standards in exchange for an appropriate bribe.

If the first of these outcomes is what is realized, it is doubtful that the government will be able to provide the displaced children seats in schools that meet the prescribed norms and standards and have the qualified teachers as stipulated in the RTE Act. Indeed, there is a good chance that rather than bring more children into the fold of elementary education, the RTE Act would wind up forcing some of the children currently enrolled in low-end private schools out of the education system altogether.

Several other provisions of the RTE Act and model rules are problematic as well. According to the latter, scales of pay and allowances, medical facilities, pension, gratuity, provident fund, and other prescribed benefits to teachers are to be those applicable to regular teachers. Once again, the vast majority of unrecognized

---

5. Indeed, it is quite unlikely that many public schools will be able to satisfy these norms and standards either.

schools will go bust if they have to pay these salaries since the children they serve come from poor families.

Ironically, while guaranteeing teachers in all schools much higher salaries and benefits than most private schools are currently able to afford, the RTE Act stops well short of providing effective measures to force the teachers to perform their duties. It simply prescribes 'disciplinary action under the service rules applicable' to the teacher for the failure to perform his or her duties. Such disciplinary actions have done precious little to discourage teachers from shirking their duties in the past and surely won't do so in the future.

The RTE Act stipulates that no child can be required to pass any board examination till the completion of elementary examination, and that automatic promotion to the next grade is guaranteed. At one level, this measure is intended to bring down the dropout rate but the other side of the coin is that it can potentially kill the value of education altogether. In a system that grants automatic promotion and where everyone has the diploma in view of the compulsory education, its value to a potential employer is hard to assess. In the absence of examinations, it will also become nearly impossible to measure the improvement in quality of education over time.

Finally, the RTE Act also prohibits schools from subjecting either the child or the parent to any kind of screening procedure for purposes of admission. While there is some merit in this provision, especially the prohibition on the screening of parents, it is not clear how else schools would make their admission decisions. Once testing of children is outlawed, the scope for arbitrariness in admissions is likely to rise unless the government forces schools to do admissions by lottery. That is, however, an unlikely prospect.

Concluding Remarks

Prospects for Continued Prosperity and Associated Assault on Poverty

India has indeed come a long way. In the 1980s, as the decade opened, pessimism about India's economic prospects was hard to refute. India, along with China, was supposed by many development experts to be the giant that would wake up from its long slumber. But this was not to be. The two giants continued to snore. Instead, the smaller countries of East Asia rapidly moved ahead of the pack. India's per capita income grew by a paltry 1.5 per cent annually; and the country therefore also failed to make the assault on poverty and on the (mis)fortunes of the underprivileged. The economic dimension of Prime Minister Jawaharlal Nehru's tryst with destiny remained elusive.

The counterproductive policy framework, most visible in the licence-and-permit raj that steadily covered India like the morning fog, had killed our aspirations in this regard. Indeed, India had become a laughing stock of the world. Could anyone take seriously a country that would not let you expand licensed capacity and would prevent diversification of production, to mention only two of the many irrational restrictions that undermined initiatives as if India had suddenly turned into the Soviet Union? These astonishingly foolish policies, and the abysmal growth rate that they entailed, were crying out to be changed, so that we would finally begin to fulfil Nehru's dream of our economic destiny.

And indeed, this did happen, within a decade. Having been converted to the view that India could not go on the way it had, Prime Minister Narasimha Rao had co-opted Dr Manmohan Singh as his finance minister. Together, this team quickly dismantled investment and import licensing, and opened the economy from virtual autarky to significant openness to direct foreign investment. Other reforms followed shortly. Tariff barriers were slashed; direct and indirect taxes were streamlined; private entry into airlines and telecommunications was permitted; private domestic and foreign entry into banking and finance was increased; and the reservation of a large number of products for exclusive manufacture by small enterprises was largely abolished. These were real, not symbolic, actions with a huge impact.[1]

As we have argued in this volume, we finally reversed the stagnation in our growth; and poverty began to fall significantly. And, as we have demonstrated (Myth 3.3), the fortunes of the Scheduled Castes and Scheduled Tribes also registered improvement. Increased prosperity went hand in hand, pretty much as we had hypothesized when Five-Year Plans began in India over half a century ago, with poverty reduction and the improvement in the lot of the underprivileged. Even on the inequality front, to which the freewheeling critics shifted in retreat, the evidence is mixed, to say the least, and favourable to reforms, at best.

Rather than join the bandwagon against reforms, the question before us, therefore, is: how do we broaden and intensify them so

1. Thus, as we have argued in this volume (Myth 3.1), the thesis advanced by Dani Rodrik and Arvind Subramanian that the dramatic turnaround in our performance was a result of 'attitudinal' changes prior to 1991 rather than the reforms begun in 1991 flies in the face of these massive changes, none of which was expected to be reversed.

that we improve upon even growth-centric Track I reforms, thereby getting better results on all fronts.

In fact, the increased revenues following Track I reforms have also meant that India can now genuinely expand social spending in what we have called Track II reforms. These are the reforms in the areas of health care and education and direct transfers of income or via employment in public works. Indian reforms are now both Track I reforms which, as our analysis in Part II showed, still require further changes to induce greater growth and still greater impact on poverty, and Track II reforms, which we have analysed in depth in Part III. We are confident that if these changes are implemented, we can be optimistic about India's medium-term and long-term economic prospects.

Why the Current Pessimism Is Misplaced

Before we consider the medium-term and long-term prospects, however, we must address the current pessimism that afflicts the vast majority of commentators about India's prospects. Some of this pessimism reflects worries about the short-term consequences of the post-2008 crisis. But the fact is that virtually every economy, certainly China, Japan, the EU and even the US, has suffered from the crisis. India is not leading the crisis-impacted decline and has indeed gone on to recover faster than most other countries.

Pessimism has also gripped many observers of India in the wake of the approximately two percentage points decline in the growth rate after the country had recovered from the financial crisis. Many commentators have expressed the view that we are now witnessing the beginning of the end of the Indian growth story. But these commentators greatly overstate their case.

What we have witnessed is a short-term decline originating in two short-term factors: thirteen consecutive hikes in the interest rates by the Reserve Bank of India (RBI), the country's central bank, and policy paralysis in the Central government. The interest-rate hikes had their origins in persistent inflation, while policy paralysis resulted from every Central ministry freezing up prudentially in response to an outbreak of massive corruption scandals.

Both factors have already begun to go into remission. The RBI has begun to ease up, allowing the interest rate to decline. Moreover, the paralysis has yielded to yet more reforms. As Panagariya (2012b) details, Prime Minister Singh has seized the initiative from the Congress party leadership to reclaim his legacy as a reformer, and announced a series of liberalizing steps, including opening multi-brand retail to FDI up to 51 per cent, and a substantial reduction in diesel subsidy. He has also opened civil aviation to FDI up to 49 per cent and raised the FDI cap in broadcasting from 49 to 74 per cent. As this book goes to press, the prime minister has even announced his decision to introduce cash subsidies, as was extensively advocated by Panagariya (2008a, 2012c) and emphasized yet again in this book.

Indeed, pessimists who base their fears on the reforms having come to a standstill misread both the history and current developments. The reforms had come to a standstill as far back as May 2004 when the United Progress Alliance first came to power. But the decline in the growth rate is quite recent. Besides, even prior to the announcements of the measures just noted, we had seen a slight progress in reforms. Reversing its 2004 decision, the government had recently deregulated petrol prices, and successfully abolished the 51 per cent FDI cap on single-brand retail, leading the Swedish retail furniture giant IKEA to announce its plans to invest nearly $2 billion in India.

Some commentators argue that coalition politics in India has led to paralysis. But this argument is not borne out by evidence. Whereas Prime Minister Rajiv Gandhi could implement only small reforms despite three-fourths majority in the Lok Sabha, Prime

Minister Narasimha Rao under a minority government and Prime Minister Vajpayee under a coalition government were able to introduce far-reaching reforms. Besides, with the emerging consensus on the importance of growth as the essential stepping stone to combating poverty and advancing other social agenda, the road to reform is likely to be smoother instead of rougher.

Reasons for Medium-term and Long-term Optimism

We, therefore, are not shaken in our optimism for India's prospects for the medium term and long term. Perhaps we are biased in our optimism because pessimism would be irrational: unless we expect that we can change the world, why turn to policy analysis? There is nothing more frustrating than banging one's head against the wall! But, forgetting this bias, we can provide objective reasons why we believe that good days lie ahead for India.

Public Opinion

1. There is little doubt that Indian reforms are irreversible and can only go forward. There are now a large number of young Indians who are conscious of the benefits that reforms have brought to them and to the country. There is no politically important constituency that can thrive on anti-reforms rhetoric in the years to come. It is telling that so many political parties tried to organize protests against the latest reforms that the prime minister announced in September 2012 but utterly failed to sustain them due to their inability to garner public support.
2. Many have also noticed that the Anna Hazare movement, bigger than the Occupy Wall Street demonstrations, was against corruption, and not against reforms. In fact, more reforms (extended to new areas like mining rights) rather than less are what the demonstrators called for.

3. Besides, as we have argued at length when dissecting the twenty-one anti-reforms myths that the critics repeat ad nauseam, the critiques rarely go beyond assertions. Increasingly, the refutation that we and the others provide are being read and the old anti-reformers are now losing the iconic status that used to be accorded readily to them in the past.

Objective Arguments

But if public opinion will not sabotage the reform process, what do 'objective' factors tell us about India's growth prospects? Here, too, there are two fundamental facts that work to India's advantage.

1. Growth depends on two underlying factors: savings (or investment) and the productivity of the investment. The Soviet Union had phenomenal savings rates but little productivity, so it went steadily downhill despite its 'blood, sweat and tears'. The East Asian economies had phenomenal savings rates but also high productivity, so they grew at 'miraculous' rates. Fortunately, India's savings rate has steadily risen. It is already 32 to 33 per cent of GDP and is expected to rise further.
2. As for productivity, India has profited, and will continue to profit, from two factors. First, India has steadily opened up to the world economy. There is ample evidence now that openness pays dividends. The second factor is India's diaspora. There are synergies, for instance, between Bangalore and Silicon Valley. The diaspora also keeps pressure steadily in favour of more reforms.

India-China Comparisons

In conclusion, what can we say about that evergreen subject: how will our growth be when compared to China's? Amartya Sen thinks this is a 'stupid' question.[2] We must reject this view. First, we can be interested as social scientists or intellectuals in anything we wish: we do not tell Sen what he should be interested in though we do have views on the subject! Besides, growth affects, as we have amply demonstrated, poverty reduction and social outcomes in which Sen professes to be interested and which, as we argued, go back to the earliest years of Indian planning and even pre-independence writings of our leaders. Finally, even if that were not true, one would have to be an innocent to think that the relative growth rates of India and China do not matter. That China's huge growth rate has produced dividends for it in international politics is beyond dispute. That it gives China an advantage over India in influencing economic outcomes in its favour should be obvious even to naïve economists. So, where do we stand vis-à-vis China?[3]

1. China has been rapidly increasing its defence spending. It is trying to match its 'hard power' to the 'soft power' that its phenomenal growth rates have earned it. But this has gone with its increasingly aggressive behaviour in the East China Sea, in the South China Sea, and in its activities in the regions surrounding India. India is thus constrained to react by spending more on its defences. Which country will be damaged more by this developing rivalry and defence spending is too early to judge.
2. China has been growing very fast, so its demand for labour in Guangdong and nearby provinces on the East coast has been rising rapidly also. But its supply of labour is not rising anywhere as fast because of its one-child policy and the

2. See James Lamont (2010), Amartya Sen (2011) and critiques by Panagariya (2011a, 2011b).
3. We do not address here the India-China comparison on social indicators, as against growth rates, that Dreze and Sen have written on. We have already demonstrated its errors (Myth 5.1).

restraints on rural migration to the urban areas. So, wages have been rising, with China transiting from a Marxian reserve army of labour available at a constant real wage to a situation of rising wages with growth. This slows down growth also. By contrast, India is behind the curve and its demographics imply that we will have an ample supply of young labour, which can place India on the growth trajectory of the earlier China with abundant labour.

3. Finally, China's authoritarian regime, compared to India's democracy, leads to two important consequences that militate in India's favour. First, China is fearful of samizdat: it cannot afford to have software develop to a point where the people can communicate freely and even dare to undermine political control. The result is that the PC (the personal computer, and all that it implies today) is incompatible with the CP (the Communist Party). But much technical progress comes today through software developments. So, India, which is a freewheeling democracy like the US, has an enormous advantage over China.
4. The other implication of China's authoritarianism is that as the bourgeoisie develops and seeks political rights, China faces a real dilemma. Will it respond to these demands in the fashion of the suppression at Tianenmen Square; or will the authorities accommodate these demands? In the former case, China will surely implode at some stage. The Chinese future, therefore, has a big question mark around it.

By contrast, India will continue to move along, albeit at a slightly less hectic pace, with its 'agitation and response' model, whereby grievances are aired and government responds to them. Her growth will be slower but surer.

And after all, democracy must be judged not just instrumentally, in terms of its economic consequences, but also as an end in itself.

Appendices

Appendix 1

Socialism under Nehru

Now, it is well known, and we have often stressed this, that production is perhaps one of the most important things before us today: that is, adding to the wealth of the country. We cannot overlook other things. Nevertheless, production comes first, and I am prepared to say that everything that we do should be judged from the point of view of production first of all. If nationalization adds to production, we shall have nationalization at every step. If it does not, let us see how to bring it about in order not to impede production. That is the essential thing.

—Prime Minister Jawaharlal Nehru in Constituent Assembly (Legislative) on 17 February 1948.

Nehru was a pragmatist first and a socialist next. The policy framework that emerged under him resulted principally from the objective of self-sufficiency. In Nehru's conception, the pursuit of self-sufficiency meant progressive reduction in the dependence on external markets for either the sales of Indian goods abroad or the purchase of foreign goods to satisfy domestic needs.[1] India having just emerged from the colonial rule, this seemed an eminently reasonable objective.

1. Nehru (1946, pp. 438-39) records this objective in clear terms when describing the deliberations of the 1938 Planning Committee in *The Discovery of India*. He states, *(Contd.…)*

Yet, what is reasonable is not necessarily rational. Self-sufficiency became an argument for import substitution and policies (such as protection) directed at promoting it.[2] It meant the recalibration of the production basket to suit domestic needs. If India needed bicycles, it must produce bicycles as well as the steel going into them. If it needed fertilizer, it must produce fertilizer and the chemicals going into them. And, of course, it must also produce the machines necessary to produce the bicycles, steel, fertilizers and chemicals.

There being general agreement at the time that the private sector lacked resources to invest in the heavy industry sectors consisting of such items as steel and machinery, it was also decided that the public sector would enter them in a major way.[3]

But reinforcing this argument for the public sector's expansion was Nehru's political belief in the desirability of progressive expansion of the public sector. In this regard he was a Fabian socialist who did not favour 'painful' nationalization but relied instead on a progressive and 'painless' shift in investment to yield a larger share of the public sector in production

---

(...contd.)

> 'The objective for the country as a whole was the attainment, as far as possible, of national self-sufficiency. International trade was certainly not excluded, but we were anxious to avoid being drawn into the whirlpool of economic imperialism. We wanted neither to be victims of an imperialist power nor to develop such tendencies ourselves.'

2. Export pessimism reinforced the self-sufficiency argument from the side of economics. If you could not export more jute to buy machinery which you needed to raise investment, then you had to produce the machinery yourself. This pessimism came from the early views that exports of traditional primary and agricultural products were under strain because of continued economizing on the use of such manufactured products and because of substitution by synthetics for them. It also came from the view that Western governments, faced with growing exports from the developing countries, would enact trade barriers.
3. The First Five-Year Plan (p. 422) stated the policy in these terms: 'The scope and need for development are so great that it is best for the public sector to develop those industries in which private enterprise is unable or unwilling to put up the resources required and run the risk involved, leaving the rest of the field free for private enterprise.'

in the economy gradually over time. It was a policy of painless, 'asymptotic' movement towards an economy dominated by public ownership of the means of production.

The last argument explains why the public sector was viewed not just as a substitute for the private sector, which could not undertake expansion in the favoured import-substituting sectors. In fact, the goal of expanding the public sector relative to the private sector progressively over time also led to the policy of reserving certain sectors exclusively for the public sector. In turn, that meant that government monopolies were created which had unfortunate consequences for efficiency since the elimination of domestic competition would be joined later by elimination of import competition as well.

In addition, one can detect some concern, starting in Nehru's administration, that the planners had to direct private investment selectively to sectors; certain sectors were socially more desirable than others and therefore encouraged even if less profitable than the latter. For example, chemicals could be less profitable than textiles and clothing but socially more desirable because they promoted development. This meant that sectoral quantities in the planning exercises were increasingly taken as not just indicative but as firm targets, to be implemented by a licensing system that would restrain investment in the less-favoured sectors such as textiles and clothing.[4] Therefore, investment licensing for large firms was adopted to allocate private investments according to the national priorities: licences would be issued more liberally for chemicals but less so for textiles and clothing.

On the external front, the policy regime during the 1950s was remarkably open. Tariffs were low; and, though import licensing had been inherited from the Second World War era controls, licences were liberally issued. Consumer goods imports were allowed and the importer

4. Later, starting with the Third Five-Year Plan, the targets were derived with more economic sophistication, in optimization models. But the optimization was academic; the targeting approach remained an albatross round the neck of Indian planners until the post-1991 reforms.

did not have to be the actual user.[5] On the foreign investment front, Nehru fought off the domestic private industry, left parties and radical socialists within the Congress to maintain and promote a liberal regime. He refused to nationalize the foreign firms and accorded them national status. He also permitted the repatriation of profits and dividends of foreign companies abroad. As late as the early 1960s, the government actively sought foreign investment in heavy electrical equipment, fertilizer and synthetic rubber, sectors in which the public sector had been active.

Investment licensing also remained relatively liberal with the decisions on the applications made without undue delay in the 1950s. This is partially evidenced by the near-absence of complaints by private entrepreneurs and also the rapid expansion of the private sector. The share of public sector in the total investment in the First Five-Year Plan was 46 per cent. The Second Plan set the explicit goal of raising this share to 61 per cent. But because private sector investment greatly exceeded its projected level, it fell well short (54 per cent) of the target in proportionate terms even while substantially achieving it in absolute terms. The Third Plan sought to push the share to 64 per cent but once again fell short at approximately 50 per cent.

The key factor behind the tightening of the import and investment licensing regimes was not ideological but the balance of payments crisis in 1957-58. That crisis led the finance ministry to introduce foreign exchange budgeting beginning in the second half of 1958. This required estimating the expected availability of foreign exchange in each forthcoming six-month period and then allocating it across its various uses. Here on, each investment licence application had to provide sufficient technical details to allow the evaluation of the foreign exchange burden it would impose for machinery and raw material imports. The licence was

---

5. According to the Third Five-Year Plan, 32 per cent of the total imports in the First Five-Year Plan (1951-52 to 1955-56) and 23 per cent in the Second Plan (1956-57 to 1960-61) were accounted for by consumer goods. 'Established importers', who were licensed to import goods for sale to other buyers, were allowed to operate relatively freely.

only issued if the product it sought to produce was judged to be sufficiently important to justify the allocation of the needed foreign exchange.

While the grip of the licence-permit raj became significantly tighter during the first half of the 1960s, radical socialists within the Congress and outside had at best limited salience while Nehru lived. Indeed, towards the end of his administration, several right-of-centre politicians such as Neelam Sanjiva Reddy, K. Kamaraj and S. Nijalingappa gained influence in the Congress organization while hardcore socialists such as Krishna Menon and K.D. Malaviya were forced out of the Union cabinet.

The 'second phase' of socialism under Indira Gandhi, the 'accidental' prime minister, was unfortunately far less pragmatic, as we note in the text: it changed the course of Indian policy until the reforms began in earnest in 1991.

Appendix 2

Measuring Inequality
The Gini Coefficient

The Gini coefficient is the commonest measure of the distribution of expenditure, income, wealth or another attribute within a given population. Since it is most common to speak in terms of income distribution among households within a population, we explain the measure in terms of inequality of income across households. The value of Gini varies between 0 and 1 with the value 0 representing a situation of perfect equality such that the income is identical across all households and 1 representing a situation of extreme inequality whereby all income is concentrated in a single household. Between 0 and 1, higher values of the Gini are associated with higher levels of inequality.

The logic behind and the limitations of the Gini can be explained with the help of the Lorenz curve (explained below), which is shown in Figure A2.1. On the horizontal axis, we arrange the households in the rising order of their incomes. Therefore, the household with the lowest income is the nearest to the origin and the one with the highest income is the farthest. We 'normalize' the total number of households to 100. On the vertical axis, we measure the cumulative incomes of households as percentage of the total income of the population. The curve representing the cumulative percentage incomes of households, depicted by OAO' in Figure A2.1, is called the Lorenz curve. A point on the Lorenz curve represents the percentage of the total income by households up to that point. The Lorenz curve begins at the origin since 0 per cent of the households account for 0 per cent of the population income. Likewise, the curve terminates at a point showing the values of 100 on both horizontal and vertical axes since 100 per cent of the households must account for 100 per cent of the population income.

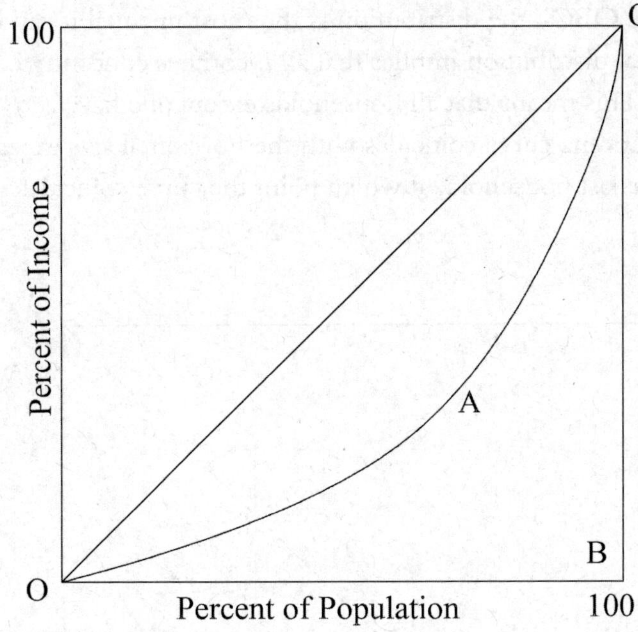

FIGURE A2.1: THE LORENZ CURVE

The Gini coefficient equals the area between the diagonal OO' and the Lorenz curve divided by the triangle OBO'. It is immediately obvious that if the Lorenz curve coincides with the diagonal OO', the Gini coefficient becomes 0 since the area between the diagonal and the Lorenz curve is 0 in this case. Alternatively, if the Lorenz curve coincides with triangle OBO', the Gini coefficient becomes 1. In this case, the area between the Lorenz curve and the diagonal is triangle OBO' and its ratio to triangle OBO' is 1. In all other cases, the value of the Gini coefficient is strictly between 0 and 1.

In the first of the above extreme cases in which the Lorenz curve coincides with the diagonal, the income is identical across all households. Identical distribution implies that the bottom 10 per cent of the households account for 10 per cent of the total income, the bottom 20 per cent for 20 per cent of the income, and so on. These points are, of course, on the diagonal. In the second extreme case in which the Lorenz curve coincides with triangle OBO', the distribution is the most unequal it can be. The most unequal distribution implies that all income is concentrated in one household. This means that all households except one have zero income so that the Lorenz curve coincides with the horizontal axis except when we get to the last household, at which point the curve coincides with the

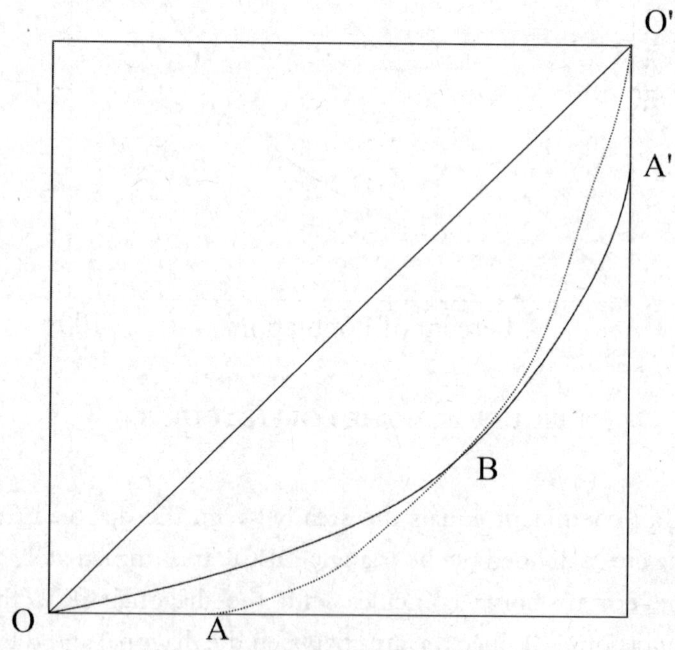

FIGURE A2.2: TWO LORENZ CURVES WITH THE SAME VALUE OF THE GINI COEFFICIENT

vertical axis. The Lorenz curve is, thus, represented by triangle OBO'. The lower the share of the households at the bottom, the closer is the Lorenz curve to the horizontal axis at the bottom. Likewise, the larger the share of the households at the top, the closer is the Lorenz curve to the vertical axis at the top. Both these factors pull the Lorenz curve away from the diagonal. Therefore, the more unequal the distribution, the farther the Lorenz curve is from the diagonal and therefore the closer is the value of the Gini coefficient to 1.

Finally, observe that any given value of the Gini coefficient is consistent with infinitely many shapes of the Lorenz curve, so that the frequent references to Gini coefficients across time or regions as measures of inequality must be handled with care. Figure A2.2 illustrates this point. Here we draw two Lorenz curves, one in solid line and the other in dotted line. Because the area between the Lorenz curve and the diagonal is the same in the two cases, the value of the Gini coefficient associated with them is the same. Yet the two Lorenz curves represent very different distributions of income. The dotted curve shows a large proportion of the bottom households as having no income and hence is associated with a significant volume of abject poverty. The solid line exhibits less poverty at the bottom but is characterized with a high degree of concentration at the top. Most observers would find the distribution represented by the solid line far more acceptable than that represented by the dotted line, though both are associated with the same value of the Gini coefficient.

Appendix 3

Key Provisions of the Right to Education Act, 2009

The following are the key provisions of the Right to Education Act, 2009:

- All children older than six years and younger than fourteen years have the legal right to free education.
- The state government in a state and the Central government in a Union territory in combination with the local authority (municipal corporation, municipal council, zila parishad, nagar panchayat or panchayat, as the case may be) has the obligation to provide every child between six and fourteen years of age elementary education meeting *specified norms and standards*, by 1 April 2013.
- Specified norms and standards that schools must meet include:

  — Student-teacher ratios of thirty at primary and thirty-five at middle level (to be enforced by the local authority beginning on 1 October 2010);

  — Provision of all-weather building consisting of one classroom per teacher, kitchen where mid-day meals can be cooked, separate toilets for boys and girls and a playground;

— Library with newspapers, magazines and books on all subjects;
— Availability of games and sports equipment; and
— 800 instructional hours per academic year at the primary and 1000 hours at the middle level.

- Duties of the local authority include:
  — Ensuring the availability of a neighbourhood school by 31 March 2013;
  — Maintaining records of children up to the age of fourteen years residing within its jurisdiction;
  — Ensuring and monitoring admission, attendance and completion of elementary education by every child residing within its jurisdiction; and
  — Ensuring admission of children of migrant families.
- Every school must achieve the specified norms and standards by 31 March 2013, failing which it will be shut down.
- No new schools should be established without a recognition certificate from the authority appointed by the state or Central government and every unrecognized school must get recognition within the time stipulated from this authority.
- No child or parent can be subject to any kind of screening procedure for purposes of admission.
- No child can be held back, expelled and required to pass the board examination till the completion of elementary education.
- No donation or capitation fee at the time of admission is permitted.
- Private schools will have to take 25 per cent of their class in grade I from the weaker section and the disadvantaged group of the society and provide free compulsory education till the completion of elementary education. Government will fund education of these children at the rate of per-child expenditure in public schools.
- Every teacher is required to attain minimum qualification specified by a Centrally appointed authority by 31 March 2015.
- The state government or local authority will set the terms and conditions of service and salary and allowances of teachers.

- No teacher is to engage in private tuition or private teaching activity.
- A teacher will be duty bound to:

  — Maintain regularity and punctuality in attending school;
  — Complete entire curriculum within the specified time;
  — Assess the learning ability of each child and accordingly, supplement additional instructions as required; and
  — Hold regular meetings with parents and guardians and apprise them about the regularity in attendance, ability to learn, progress made in learning and any other relevant information about the child.
  — A teacher in default of duties is liable to disciplinary action under the service rules applicable to him or her.

References

Ahluwalia, Deepak (1993): 'Public Distribution of Food in India: Coverage, Targeting and Leakages,' *Food Policy*, 18(1): pp. 33-54

Ahmad, Zainon (1995): 'India to Push on with Economic Reforms,' *New Straits Times* (Malaysia), 3 August, p. 16.

Alfaro, Laura and Anusha Chari (2012): 'Does Liberalization Promote Competition?' In Bhagwati, Jagdish and Arvind Panagariya, eds., *Reforms and Economic Transformation in India*, New York: Oxford University Press, pp. 200-26.

Balachandran, Kamala (2010): 'Understanding RTE,' *Deccan Herald*, 10 August 2010.

Bhagwati, Jagdish (1958): 'Immiserizing Growth: A Geometrical Note,' *Review of Economic Studies* 25, pp. 201-05.

Bhagwati, Jagdish (1988): 'Poverty and Public Policy,' *World Development*, vol. 16, issue 5, pp. 539-55.

Bhagwati, Jagdish (1998): 'Review of India's Economic Reforms: 1991-2001' by Vijay Joshi and I.M.D. Little, and 'India: Economic Development and Social Opportunity' by Jean Dreze and Amartya Sen. *Economic Journal* 108, pp. 196-200.

Bhagwati, Jagdish (2010): 'Indian Reforms: Yesterday and Today,' The 3rd Professor Hiren Mukherjee Memorial Annual Parliamentary Lecture, 2 December 2010. Available at http://www.columbia.edu/~jb38/papers/pdf/Lok-Sabha-speech-FINAL-EXPANDED-December-14.pdf (accessed on 13 April 2012).

Bhagwati, Jagdish (2011): 'Designing Institutions for Governance Reforms,' 24th Intelligence Bureau (IB) Centenary Endowment Lecture, home ministry, Government of India. Available at http://www.equilibri.net/nuovo/es/node/2011 (accessed on 13 April 2012).

Bhagwati, Jagdish and Padma Desai (1970): *India: Planning for Industrialization*, London: Oxford University Press.

Bhagwati, Jagdish and Padma Desai (1975): 'Socialism and Indian Economic Policy,' *World Development* 3(4).

Bhagwati, Jagdish and Rajeev Kohli (2011): 'Selling the Wrong Idea,' *The Times of India*, 12 December 2011.

Bhagwati, Jagdish and Arvind Panagariya (2004): 'Great Expectations,' *The Wall Street Journal*, 24 May 2004.

Bhagwati, Jagdish and Arvind Panagariya (2012): 'Introduction: Trade, Poverty, Inequality, and Democracy.' In Bhagwati, Jagdish and Arvind Panagariya, eds., *India's Reforms: How They Produced Inclusive Growth*, New York: Oxford University Press, pp. 3-17.

Cain, J., Rana Hasan and Devashish Mitra (2012): 'Trade Liberalization and Poverty Reduction: New Evidence from Indian States.' In Bhagwati, J. and Arvind Panagariya, eds., *India's Reforms: How They Produced Inclusive Growth*, New York: Oxford University Press, pp. 91-185.

Chakrabarty, Bidyut (1992): 'Jawaharlal Nehru and Planning, 1938-41: India at the Crossroads,' *Modern Asian Studies* 26(2), pp. 275-87.

Chakraborty, Pinaki, Sudipto Mundle, Arvind Panagariya and Govinda Rao (2011): *Economic Policies and Outcomes in the Largest Fifteen States in India*, Columbia University, New York and National Institute of Public Finance and Policy, New Delhi.

Chaudhuri, Sudip (2002): 'Economic Reforms and Industrial Structure in India,' *Economic & Political Weekly,* 37 (2): pp. 155–62.

Das, Deb Kusum, Deepika Wadhwa, and Gunajit Kalita (2009): 'The Employment Potential of Labour Intensive Industries in India's Organized Manufacturing,' ICRIER Working Paper 236, June.

Das Gupta, Monica, Shukla, Rajendra, Somanathan, T.V. and Datta, K.K. (2009): 'How Might India's Public Health Systems Be Strengthened?', World Bank Policy Research Working Paper Series, Paper No. 5140.

Das, Jishnu & Hammer, Jeffrey, 2007: 'Money for Nothing: The Dire Straits of Medical Practice in Delhi, India,' *Journal of Development Economics*, Elsevier, vol. 83(1), pp. 1-36, May.

Deaton, Angus and Jean Drèze (2002). 'Poverty and Inequality in India: A Reexamination,' *Economic & Political Weekly*, 7 September: 3729-48.

Deaton, Angus and Jean Dreze. (2008): 'Food and Nutrition in India: Facts and Interpretations,' *Economic & Political Weekly*, Vol. XLIV, No 7, pp. 42-65.

Debroy, Bibek (2001): 'Why We Need Law Reform,' *Seminar*, January 2001. Available at http://www.india-seminar.com/2001/497/497%20bibek%20debroy.htm (accessed on 4 November 2011).

Dehejia, Rajeev and Arvind Panagariya (2012): 'Services Growth in India: A Look Inside the Black Box.' In Bhagwati, Jagdish and Arvind Panagariya, eds., *Reforms and Economic Transformation in India,* New York: Oxford University Press, pp. 86-118.

Dehejia, Rajeev and Arvind Panagariya (2012): 'Entrepreneurship in Services and the Socially Disadvantaged.' In Bhagwati, Jagdish and Arvind Panagariya, eds., *Reforms and Economic Transformation in India,* New York: Oxford University Press, pp. 253-77.

DeLong, J. Bradford (2003): 'India since Independence: An Analytic Growth Narrative.' In Dani Rodrik (ed.), *In Search of Prosperity: Analytic Narratives of Economic Growth*, Princeton, NJ: Princeton University Press, pp. 183-204.

Deshpande, R.S. (2002): 'Suicide by Farmers in Karnataka: Agrarian Distress and Possible Alleviatory Steps,' *Economic & Political Weekly*, 37 (25): pp. 2601-10.

Dev, S. M. and M.H. Suryanarayana (1991): 'Is PDS Urban Biased and Pro-Rich: An Evaluation,' *Economic & Political Weekly,* 26(41): pp. 2357-66.

Drèze Jean (2004): 'Bangladesh Shows the Way,' *The Hindu*, 17 September.

Drèze, Jean and Reetika Khera (2010): 'The BPL Census and a Possible Alternative,' *Economic & Political Weekly*, 45(9): pp. 54-63.

Drèze J. and Sen, A.K. (1995): *India: Economic Development and Social Opportunity*, Oxford: Clarendon Press.

Drèze J. and Sen, A.K. (2011): 'Putting Growth in its Place,' *Outlook*, 14 November.

Dutta, B. and B. Ramaswami (2001): 'Targeting and Efficiency in the Public Distribution System: Case of Andhra Pradesh and Maharashtra,' *Economic & Political Weekly*, 36(18): pp. 1524-32.

Fields, Gary (1980): *Poverty, Inequality and Development*, Cambridge: Cambridge University Press.

Ghate, Chetan and Stephen Wright (2008): 'The "V-factor": Distribution, Timing and Correlates of the Great Indian Growth Turnaround,' Discussion Papers of DIW Berlin 783, DIW Berlin, German Institute for Economic Research. Revised version forthcoming in the *Journal of Development Economics*.

Government of India (2005): *Report of the National Commission on Macroeconomics and Health*, New Delhi: Ministry of Health and Family Welfare.

Government of India (2007): *Report on Conditions of Work and Promotion of Livelihoods in the Unorganized Sector*, New Delhi: National Commission for Enterprises in the Unorganized Sector.

Government of India (2009a): *Nutrition in India: National Family Health Survey (NFHS-3) 2005-06*, Mumbai: International Institute for Population Sciences.

Government of India (2009b): *Guidelines for Implementation of Works on Individual Land Under NREGA*, January draft, New Delhi: Ministry of Rural Development. The document is available at http://nrega.nic.in/draft_guidelines.pdf (accessed on 19 November 2011).

Gruere, Guillaume P., Purvi Mehta-Bhatt, and Debdatta Sengupta (2008): 'Bt cotton and Farmer Suicides in India: Reviewing the Evidence,' IFPRI Discussion paper 00808, October.

Gupta, Poonam and Arvind Panagariya. (2011a). 'Rich, Educated and Criminal?', *The Times of India*, 5 April.

Gupta, Poonam and Arvind Panagariya (2011b): 'Crime Tainted MPs Have Little to Do with Corruption,' *The Economic Times*, 21 September.

Gupta, Poonam and Arvind Panagariya (2012): 'Economic Reforms and Election Outcomes.' In Bhagwati, J. and Arvind Panagariya, eds.,

India's Reforms: How they Produced Inclusive Growth, New York: Oxford University Press, pp. 51-87.

Hasan, Rana and Karl Robert L. Jandoc (2012): 'Labour Regulations and Firm Size Distribution in Indian Manufacturing.' In Bhagwati, Jagdish and Arvind Panagariya, *Reforms and Economic Transformation in India*, New York: Oxford University Press, pp. 15-48.

Hasan, Rana, Devashish Mitra, and Asha Sundaram 2010: 'The Determinants of Capital Intensity in Manufacturing: The Role of Factor Endowments and Factor Market Imperfections,' Mimeo, New York: Syracuse University.

Hasan, Rana, Devashish Mitra, and Beyza P. Ural (2006-07): 'Trade Liberalization, Labour Market Institutions, and Poverty Reduction: Evidence from Indian States,' *India Policy Forum*, pp. 70-135.

Haq, Mahbub ul. (1972): 'Let Us Stand Economic Theory on Its Head: Joining the GNP Rat Race Won't Wipe Out Poverty,' *Insight*, January.

Himanshu and Abhijit Sen (2011): 'Why Not a Universal Food Security Legislation?', *Economic & Political Weekly,* 46(12): pp. 38-47.

Hnatkovska, Viktoria, Amartya Lahiri and Sourabh B. Paul (2012): 'Castes and Labor Mobility,' *American Economic Journal: Applied Economics*, Volume 4, No. 2, pp. 274-305.

Howes, Stephan and Shikha Jha (1992): 'Urban Bias in Indian Public Distribution System,' *Economic & Political Weekly,* 27(19): pp. 1022-30.

Howes, Stephan and Shikha Jha (1994): 'Public Distribution of Food in India: A Comment,' *Food Policy,* 19(1): pp. 65-68.

International Institute for Population Sciences (IIPS) and Macro International (2007): *National Family Health Survey (NFHS-3), 2005-06: India*, Mumbai: IIPS.

Jeffrey, Robin 1992: *Politics, Women and Well-Being: How Kerala Became 'a Model'*, Hampshire: The Macmillan Press Ltd.

Jha, Shikha (1992): 'Consumer Subsidies in India: Is Targeting Effective?', *Development and Change,* 23(4): pp. 101-28.

Jha, Shikha and Bharat Ramaswami (2011): 'The Percolation of Public Expenditure: Food Subsidies and the Poor in India and the

Philippines,' Paper presented at the India Policy Forum Conference, 12-13 July 2011 and available at the website http://www.ncaer.org/popuppages/EventDetails/IPF_2011/Shikha_Jha&Bharat_Ramaswami.pdf (accessed on 5 December 2011).

Kingdon, Geeta Gandhi (2005): 'Private and Public Schooling: The Indian Experience,' paper presented at the conference 'Mobilizing the Private Sector for Public Education,' Kennedy School of Government, Harvard University, 5-6 October 2005.

Kohli, Atul (2006): 'Politics of Economic Growth in India, 1980-2005—I,' *Economic & Political Weekly*, Vol. 41, No. 13: pp. 1251-59.

Kohli, Rajeev and Jagdish Bhagwati (2012): 'Organized Retailing in India: Issues and Outlook.' In Bhagwati, Jagdish and Arvind Panagariya, eds., *Reforms and Economic Transformation in India,* New York: Oxford University Press, pp. 119-37.

Krishna, Pravin and Guru Sethupathy (2012): 'Trade and Inequality in India.' In Bhagwati, J. and Arvind Panagariya, eds., *India's Reforms: How They Produced Inclusive Growth*, New York: Oxford University Press, pp. 247-78.

Lamont, James (2010): 'Nobel Laureate Attacks India on Growth,' *Financial Times*, 21 December. Available at http://www.ft.com/cms/s/0/554eab3e-0d33-11e0-82ff-00144feabdc0.html#axzz1sDTPdVyV (accessed on 16 April 2012).

Marathe, S. S. (1989): *Regulation and Development: India's Policy Experience of Controls over Industry*, Second edition, New Delhi: Sage Publications.

Mathew, George (2001): 'Amartya Sen and the Kerala "Model",' *The Hindu*, 9 January.

Mazumdar, D., and S. Sarkar (2008): *Globalization, Labor Markets and Inequality in India*,' London and New York: Routledge.

Mukim, Megha and Arvind Panagariya (2012): 'Growth, Openness and the Socially Disadvantaged.' In Bhagwati, J. and Arvind Panagariya, eds., *India's Reforms: How They Produced Inclusive Growth*, New York: Oxford University Press, pp. 186-246.

Muralidharan, Karthik and Michael Kremer (2006): 'Public and Private Schools in Rural India,' mimeo, Department of Economics, Harvard University.

Nagaraj, K. (2008): 'Farmers' Suicide in India: Magnitudes, Trends and Spatial Patterns,' Available at http://www.macroscan.org/anl/mar08/pdf/farmers_suicides.pdf (accessed on 20 December 2011).

National Sample Survey Organization (1996): *Nutritional Intake in India NSS 50th Round: July 1993-June 1994*, Report No. 405, New Delhi.

National Sample Survey Organization (2001a): *Nutritional Intake in India 1999-2000: NSS 55th Round (July 1999-June 2000)*, Report No. 471 (55/1.0/9), New Delhi.

National Sample Survey Organization (2001b): *Reported Adequacy of Food Intake in India 1999-2000: NSS 55th Round (July 1999-June 2000)*, Report No. 466 (55/1.0/7), New Delhi.

National Sample Survey Organization (2006): *Morbidity, Health Care and the Condition of the Aged: NSS 60th Round (January-June 2004)*, Report No. 507 (60/25.0/1), New Delhi.

National Sample Survey Organization (2007a): *Nutritional Intake in India 2004-05: NSS 61st Round (July 2004-June 2005)*, Report No. 513 (61/1.0/6), New Delhi.

National Sample Survey Organization (2007b): *Perceived Adequacy of Food Intake in India 2004-05: NSS 61st Round (July 2004-June 2005)*, Report No. 512 (61/1.0/5), New Delhi.

National Sample Survey Organization (2007c): *Public Distribution System and Other Sources of Household Consumption 2004-05*, Report No 510, Ministry of Statistics and Programme Implementation, GOI, New Delhi.

Nayyar, Deepak (2006): 'Economic Growth in Independent India: Lumbering Elephant or Running Tiger?', *Economic & Political Weekly*, Vol. 41, No. 15: pp. 1451-58.

Nundy, Madhurima (2005): 'Primary Health Care in India: Review of Policy, Plan and Committee Reports.' In Government of India, *Background Papers of the National Commission on Macroeconomics and Health*, New Delhi: Ministry of Health and Family Welfare, pp. 39-42.

Nehru, Jawaharlal (1946): *The Discovery of India*, New Delhi: Penguin Books India, 2004 edition.

Palmer-Jones, Richard, and Kunal Sen (2001): 'On Indian Poverty Puzzles and Statistics of Poverty,' *Economic & Political Weekly,* 36(3), 20 January, pp. 211-17.

Panagariya, Arvind (2004): 'Growth and Reforms during 1980s and 1990s,' *Economic & Political Weekly* 39 (25): pp. 2581–94.

Panagariya, Arvind (2008a): 'India: The Emerging Giant,' New York: Oxford University Press.

Panagariya, Arvind (2008b): 'El Nano: A Perfect Storm,' *The Economic Times*, 25 September.

Panagariya, A. (2009a): 'Is Anti-incumbency Really Passé?', *The Economic Times*, 28 May.

Panagariya, A. (2009b): 'The Fall of the Holy Trinity,' *The Economic Times*, 26 March.

Panagariya, Arvind. (2010a): 'India on the Growth Turnpike: No State Left Behind,' In Kochhar, Samir, ed., *India on the Growth Turnpike*, New Delhi Academic Foundation.

Panagariya, Arvind (2010b): 'Raising Investment in Higher Education,' *The Economic Times*, 27 October.

Panagariya, Arvind (2010c): 'Pursuing Excellence and Equity,' *The Times of India*, 10 April.

Panagariya, Arvind (2011a): 'I Beg to Differ, Professor Amartya Sen,' *The Economic Times*, 23 February.

Panagariya, Arvind (2011b): 'Does India Compare Poorly with China on People's Well Being?', *The Economic Times*, 23 March.

Panagariya, Arvind (2011c): 'Trade Openness and Growth Miracles: A Fresh Look at Taiwan.' In Ken Heyden and Stephen Woolcock, eds., *Ashgate Research Companion to International Trade Policy*, London: Ashgate Publishing Limited, pp. 309-26.

Panagariya, Arvind (2011d): 'Are We Living in a Gilded Age?', *The Economic Times*, 19 May.

Panagariya, Arvind (2011e): 'Reforms to the Rescue,' *The Times of India*, 8 September.

Panagariya, Arvind (2011f): 'The Problem with the Food Bill,' *The Economic Times*, 28 December.

Panagariya, Arvind (2011g): 'The Art of Graft,' *The Times of India*, 9 May.

Panagariya, Arvind. (2012a): 'Myths About Poverty Lines,' *The Times of India*, 30 March 2012.

Panagariya, Arvind (2012b): 'Slew of Reforms: Manmohan Singh Scores a Decisive Victory, Stakes Claim to His Legacy,' *The Economic Times*, 19 September.

Panagariya, Arvind (2012b): 'Empowering the Poor: Abandon the Broken Model,' *The Times of India*, 25 August.

Pant, Pitambar (1962): 'Perspective of Development, 1961-1976, Implications of Planning for a Minimum Level of Living,' Paper originally circulated in August 1962 by the Perspective Planning Division, Planning Commission and reproduced in T.N. Srinivasan and P.K. Bardhan, eds., *Poverty and Income Distribution in India*, Calcutta: Statistical Publishing Society.

Parikh, K.S. (1994): 'Who Get How Much from the PDS—How Effectively Does It Reach the Poor?', *Sarvekshana*, 17(3): p. 34.

Planning Commission. (2011): *Report on Universal Coverage for India*, New Delhi: Planning Commission.

PROBE Team, 1999, *Public Report on Basic Education in India*, New Delhi: Oxford University Press.

Ranadive, K.R. (1973): 'Growth and Social Justice: Political Economy of "Garibi Hatao,"' *Economic & Political Weekly*, Vol. 8, No. 18 (5 May), pp. 834-41.

Rani, Uma and Jeemol Unni (2004): 'Unorganized and Organized Manufacturing in India: Potential for Employment Generating Growth,' *Economic & Political Weekly*, 39 (41): pp. 4568–80.

Rao, Sujatha (2012): 'Long on Aspiration, Short on Detail: Report on Universal Health Coverage,' *Economic & Political Weekly* 47(6):12-16.

Ray, Ranjan and Geoffrey Lancaster (2005): 'On Setting the Poverty Line Based on Estimated Nutrient Prices: Condition of Socially Disadvantaged Groups during the Reform Period,' *Economic & Political Weekly*, 40(1), 1 January, pp. 46-56.

Rodrik, Dani (2003): 'Institutions, Integration, and Geography: In Search of the Deep Determinants of Economic Growth.' In Dani Rodrik (ed.), *In Search of Prosperity: Analytic Narratives of Economic Growth*, Princeton, NJ: Princeton University Press, 1-19.

Rodrik, Dani, and Arvind Subramanian (2005): 'From "Hindu Growth" to Productivity Surge: The Mystery of the Indian Growth Transition,' *IMF Staff Papers* 52(2), pp. 193-228.

Sainath, P. (2009): 'The Largest Wave of Suicides in History,' Available at http://85.92.88.218/the-largest-wave-of-suicides-in-history-by-p-sainath.pdf (accessed on 20 December 2011).

Sanyal, Sanjeev (2006): 'Post-liberalization India and the Importance of Legal Reform,' http://www.idfresearch.org/gov_parent/Sanjeev%20Sanyal%20Indian%20Legal%20Reforms%20Jul06.pdf (accessed on 20 December 2011).

Sau, Ranjit (1972): 'The "New Economics,"' *Economic & Political Weekly*, Vol. 7, No. 31/33, Special Number (August), pp.1571-73.

Sen, Amartya (2011): 'Growth and Other Concerns,' *The Hindu*, 14 February.

Sen, Amartya and James D. Wolfensohn (1999): 'Development: a Coin with Two Sides,' *The Hindu*, Opinion section, 6 May.

Sharma, Anil (2009): *Evaluating the Performance of the National Rural Employment Guarantee Scheme*, New Delhi: National Council of Applied Economic Research. Also at http://www.ncaer.org/downloads/Reports/NCAER-PIFStudyNREGA.pdf (accessed on 19 November, 2011).

Shiva, Vandana (2004): 'The Suicide Economy of Corporate Globalization,' Available at http://www.zcommunications.org/the-suicide-economy-of-corporate-globalisation-by-vandana2-shiva.pdf (accessed on 20 December 2011).

Sinha, Jayant and Ashutosh Varshney (2011): 'It is Time for India to Rein in its Robber Barons,' Comments and Analysis, *Financial Times*, 6 January.

Srinivasan, T.N. (2005): 'Comments on "From Hindu Growth to Productivity Surge: The Mystery of the Indian Growth Transition,"' *IMF Staff Papers*, 52(2). pp. 229-33.

Sukumaran, Ajay and Dilip Bisoi. (2011). Not Too Much of a Stretch,' *The Financial Express*, 29 July.

Svedberg, Peter (2912): 'Reforming or Replacing the Public Distribution System with Cash Transfers?', *Economic & Political Weekly* XLVII, No. 7, 18 February, pp. 53-62.

Tarozzi, Alessandro (2008): 'Growth Reference Charts and the Status of Indian Children,' *Economics and Human Biology*, 6(3), pp. 455-68.

Thorat, Sukhdeo and Amaresh Dubey (2012): 'Has Growth Been Socially Inclusive During 1993-94—2009-10?', *Economic & Political Weekly*, vol. XLVII, No. 10, 10 March, pp. 43-53.

Tooley, James, and Pauline Dixon (undated): 'Private Schools Serving the Poor: A Study from Delhi, India,' Working Paper, Viewpoint 8, Centre for Civil Society, New Delhi.

Topalova, Petia (2007): 'Trade Liberalization, Poverty and Inequality: Evidence from Indian Districts,' In Ann Harrison (ed.), *Globalization and Poverty*, Chicago: University of Chicago Press, pp. 291–336.

United Nations (1975): 'Poverty, Unemployment and Development Policy: A Case Study of Selected Issues with Reference to Kerala,' New York: United Nations Publication No. ST/ESA/29.

United Nations Development Program (1990): *Human Development Report*, New York: Oxford University Press.

Wallack, Jessica (2003): 'Structural Breaks in Indian Macroeconomic Data,' *Economic & Political Weekly*, Vol. 38, No. 41, pp. 4312-15.

Weisskopf, Thomas E. (2011). 'Why Worry about Inequality in the Booming Indian Economy?' *Economic & Political Weekly*, Vol. XLVI, No. 47, 19 November.

Wolfensohn, James and Joseph Stiglitz. (1999): 'Growth is Not Enough,' *Financial Times*, Comments and Analysis, p. 22, 22 September.

World Health Organization (WHO) (2011): 'World Health Statistics 2011,' Available at http://www.who.int/gho/publications/world_health_statistics/2011/en/index.html (accessed on 19 December 2011).

Index